Hands-On High Performance with Spring 5

Techniques for scaling and optimizing Spring and Spring Boot applications

Chintan Mehta
Subhash Shah
Pritesh Shah
Prashant Goswami
Dinesh Radadiya

BIRMINGHAM - MUMBAI

Hands-On High Performance with Spring 5

Commissioning Editor: Richa Tripathi
Acquisition Editor: Nitin Dasan
Content Development Editor: Rohit Kumar Singh
Technical Editor: Gaurav Gala
Copy Editor: Safis Editing
Project Coordinator: Vaidehi Sawant
Proofreader: Safis Editing
Indexer: Mariammal Chettiyar
Graphics: Jason Monteiro
Production Coordinator: Aparna Bhagat

First published: June 2018

Production reference: 1080618

Published by Packt Publishing Ltd.
Livery Place
35 Livery Street
Birmingham
B3 2PB, UK.

ISBN 978-1-78883-838-2

www.packtpub.com

`mapt.io`

Mapt is an online digital library that gives you full access to over 5,000 books and videos, as well as industry leading tools to help you plan your personal development and advance your career. For more information, please visit our website.

Why subscribe?

- Spend less time learning and more time coding with practical eBooks and Videos from over 4,000 industry professionals

- Improve your learning with Skill Plans built especially for you

- Get a free eBook or video every month

- Mapt is fully searchable

- Copy and paste, print, and bookmark content

PacktPub.com

Did you know that Packt offers eBook versions of every book published, with PDF and ePub files available? You can upgrade to the eBook version at `www.PacktPub.com` and as a print book customer, you are entitled to a discount on the eBook copy. Get in touch with us at `service@packtpub.com` for more details.

At `www.PacktPub.com`, you can also read a collection of free technical articles, sign up for a range of free newsletters, and receive exclusive discounts and offers on Packt books and eBooks.

Contributors

About the authors

Chintan Mehta is a co-founder of KNOWARTH Technologies and heads the cloud/RIMS/DevOps team. He has rich, progressive experience in server administration of Linux, AWS Cloud, DevOps, RIMS, and on open source technologies. He is also an AWS Certified Solutions Architect. Chintan has authored *MySQL 8 for Big Data*, *Mastering Apache Solr 7.x*, *MySQL 8 Administrator's Guide*, and *Hadoop Backup and Recovery Solutions*. Also, he has reviewed *Liferay Portal Performance Best Practices* and *Building Serverless Web Applications*.

Subhash Shah works as a Principal Consultant at KNOWARTH Technologies. He holds a degree in Information Technology from HNGU. He is experienced in developing web-based solutions using various software platforms. He is a strong advocate of open source software development and its use by businesses to reduce risk and cost. His interests include designing sustainable software solutions. His technical skills include requirement analysis, architecture design, project delivery, application setup, and execution processes. He admires quality code and test-driven development.

Pritesh Shah is a Solutions Architect at CentralBOS LLC. Pritesh is responsible for integrating technologies with best practices to translate business requirements into business change. He holds a degree in Computer Engineering from Dharmsinh Desai University. His expertise lies in, but is not limited to, designing, developing, deploying, and testing N-tier applications, and leading teams. He is very good at debugging problems and finding the best solution. Pritesh believes in constant improvement by quickly adapting new technologies suitable for building solutions.

Prashant Goswami works as a Senior Consultant at KNOWARTH Technologies and handles enterprise projects with regard to software design, development, deployment, and building processes to provide customers with affordable software solutions. He holds a master's degree in Computer Applications from Gujarat Technological University. He is able to adapt quickly to any technology and has a keen desire for constant improvement. Prashant has proven experience in working with various technologies in web application development, design patterns, enterprise architectures, and open source technologies.

Dinesh Radadiya works as a Lead Consultant and Architect at KNOWARTH Technologies, a leading open source software development company. He is a software architect with over 10 years of professional experience in developing web-based applications using various software platforms. He has proven expertise in leading and delivering software projects with varying degrees of complexity in domains such as ERP, HR, healthcare, CRM, and manufacturing. He has a keen interest in requirement analysis, progressive design, high-quality code, microservices, and refactoring.

About the reviewer

Mohamed Sanaulla is a software developer with more than 7 years of experience in developing enterprise applications and Java-based backend solutions for e-commerce applications. His interests include enterprise software development, refactoring and redesigning applications, designing and implementing RESTful web services, troubleshooting Java applications for performance issues, and TDD.
He is also a Sun-Certified Java programmer for the Java 6 platform. He is a moderator for JavaRanch, and he likes to share his findings on his blog. He has co-authored *Java 9 Cookbook*.

Packt is searching for authors like you

If you're interested in becoming an author for Packt, please visit authors.packtpub.com and apply today. We have worked with thousands of developers and tech professionals, just like you, to help them share their insight with the global tech community. You can make a general application, apply for a specific hot topic that we are recruiting an author for, or submit your own idea.

Table of Contents

Preface

The mission of this book is to introduce developers to application monitoring and performance tuning to create highly performant applications. The book starts with the basic details of Spring Framework, including various Spring modules and projects, Spring bean and BeanFactory implementation, and aspect-oriented programming. It also explores Spring Framework as an IoC bean container. We will be discussing Spring MVC, which is a commonly used Spring module for building a user interface in detail with Spring Security authentication part with a stateless API. This book also emphasizes the importance of building optimized Spring applications for interacting with relational databases. Then, we will walk through some of the advanced ways of accessing databases using object-relational mapping (ORM) frameworks, such as Hibernate. The book moves on to the details of new Spring features, such as Spring Boot and reactive programming, with best practices suggestions. An important aspect of the book is its focus on building highly performant applications. The latter part of the book includes details for application monitoring, performance optimization, JVM internals, and garbage collection optimization. Finally, how to build microservices is explained to help you understand the challenges faced in the process and how to monitor its performance.

Who this book is for

This book is suitable for Spring developers who would like to build high-performance applications and have more control over their application's performance in production and development. This book requires developers to have some familiarity with Java, Maven, and Eclipse.

What this book covers

Chapter 1, *Exploring Spring Concepts*, focuses on gaining a clear understanding of the core features of Spring Framework. It briefly outlines the Spring modules and explores the integration of different Spring projects, and gives a clear explanation of the Spring IoC container. It ends by introducing the new features of Spring 5.0.

Chapter 2, *Spring Best Practices and Bean Wiring Configurations*, explores different bean wiring configurations with Java, XML, and annotations. The chapter also helps us learn different best practices when it comes to bean wiring configuration. It also helps us understand performance assessment with different configurations, as well as DI pitfalls.

Chapter 3, *Tuning Aspect-Oriented Programming*, explores the concepts of the Spring Aspect-Oriented Programming (AOP) module and its various terminologies. It also covers the concept of proxy. It ends by going through the best practices for achieving quality and performance with the Spring AOP module.

Chapter 4, *Spring MVC Optimization*, starts by giving a clear understanding of the Spring MVC module with different Spring MVC configuration methods. It also covers the concept of asynchronous processing in Spring. Then it explains Spring Security configuration and authentication part with a stateless API. It finishes by going through the monitoring part of Tomcat with JMX, and Spring MVC performance improvements.

Chapter 5, *Understanding Spring Database Interactions*, helps us learn about database interaction with Spring Framework. It then walks through Spring transaction management and optimal connection pooling configuration. It ends by going through database design best practices.

Chapter 6, *Hibernate Performance Tuning and Caching*, describes some of the advanced ways of accessing the database using ORM frameworks, such as Hibernate. It ends by explaining how we can remove the boilerplate code of implementing the Data Access Object (DAO) interface using Spring Data.

Chapter 7, *Optimizing Spring Messaging*, starts by exploring the concepts of messaging in Spring and talks through its advantages. It then walks through the RabbitMQ configuration for using messaging in the Spring application. Finally, it describes the parameters for improving the performance and scalability to maximize throughput.

Chapter 8, *Multithreading and Concurrent Programming*, covers the core concepts of Java threads and advanced thread support. It also covers the concept of Java thread pooling to improve performance. Before its close, it will explore Spring transaction management with threads and various best practices for programming threads.

Chapter 9, *Profiling and Logging*, focuses on concepts surrounding profiling and logging. This chapter starts by defining profiling and logging and how they are useful for assessing application performance. In the latter part of the chapter, the focus will be on learning about software tools that can be used to study application performance.

Chapter 10, *Application Performance Optimization*, focuses on optimizing application performance. It also covers details for identifying the symptoms of performance issues, the performance tuning life cycle, and JMX support in Spring.

Chapter 11, *Inside JVM*, walks through the insides of JVM and tuning JVM to achieve high performance. It also covers the topics related to memory leaks and common misunderstandings related to garbage collection, before moving onto different garbage collection methods and discussion of their importance.

Chapter 12, *Spring Boot Microservice Performance Tuning*, covers the concept of Spring Boot microservices and their performance tuning. It also clearly describes how to use actuators and health checks in order to monitor Spring Boot applications. It also covers the different techniques in order to tune the performance of Spring Boot applications.

To get the most out of this book

This book requires developers to have some familiarity with Java, Maven, and Eclipse.

Download the example code files

You can download the example code files for this book from your account at www.packtpub.com. If you purchased this book elsewhere, you can visit www.packtpub.com/support and register to have the files emailed directly to you.

You can download the code files by following these steps:

1. Log in or register at www.packtpub.com.
2. Select the **SUPPORT** tab.
3. Click on **Code Downloads & Errata**.
4. Enter the name of the book in the **Search** box and follow the onscreen instructions.

Once the file is downloaded, please make sure that you unzip or extract the folder using the latest version of:

- WinRAR/7-Zip for Windows
- Zipeg/iZip/UnRarX for Mac
- 7-Zip/PeaZip for Linux

The code bundle for the book is also hosted on GitHub at `https://github.com/PacktPublishing/Hands-On-High-Performance-with-Spring-5`. In case there's an update to the code, it will be updated on the existing GitHub repository.

We also have other code bundles from our rich catalog of books and videos available at `https://github.com/PacktPublishing/`. Check them out!

Download the color images

We also provide a PDF file that has color images of the screenshots/diagrams used in this book. You can download it from `https://www.packtpub.com/sites/default/files/downloads/HandsOnHighPerformancewithSpring5_ColorImages.pdf`.

Conventions used

There are a number of text conventions used throughout this book.

`CodeInText`: Indicates code words in text, database table names, folder names, filenames, file extensions, pathnames, dummy URLs, user input, and Twitter handles. Here is an example: "To avoid `LazyInitializationException`, one of the solutions is an open session in view. "

A block of code is set as follows:

```
PreparedStatement st = null;
try {
    st = conn.prepareStatement(INSERT_ACCOUNT_QUERY);
    st.setString(1, bean.getAccountName());
    st.setInt(2, bean.getAccountNumber());
    st.execute();
}
```

When we wish to draw your attention to a particular part of a code block, the relevant lines or items are set in bold:

```
@Configuration
@EnableTransactionManagement
@PropertySource({ "classpath:persistence-hibernate.properties" })
@ComponentScan({ "com.packt.springhighperformance.ch6.bankingapp" })
    @EnableJpaRepositories(basePackages =
"com.packt.springhighperformance.ch6.bankingapp.repository")
public class PersistenceJPAConfig {

}
```

Any command-line input or output is written as follows:

```
curl -sL --connect-timeout 1 -i
http://localhost:8080/authentication-cache/secure/login -H "Authorization:
Basic Y3VzdDAwMTpUZXN0QDEyMw=="
```

Bold: Indicates a new term, an important word, or words that you see onscreen. For example, words in menus or dialog boxes appear in the text like this. Here is an example: "Inside the **Applications** window, we can see a menu for **Local** nodes."

 Warnings or important notes appear like this.

 Tips and tricks appear like this.

Get in touch

Feedback from our readers is always welcome.

General feedback: Email feedback@packtpub.com and mention the book title in the subject of your message. If you have questions about any aspect of this book, please email us at questions@packtpub.com.

Errata: Although we have taken every care to ensure the accuracy of our content, mistakes do happen. If you have found a mistake in this book, we would be grateful if you would report this to us. Please visit www.packtpub.com/submit-errata, selecting your book, clicking on the Errata Submission Form link, and entering the details.

Piracy: If you come across any illegal copies of our works in any form on the Internet, we would be grateful if you would provide us with the location address or website name. Please contact us at copyright@packtpub.com with a link to the material.

If you are interested in becoming an author: If there is a topic that you have expertise in and you are interested in either writing or contributing to a book, please visit authors.packtpub.com.

Reviews

Please leave a review. Once you have read and used this book, why not leave a review on the site that you purchased it from? Potential readers can then see and use your unbiased opinion to make purchase decisions, we at Packt can understand what you think about our products, and our authors can see your feedback on their book. Thank you!

For more information about Packt, please visit `packtpub.com`.

Exploring Spring Concepts
1

The **Spring Framework** provides extensive support for managing large enterprise Java applications and also addresses the complexities of enterprise application development. Spring provides a complete set of API and configuration models for modern enterprise applications so that programmers just need to focus on the business logic of the application.

Introduced as a lightweight framework, the Spring Framework was aimed at providing a way of making the development of Java enterprise applications easy and simple.

This chapter will help you gain a better understanding of the core features of the Spring Framework. We will start with an introduction to the Spring Framework. This chapter will also give you a clear understanding of every major module of the Spring Framework. After having a quick look at the important modules in the Spring Framework, we will dive into the world of Spring projects. We will also have a clear understanding of the Spring **Inversion of Control** (**IoC**) container. At the end, we will have a look at the new features and enhancements introduced in Spring 5.0.

In this chapter, we will be looking at the following topics:

- Introducing the Spring Framework
- Understanding Spring modules
- Spring projects
- Spring IoC container
- New features in Spring Framework 5.0

Introducing the Spring Framework

The Spring Framework is one of the most popular open source Java application frameworks and IoC containers. Spring was originally developed by Rod Johnson and Jurgen Holler. The first milestone version of Spring Framework was released in March 2004. Though it has been a decade and a half, the Spring Framework remains the framework of choice to build any Java application.

The Spring Framework provides comprehensive infrastructure support for developing enterprise Java applications. So, developers don't need to worry about the infrastructure of the application; they can focus on the business logic of the application, rather than handling the configuration of the application.

All infrastructure, configuration, and meta configuration files, either Java-based or XML-based, are handled by the Spring Framework. So, this framework gives you more flexibility in building an application with a **Plain Old Java Object** (**POJO**) programming model rather than a non-invasive programming model.

The Spring IoC container forms the core of the entire framework by putting together any application's various components. Spring **Model-View-Controller** (**MVC**) components can be used to build a very flexible web tier. The IoC container simplifies the development of the business layer with POJOs.

Problems with EJB

In the early days, it was very difficult for programmers to manage enterprise applications, because the enterprise Java technologies like **Enterprise JavaBeans** (**EJB**) were much heavier to provide the enterprise solutions to programmers.

When EJB technology was first announced, it was offering a distributed component model that would allow the developers to focus only on the business side of the system while ignoring the middleware requirements, such as wiring of components, transaction management, persistence operations, security, resource pooling, threading, distribution, remoting, and so on; however, it was a very cumbersome process for developing, unit testing, and deploying EJB applications. Some of the following complexities were faced while using EJB:

- Forcing implementation of unnecessary interfaces and methods
- Making unit testing difficult, especially outside the EJB container
- Inconveniences in managing deployment descriptors
- Tedious exception handling

At that time, Spring was introduced as an alternative technology especially made for EJB, because Spring provided a very simple, leaner, and lighter programming model compared with other existing Java technologies. Spring makes it possible to overcome the preceding complexities, and also to avoid the use of some other heavier enterprise technologies by using many available design patterns. The Spring Framework focused on the POJO programming model rather than a non-invasive programming model. This model provided the simplicity to the Spring Framework. It also empowered ideas such as the **dependency injection** (**DI**) pattern and **Aspect-Oriented Programming** (**AOP**), using the proxy pattern and decorator pattern.

Simplifying implementation using POJO

The most important advantage of the POJO programming model is that coding application classes is very fast and simple. This is because classes don't need to depend on any particular API, implement any special interface, or extend from a particular framework class. You do not have to create any special callback methods until you really need them.

Benefits of the Spring Framework

The important benefits of the Spring Framework are as follows:

- No need to reinvent the wheel
- Ease of unit testing
- Reduction in implementing code
- Inversion of control and API
- Consistency in transaction management
- Modular architecture
- Up to date with time

Let's discuss each in detail.

No need to reinvent the wheel

No need to reinvent the wheel is one of the most important benefits that developers can leverage from the Spring Framework. It facilitates the practical use of the well-known technologies, ORM frameworks, logging frameworks, JEE, JDK timers, Quartz, and so on. So, developers don't have to learn any new technologies or frameworks.

It facilitates good programming practices, such as programming using interfaces instead of classes. Spring enables developers to develop enterprise applications using POJO and **Plain Old Java Interface** (**POJI**) model programming.

Ease of unit testing

If you want to test the applications developed using Spring, it is quite easy. The main reason behind this is that the environment-dependent code is available in this framework. Earlier versions of EJBs were very difficult to unit test. It was difficult to even run EJBs outside the container (as of version 2.1). The only way to test them was to deploy them in a container.

The Spring Framework introduced the DI concept. We will discuss DI in complete detail in `Chapter 2`, *Spring Best Practices and Bean Wiring Configurations*. The DI enables unit testing. This is done by replacing the dependencies with their mocks. The entire application need not be deployed to unit test.

Unit testing has multiple benefits:

- Improving the productivity of programmers
- Detecting defects at earlier stages, thereby saving the cost of fixing them
- Preventing future defects by automating unit tests in applications that are running in **continuous integration** (**CI**) builds

Reduction in implementing code

All application classes are simple POJO classes; Spring is not invasive. It does not require you to extend framework classes or implement framework interfaces for most use cases. Spring applications do not require a Jakarta EE application server, but they can be deployed on one.

Before the Spring Framework, typical J2EE applications contained a lot of plumbing code. For example:

- Code for getting a database connection
- Code for handling exceptions
- Transaction management code
- Logging code and a lot more

Let's look at the following simple example of executing a query using
`PreparedStatement`:

```
PreparedStatement st = null;
try {
    st = conn.prepareStatement(INSERT_ACCOUNT_QUERY);
    st.setString(1, bean.getAccountName());
    st.setInt(2, bean.getAccountNumber());
    st.execute();
}
catch (SQLException e) {
    logger.error("Failed : " + INSERT_ACCOUNT_QUERY, e);
} finally {
    if (st != null) {
        try {
            st.close();
        } catch (SQLException e) {
            logger.log(Level.SEVERE, INSERT_ACCOUNT_QUERY, e);
        }
    }
}
```

In the preceding example, there are four lines of business logic and more than 10 lines
of plumbing code. The same logic can be applied in a couple of lines using the Spring
Framework, as follows:

```
jdbcTemplate.update(INSERT_ACCOUNT_QUERY,
bean.getAccountName(), bean.getAccountNumber());
```

Using Spring, you can use a Java method as a request handler method or remote method,
like a `service()` method of a servlet API, but without dealing with the servlet API of the
servlet container. It supports both XML-based and annotation-based configuration.

Spring enables you to use a local Java method as a message handler method, without using
a **Java Message Service** (**JMS**) API in the application. Spring serves as a container for your
application objects. Your objects do not have to worry about finding and establishing
connections with each other. Spring also enables you to use the local Java method as a
management operation, without using a **Java Management Extensions** (**JMX**) API in the
application.

Inversion of control and API

Spring also helps developers to get rid of the necessity of writing a separate compilation unit, or a separate class loader to handle exceptions. Spring converts technology-dependent exceptions, particularly thrown by **Java Database Connectivity (JDBC)**, Hibernate or **Java Data Objects (JDO)**, into unchecked and consistent exceptions. Spring does this magic using inversion of control and APIs.

Also, it uses IoC for DI, which means aspects can be configured normally. If we want to add our own behavior, we need to extend the classes of the framework or plug in our own classes. The following is a list of advantages for this kind of architecture:

- Decoupling the execution of a task from its implementation
- Making it easier to switch between different implementations
- Greater modularity of a program
- Greater ease in testing a program by isolating a component or mocking it
- Dependencies and allowing components to communicate through contracts

Consistency in transaction management

Spring also provides support for transaction management with consistency. It provides an easy and flexible way to configure local transactions for small applications as well as global transactions for large applications using the **Java Transaction API (JTA)**. So we do not need to use any third-party transactional API to execute a database transaction; Spring will take care of it with the transaction management feature.

Modular architecture

Spring provides a modular architecture that helps developers to identify the packages or classes which are to be used and which are to be ignored. Hence, in this way, we can keep only those things which we really need. So that makes it easy to identify and utilize the usable packages or classes even if there are many packages or classes.

Spring is a powerful framework that addresses many common problems in Jakarta EE. It includes support for managing business objects and exposing their services to presentation tier components.

Spring instantiates the beans and injects the dependencies of your objects into the application it serves as a life cycle manager of the beans.

Up to date with time

When the first version of the Spring Framework was built, its main focus was to make applications testable. There were also new challenges in the later versions, but the Spring Framework managed to evolve and stay ahead and on track with the architectural flexibility and modules that are offered. Some examples are listed as follows:

- The Spring Framework introduced a number of abstractions ahead of Jakarta EE to keep the application decoupled from the specific implementation
- The Spring Framework also provided transparent caching support in Spring 3.1
- Jakarta EE was introduced with JSR-107 for JCache in 2014, so it was provided in Spring 4.1

Another major evolution that Spring was involved with was to provide different Spring projects. The Spring Framework is just one of the many projects among Spring projects. The following example illustrates how the Spring Framework managed to remain up to date in terms of Spring projects:

- As architecture evolved toward cloud and microservices, Spring came up with new cloud-oriented Spring projects. The Spring Cloud project simplifies development and deployment of microservices.
- To build Java batch applications, a new approach was introduced as the Spring Batch project by the Spring Framework.

In the next section, we will dive deep into the different Spring Framework modules.

Understanding Spring modules

Spring provides a modular architecture that is one of the most important reasons for the popularity of the Spring Framework. Its layered architecture enables integration of other frameworks easily and without hassle. These modules provide everything that a developer may need to use in enterprise application development. The Spring Framework is organized into 20 different modules that are built on the top of its Core Container.

The following diagram illustrates different Spring modules organized in a layered architecture:

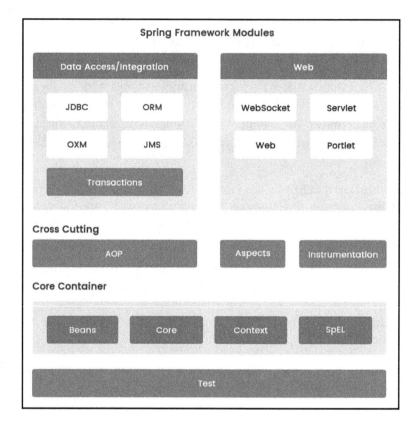

Spring Framework modules

We will start with discussing the Core Container before moving on to other modules.

Core Container

The **Spring Core Container** provides the core features of the Spring Framework, namely as Core, Beans, Context, and Expression Language, the details of which are as follows:

Artifact	Module Usage
spring-core	This module facilitates all the utilities used by other modules and it also provides a way for managing the different bean life cycle operations.

`spring-beans`	This module is mainly used to decouple code dependencies from your actual business logic and eliminates the use of singleton classes using DI and IoC features.
`spring-context`	This module provides features like internationalization, and resource loading, and also underpins Java EE features like EJB, JMS, and remoting.
`spring-expression`	This module provides support for accessing properties of beans at runtime and also allows us to manipulate them.

Crosscutting concerns

Crosscutting concerns are applicable to all the layers of an application, including logging and security, among others. Important Spring modules related to crosscutting concerns are as follows:

Artifact	Module Usage
`spring-aop`	This module is mainly used to perform the tasks which are common amongst different parts of a system like transaction management, logging, and security. To enable this we can implement method-interceptors and pointcuts.
`spring-aspects`	This module is used to integrate any custom object type. It is possible using AspectJ, and the main use of this module is to integrate the objects which are not in the control of the container.
`spring-instrument`	This module is used to measure the application's performance and also helps to perform error diagnosis using trace information.
`spring-test`	This module is used to integrate testing support in a Spring application.

Data Access/Integration

The **Data Access/Integration** layer in applications interacts with the database and/or the external interfaces. It consists of JDBC, ORM, OXM, JMS, and Transaction modules. These modules are `spring-jdbc`, `spring-orm`, `spring-oxm`, `spring-jms`, and `spring-tx`.

Web

The **Web** layer contains the Web, Web-MVC, Web-Socket, and other Web-Portlet modules. The respective module names are `spring-web`, `spring-webmvc`, `spring-websocket`, `spring-webmvc-portlet`.

In the next section, we will go through different kinds of Spring projects.

Spring projects

The Spring Framework provides different kinds of projects for different infrastructure needs, and also helps to explore solutions to other problems in the enterprise application: deployment, cloud, big data, and security, among others.

Some of the important Spring projects are listed as follows:

- Spring Boot
- Spring Data
- Spring Batch
- Spring Cloud
- Spring Security
- Spring HATEOAS

Let's discuss them in detail.

Spring Boot

Spring Boot provides support to create standalone, production-grade, Spring-based applications that you can just run.

Spring Boot also provides some of the following features out of the box, by taking an opinionated view of how applications have to be developed:

- Provides support for developing standalone Spring applications
- Embeds Tomcat, Jetty, or Undertow directly, with no need to deploy WAR files
- Allow us to externalize configuration to work in different environments with the same application code
- Simplifies Maven configuration by providing opinionated starter POMs

- Eliminates the need for code generation and the requirement for XML configuration
- Provides support for production features like metrics, health checks, and application monitoring

We will look at Spring Boot in depth in `Chapter 12`, *Spring Boot Microservice Performance Tuning*.

Spring Data

The main goal of the **Spring Data** project is to provide an easy and consistent Spring-based model to access data and other special features, to manipulate SQL-and NoSQL-based data stores. It also tries to provide an easy way to use data access technologies, map-reduce frameworks, relational and non-relational databases, and cloud-based data services.

Some of the important features are as follows:

- Provides support for integration with custom repository code
- Provides repository and object-mapping abstractions by deriving dynamic queries using repository method names
- Advanced integration support with Spring MVC controllers
- Advanced support for transparent auditing features such as created by, created date, last changed by, and last changed date
- Experimental integration support for cross-store persistence

Spring Data provides integration support for the following data sources:

- JPA
- JDBC
- LDAP
- MongoDB
- Gemfire
- REST
- Redis
- Apache Cassandra
- Apache Solr

Spring Batch

Spring Batch facilitates essential processing for large volumes of records, including logging/tracing, transaction management, job processing statistics, job restart, skip, and resource management, by providing reusable functions. It also provides more advanced technical services and features that will enable extremely high-volume and high-performance batch jobs using optimization and partitioning techniques.

Important features of Spring Batch are as follows:

- The ability to process data in chunks
- The ability to start, stop and restart jobs, including the ability to restart, in the case of failed jobs, from the point where they failed
- The ability to retry steps or to skip steps on failure
- Web-based administration interface

Spring Cloud

It is not an overstatement to say *the world is moving to the cloud*.

Spring Cloud provides tools for developers to build common patterns in distributed systems. Spring Cloud enables developers to quickly build services and applications that implement common patterns to work in any distributed environment.

Some of the common patterns implemented in Spring Cloud are as follows:

- Distributed configuration
- Service registration and discovery
- Circuit breakers
- Load balancing
- Intelligent routing
- Distributed messaging
- Global locks

Spring Security

Authentication and authorization are the essential parts of enterprise applications, both web applications and web services. **Spring Security** is a powerful and highly customizable authentication and access control framework. Spring Security focuses on providing declarative authentication and authorization to Java applications.

Important features in Spring Security are as follows:

- Comprehensive support for both authentication and authorization
- Good support for integration with servlet APIs and Spring MVC
- Module support for integration with **Security Assertion Markup Language (SAML)** and **Lightweight Directory Access Protocol (LDAP)**
- Providing support for common security attacks such as **Cross-Site Forgery Request (CSRF)**, session fixation, clickjacking, and so on

We will discuss how to secure web applications with Spring Security in `Chapter 4`, *Spring MVC Optimization*.

Spring HATEOAS

The main purpose of **Hypermedia As The Engine Of Application State (HATEOAS)** is to decouple the server (the service provider) from the client (the service consumer). The server provides the client with information on other possible actions that can be performed on the resource.

Spring HATEOAS provides a HATEOAS implementation, especially for the **REpresentational State Transfer (REST)** services implemented with Spring MVC.

Spring HATEOAS has the following important features:

- A simplified definition of links pointing to service methods, making the links less fragile
- Support for JSON and JAXB (XML-based) integration
- Support for hypermedia formats such as **Hypertext Application Language (HAL)**

In the next section, we will understand the mechanism of Spring's IoC container.

Spring's IoC container

Spring's **IoC container** is built as the core module of the Spring architecture. IoC is also known as DI. It is a design pattern which eliminates the dependency of the code to provide ease in managing and testing the application. In DI, the objects themselves characterize their dependencies with the other objects they work, just through constructor arguments, arguments to a factory method, or properties that are set on the object instance after it is created or returned from a factory method.

The container is then responsible to inject those dependencies when it creates the bean. This process is basically the inverse (so it is known as IoC) of the bean itself controlling the instantiation or location of its dependencies, by using the direct construction of classes, or a mechanism.

There are two main base packages of the Spring Framework's IoC container: `org.springframework.beans`, and `org.springframework.context`. The `BeanFactory` interface provides some of the advanced-level configuration mechanisms to manage any type of object. `ApplicationContext` includes all the functionalities of `BeanFactory`, and acts as a subinterface of it. In fact, `ApplicationContext` is also recommended over `BeanFactory`, and provides more supporting infrastructure that enables: easier integration with Spring's AOP features and transaction; message resource handling in terms of internationalization and event publication; and application layer-specific contexts such as `WebApplicationContext` for use in web applications.

The interface `org.springframework.context.ApplicationContext` is represented as the Spring IoC container, and it is in complete control of a bean's life cycle and responsible for instantiating, configuring, and assembling the beans.

The container gets all the instructions to instantiate, configure, and assemble, by scanning bean configuration metadata. The configuration metadata can be represented using the following methods:

- XML-based configuration
- Annotation-based configuration
- Java-based configuration

We will learn these methods in more detail in Chapter 2, *Spring Best Practices and Bean Wiring Configurations*.

The following diagram represents a simple representation of the **Spring Container** process towards creating a fully configured application:

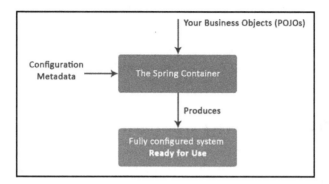

The Spring IoC container

The following example shows the basic structure of XML-based configuration metadata:

```xml
<?xml version="1.0" encoding="UTF-8"?>
<beans xmlns="http://www.springframework.org/schema/beans"
  xmlns:xsi="http://www.w3.org/2001/XMLSchema-instance"
  xsi:schemaLocation="http://www.springframework.org/schema/beans
  http://www.springframework.org/schema/beans/spring-beans.xsd">

  <!-- All the bean configuration goes here -->
  <bean id="..." class="...">

  </bean>

  <!-- more bean definitions go here -->

</beans>
```

The id attribute is a string that you use to identify the individual bean definition. The class attribute defines the type of bean, and uses the fully qualified class name. The value of the id attribute refers to collaborating objects.

What are Spring beans?

You can consider a **Spring bean** as a simple Java object, instantiated, configured, and managed by a Spring IoC container. It is called a bean instead of an object or component because it is a replacement for complex and heavy enterprise JavaBeans with respect to the origin of the framework. We will learn more about Spring bean instantiation methods in Chapter 2, *Spring Best Practices and Bean Wiring Configurations*.

Instantiating a Spring container

For creating bean instances, we first need to instantiate a Spring IoC container by reading the configuration metadata. After initialization of an IoC container, we can get the bean instances using the bean name or ID.

Spring provides two types of IoC container implementations:

- BeanFactory
- ApplicationContext

BeanFactory

The BeanFactory container acts as the simplest container providing basic support for DI, and it is defined by the org.springframework.beans.factory.BeanFactory interface. BeanFactory is responsible to source, configure, and assemble the dependencies between objects. BeanFactory mainly acts as an object pool, where object creation and destruction is managed through configuration. The most popular and useful implementation of BeanFactory is the org.springframework.context.support.ClassPathXmlApplicationContext. The ClassPathXmlApplicationContext uses XML configuration metadata to create a fully configured application.

The following sample defines a simple `HelloWorld` application
using `ClassPathXmlApplicationContext`. The content of `Beans.xml` looks as follows:

```xml
<?xml version="1.0" encoding="UTF-8"?>
<beans xmlns="http://www.springframework.org/schema/beans"
  xmlns:xsi="http://www.w3.org/2001/XMLSchema-instance"
  xsi:schemaLocation="http://www.springframework.org/schema/beans
  http://www.springframework.org/schema/beans/spring-beans.xsd">

  <bean id="bankAccount"
    class="com.packt.springhighperformance.ch1.bankingapp.BankAccount">
    <property name="accountType" value="Savings Bank Account" />
  </bean>
</beans>
```

The preceding XML code represents the content of `bean` XML configuration. It has a single
`bean` configured, which has a single property with the `name` message. It has a default
`value` set for the property.

Now, the following Java class represents `bean` configured in the preceding XML.

Let's have a look at `HelloWorld.java`:

```java
package com.packt.springhighperformance.ch1.bankingapp;

public class BankAccount {
  private String accountType;

  public void setAccountType(String accountType) {
    this.accountType = accountType;
  }

  public String getAccountType() {
    return this.accountType;
  }
}
```

At the end, we need to use `ClassPathXmlApplicationContext` to create the
`HelloWorld` bean and invoke a method in the created Spring bean.

`Main.java` looks as follows:

```
package com.packt.springhighperformance.ch1.bankingapp;

import org.apache.log4j.Logger;
import org.springframework.beans.factory.BeanFactory;
import org.springframework.context.
support.ClassPathXmlApplicationContext;

public class Main {

  private static final Logger LOGGER = Logger.getLogger(Main.class);

  @SuppressWarnings("resource")
  public static void main(String[] args) {
    BeanFactory beanFactory = new
    ClassPathXmlApplicationContext("Beans.xml");
    BankAccount obj = (BankAccount) beanFactory.getBean("bankAccount");
    LOGGER.info(obj.getAccountType());
  }
}
```

ApplicationContext

The `ApplicationContext` container provides support to access application components using `BeanFactory` methods. This includes all functionality of `BeanFactory`. In addition, `ApplicationContext` can also perform more enterprise functionalities, like transaction, AOP, resolving text messages from properties files, and pushing application events to interested listeners. It also has the ability to publish events to the registered listeners.

The mostly-used implementations of `ApplicationContext` are `FileSystemXmlApplicationContext`, `ClassPathXmlApplicationContext`, and `AnnotationConfigApplicationContext`.

Spring also provides us with a web-aware implementation of the `ApplicationContext` interface, as shown:

- `XmlWebApplicationContext`
- `AnnotationConfigWebApplicationContext`

We can use either one of these implementations to load beans into a `BeanFactory`; it depends upon our application configuration file locations. For example, if we want to load our configuration file `Beans.xml` from the filesystem in a specific location, we can use a `FileSystemXmlApplicationContext` class that looks for the configuration file `Beans.xml` in a specific location within the filesystem:

```
ApplicationContext context = new
FileSystemXmlApplicationContext("E:/Spring/Beans.xml");
```

If we want to load our configuration file `Beans.xml` from the classpath of our application, we can use `ClassPathXmlApplicationContext` class provided by Spring. This class looks for the configuration file `Beans.xml` anywhere in the classpath, including JAR files:

```
ApplicationContext context = new
ClassPathXmlApplicationContext("Beans.xml");
```

If you are using a Java configuration instead of an XML configuration, you can use `AnnotationConfigApplicationContext`:

```
ApplicationContext context = new
AnnotationConfigApplicationContext(AppConfig.class);
```

After loading the configuration files and getting an `ApplicationContext`, we can fetch beans from the Spring container by calling the `getBean()` method of the `ApplicationContext`:

```
BankAccountService bankAccountService =
context.getBean(BankAccountService.class);
```

In the following section, we will learn about the Spring bean life cycle, and how a Spring container reacts to the Spring bean to create and manage it.

Spring bean life cycle

The factory method design pattern is used by the Spring `ApplicationContext` to create Spring beans in the container in the correct order, as per the given configuration. So, the Spring container is responsible for managing the life cycle of the bean, from creation to destruction. In a normal Java application, a `new` keyword of Java is used to instantiate the bean, and it's ready to use. Once the bean is no longer in use, it's eligible for garbage collection. But in a Spring container, the life cycle of the bean is more elaborate.

The following diagram illustrates the life cycle of a typical Spring bean:

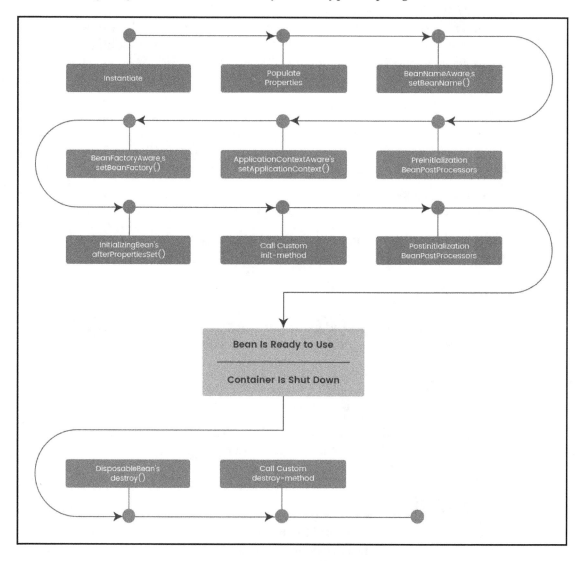

Spring bean life cycle

In the next section, we will see the new features of the Spring Framework 5.0.

New features in the Spring Framework 5.0

The **Spring Framework 5.0** is the first major upgrade in the Spring Framework, almost four years after the Spring Framework 4.0. In this time frame, one of the major developments has been the evolution of the Spring Boot project. We will discuss the new features in Spring Boot 2.0 in the next section. One of the biggest features of the Spring Framework 5.0 is **reactive programming**.

Core reactive programming features and support for reactive endpoints are available out of the box with the Spring Framework 5.0. The list of important changes includes the following:

- Baseline upgrades
- Reactive programming support
- Core features upgrades
- Spring Web MVC upgrades
- Spring's new functional web framework, **WebFlux**
- Modularity support
- Kotlin language support
- Improved testing support
- Dropped or deprecated features

We will discuss these changes in detail in the following sections.

Baseline upgrades

The entire Spring Framework 5.0 has a JDK 8 and Jakarta EE 7 baseline. Basically, it means that to work on the Spring Framework 5.0, Java 8 is the minimum requirement.

Some of the important baseline Jakarta EE 7 specifications for the Spring Framework 5.0 are as follows:

- The code base of the Spring Framework 5.0 is based on Java 8 source code level now. So, the code readability is improved using inferred generics, lambdas, and so on. It also has the stability in the code for conditional support for Java 8 features.
- The Spring Framework requires at least Jakarta EE 7 API level to run any of the Spring Framework 5.0 applications. It requires Servlet 3.1, Bean Validation 1.1, JPA 2.1, and JMS 2.0.

- The development and deployment process is fully compatible with JDK 9 as follows:
    - Compatible with classpath and module path, with stable automatic module names
    - The Spring Framework's build and test suite also pass on JDK 9, and by default, it can be run on JDK 8

Reactive programming support

The reactive programming model stands out among the most exciting feature of Spring 5.0. The Spring 5.0 Framework is based on a reactive foundation and is completely asynchronous and non-blocking. The new event-loop execution model can scale vertically using few threads.

The framework procures reactive streams to provide a system for conveying **backpressure** in a pipeline of reactive components. Backpressure is an idea that guarantees consumers do not get overpowered with data originating from different producers.

While Java 8 does not have built-in support for reactive programming, there are a number of frameworks that provide support for reactive programming:

- **Reactive Streams**: Language-neutral attempt to define reactive APIs
- **Reactor**: Java implementation of Reactive Streams provided by the Spring Pivotal team
- **Spring WebFlux**: Enables the development of web applications based on reactive programming; provides a programming model similar to Spring MVC

Core features upgrades

As a part of the new features introduced in Java 8, the core of the Spring Framework 5.0 has been revised to provide some of the following key features:

- Java 8 reflection enhancements include a provision of accessing method parameters in the Spring Framework 5.0 efficiently.
- Provision of selective declaration support of Java 8 default methods in Spring Core interfaces.

- Supports `@Nullable` and `@NotNull` annotations to explicitly mark nullable arguments and return values. This eliminates the cause of `NullPointerExceptions` at runtime and enables us to deal with null values at compile time.

For the logging side, the Spring Framework 5.0 provides out-of-the-box support with the Commons Logging Bridge module, named `spring-jcl` instead of the standard Commons Logging. Also, this new version will be able to detect Log4j 2.x, the **Simple Logging Facade for Java (SLF4J)**, **JUL** (short for `java.util.logging`), without any extra amendments.

It also supports `Resource` abstraction by providing the `isFile` indicator for the `getFile` method.

Spring Web MVC upgrades

Spring 5.0 fully supports the Servlet 3.1 signature in Spring-provided `Filter` implementations. It also provides support for the Servlet 4.0 `PushBuilder` argument in Spring MVC controller methods.

Spring 5.0 also provides unified support for common media types through the `MediaTypeFactory` delegate, including the use of the Java Activation Framework.

The new `ParsingPathMatcher` will act as an alternative to `AntPathMatcher`, with more efficient parsing and extended syntax.

Spring 5.0 will also be providing support for `ResponseStatusException` as a programmatic alternative to `@ResponseStatus`.

Spring's new functional web framework – WebFlux

Another exciting feature to support reactive HTTP and WebSocket clients, the Spring Framework 5.0 provides the `spring-webflux` module. The Spring Framework 5.0 also provides support for REST, HTML, and WebSocket-style interactions for reactive web applications running on servers.

In `spring-webflux`, there are two major programming models on the server side:

- Support for `@Controller` annotation including other Spring MVC annotations
- Provision for functional style routing and handling with Java 8 Lambda

Spring `spring-webflux` also provides support for creating `WebClient`, which is reactive and non-blocking, as an alternative to `RestTemplate`.

Modularity support

The modular framework is trending on the Java platform. From Java 9, the Java platform became modular, and that helps to remove the flaws in encapsulation.

There are certain problems resulted to have modularity support, as explained here:

- Java platform size: Since the last couple of decades, there was no need to add modularity support in Java. But there are many new lightweight platforms available on the market, like the **Internet of Things** (**IoT**), and Node.js. So, it was an urgent need to reduce the size of JDK version, because initial versions of JDK were less than 10 MB in size, whereas recent versions need more than 200 MB.
- `ClassLoader` difficulty: When the Java `ClassLoader` searches for the classes, it will pick the class definition that is around itself, and immediately load the first class available. So, if there is the same class available in different JARs, then it is not possible for `ClassLoader` to specify the JAR from which the class is to be loaded.

To make Java applications modular, **Open System Gateway initiative (OSGi)** is one of the initiatives to bring modularity into the Java platform. In OSGi, each module is denoted as a **bundle**. Each bundle has its own life cycle, with different states as installed, started, and stopped.

The **Jigsaw** project is a primary motivation under the **Java Community Process** (**JCP**), to bring modularity into Java. Its main purpose is to define and implement a modular structure for JDK and to define a module system for Java applications.

Kotlin language support

The Spring Framework 5.0 introduces a statically typed JVM language support the **Kotlin language** (https://kotlinlang.org/), which enables code that is short, readable, and expressive. Kotlin is basically an object-oriented language that runs on top of the JVM, and also supports functional programming style.

With Kotlin support, we can dive into functional Spring programming, especially for functional web endpoints and bean registration.

In Spring Framework 5.0, we can write clean and readable Kotlin code for web-functional APIs as follows:

```
{
    ("/bank" and accept(TEXT_HTML)).nest {
        GET("/", bankHandler::findAllView)
        GET("/{customer}", bankHandler::findOneView)
    }
    ("/api/account" and accept(APPLICATION_JSON)).nest {
        GET("/", accountApiHandler::findAll)
        GET("/{id}", accountApiHandler::findOne)
    }
}
```

With the Spring 5.0 version, Kotlin's null-safety support is also provided with the indicating annotations using `@NonNull`, `@Nullable`, `@NonNullApi`, and `@NonNullFields` from the `org.springframework.lang` package.

There are some newly added Kotlin extensions that basically add function extensions to the existing Spring APIs. For example, the extension `fun <T : Any> BeanFactory.getBean(): T` from the package `org.springframework.beans.factory` adds the support in `org.springframework.beans.factory.BeanFactory` for searching a bean by just specifying the bean type as Kotlin's reified type parameter without class argument:

```
@Autowired
lateinit var beanFactory : BeanFactory

@PostConstruct
fun init() {
 val bankRepository = beanFactory.getBean<BankRepository>()

}
```

One more extension can be found in `org.springframework.ui`, which provides operator overloading support to add an array-like getter and setter to the `model` interface:

```
model["customerType"] = "Premium"
```

Improved testing support

On the testing front, the Spring Framework 5.0 likewise accompanies JUnit Jupiter (`https:/ /junit.org/junit5/docs/current/user-guide/`). It helps in writing tests and extensions in JUnit 5. It also gives a test engine to run Jupiter-constructed tests with respect to Spring and also provides a programming and extension model.

The Spring Framework 5.0 additionally underpins parallel test execution in the Spring `TestContext` Framework. For Spring WebFlux, `spring-test` likewise incorporates bolster for `WebTestClient` to integrate testing support for the reactive programming model.

There is no compelling reason to run a server for testing scenarios. By utilizing a new `WebTestClient`, which is like `MockMvc`, `WebTestClient` can bind specifically to the WebFlux server infrastructure using a mock request and response.

Dropped or deprecated features

In Spring 5.0, there are some of the packages that have been either removed or deprecated at the API level. The `mock.staticmock` package of the `spring-aspects` module is no longer available. The `BeanFactoryLocator` is also not available along with the `bean.factory.access` package. The `NativeJdbcExtractor` is also no longer available along with the `jdbc.support.nativejdbc` package. The packages `web.view.tiles2`, `orm.hibernate3`, and `orm.hibernate4` are also replaced with Tiles 3 and Hibernate 5.

Many other bundles like JasperReports, Portlet, Velocity, JDO, Guava, XMLBeans are no longer supported in Spring 5. If you are utilizing any of the preceding bundles, it is advised to remain on the Spring Framework 4.3.x.

Summary

In this chapter, we gained a clear understanding of the core features of the Spring Framework. We also covered different kinds of Spring modules. After that, we went through different types of Spring projects in the Spring Framework. We also understood the mechanisms of a Spring IoC container. At the end of the chapter, we looked at the new features and enhancements introduced in Spring 5.0.

In the next chapter, we will understand the concept of DI in detail. We will also cover the different types of configurations using DI, including performance assessment. And finally, we will go through the pitfalls of DI.

2
Spring Best Practices and Bean Wiring Configurations

In the previous chapter, we learned how Spring Framework implements the **Inversion of Control (IoC)** principle. Spring IoC is the mechanism to achieve loose coupling between object dependencies. A Spring IoC container is the program that injects dependencies into an object and makes it ready for our use. Spring IoC is also known as dependency injection. In Spring, the objects of your application are managed by the Spring IoC container and are also known as **beans**. A bean is an object that is instantiated, assembled, and managed by a Spring IoC container. So, a Spring container is responsible for creating the beans in your application and coordinating the relationships between those objects via dependency injection. But, it is the developer's responsibility to tell Spring which beans to create and how to configure them together. When it comes to conveying a bean wiring configuration, Spring is very flexible, offering different writing configurations.

In this chapter, we first start exploring different bean wiring configurations. This includes a configuration with Java, XML, and annotations, and also learning different best practices of bean wiring configuration. We will also understand the performance assessment with different configurations, as well as dependency injection pitfalls.

This chapter will cover the following topics:

- Dependency injection configurations
- Performance assessment with different configurations
- Dependency injection pitfalls

Dependency injection configurations

In any application, objects collaborate with other objects to perform some useful task. This relationship between one object and another in any application creates a dependency, and such dependencies between objects create tight-coupled programming in the application. Spring provides us with a mechanism to convert tight-coupled programming to loosely-coupled programming. This mechanism is called **dependency injection (DI)**. DI is a concept or design pattern that describes how to create loosely-coupled classes where objects are designed in a manner where they receive instances of the objects from other pieces of code, instead of constructing them internally. This means that objects are given their dependencies at runtime, rather than compile time. So, with DI, we can get a decoupled structure that offers us simplified testing, greater reusability, and improved maintainability.

In the following section, we will learn about different types of DI configurations, which you can use in any of the configurations in your application, as per business requirement.

Types of DI patterns

In Spring, the following types of DI are performed:

- Constructor-based DI
- Setter-based DI
- Field-based DI

We will learn more about these in the next sections.

Constructor-based DI

Constructor-based DI is a design pattern to resolve the dependencies of a dependent object. In a constructor-based DI, a constructor is used to inject a dependent object. It is accomplished when the container invokes a constructor with a number of arguments.

Let's look at the following example for a constructor-based DI. In the following code, we show how to use a constructor for injecting a `CustomerService` object in a `BankingService` class:

```
@Component
public class BankingService {

    private CustomerService customerService;
```

```
// Constructor based Dependency Injection
@Autowired
public BankingService(CustomerService customerService) {
  this.customerService = customerService;
}

public void showCustomerAccountBalance() {
  customerService.showCustomerAccountBalance();
}

}
```

The following is the content of another dependent class file, `CustomerServiceImpl.java`:

```
public class CustomerServiceImpl implements CustomerService {

  @Override
  public void showCustomerAccountBalance() {
    System.out.println("This is call customer services");
  }
}
```

The content for the `CustomerService.java` interface is as follows:

```
public interface CustomerService {
  public void showCustomerAccountBalance();
}
```

Advantages of the constructor-based DI

The following are the advantages of a constructor-based DI in your Spring application:

- It's suitable for mandatory dependencies. In a constructor-based DI, you can be sure that the object is ready to be used the moment it is constructed.
- The code structure is very compact and clear to understand.
- When you need an immutable object then, through constructor-based dependency, you can ensure you get the immutable nature of the object.

Disadvantages of the constructor-based DI

The only disadvantage of the constructor-based injection is that it may cause **circular dependency** between objects. Circular dependency means two objects depend on each other. For resolving that, we should use a setter injection instead of a constructor injection.

Let's see a different type of DI in Spring, which is a setter-based injection.

Setter-based DI

In a constructor-based DI, we saw a dependent object injecting through a constructor argument. In a setter-based DI, the dependent object is provided by a setter method in the dependent class. Setter-based DI is accomplished by calling setter methods on beans after invoking `no-args` constructors through the container.

In the following code, we show how to use a setter method for injecting a `CustomerService` object in the `BankingService` class:

```
@Component
public class BankingService {

  private CustomerService customerService;

  // Setter-based Dependency Injection
  @Autowired
  public void setCustomerService(CustomerService customerService) {
  this.customerService = customerService;
  }

  public void showCustomerAccountBalance() {
    customerService.showCustomerAccountBalance();
  }

}
```

Advantages of the setter-based DI

The following are the advantages of the setter-based DI in your Spring application:

- It's more readable than the constructor injection.
- This is useful for non-mandatory dependencies.
- It solves the circular dependency problem in the application.
- It helps us to inject the dependency only when it is required.
- It's possible to reinject dependencies. It is not possible in a constructor-based injection.

Disadvantages of the setter-based DI

Although the setter-based DI has higher priority than the constructor-based DI, the following are the disadvantages of the former:

- There is no guarantee in a setter-based DI that the dependency will be injected.
- One can use a setter-based DI to override another dependency. This can cause security issues in a Spring application.

Field-based DI

In the preceding sections, we saw how we can use constructor-based and setter-based dependencies in our application. In the following example, we will see field-based DI. Actually, field-based DI is easy to use, and it has clean code compared to the other two types of injection method; however, it has several serious trade-offs, and should generally be avoided.

Let's look at the following example of a field-based DI. In the following code, we will see how to use a field for injecting a `CustomerService` object in the `BankingService` class:

```
@Component
public class BankingService {

  //Field based Dependency Injection
  @Autowired
  private CustomerService customerService;

  public void showCustomerAccountBalance() {
    customerService.showCustomerAccountBalance();
  }

}
```

As we discussed, this type of DI has the benefit of removing clutter code over setter-or constructor-based dependencies, but it has many drawbacks, such as dependencies are invisible from the outside. In constructor-based and setter-based dependencies, classes clearly expose these dependencies using the `public` interface or setter method. In a field-based DI, the class is inherently hiding the dependencies from the outside world. Another difficulty is that field injection cannot be used to assign dependencies to final/immutable fields, as these fields must be instantiated at class instantiation.

Generally, Spring discourages the use of the field-based dependency.

Here is a diagram with the different types of DI that we have learned about so far:

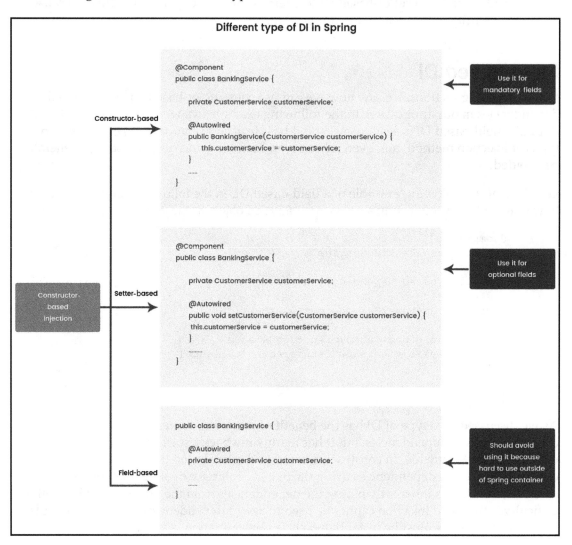

Constructor versus setter injection

As we can see, Spring supports three types of DI methods; however, field-based dependency is not recommended by Spring. So, constructor-based and setter-based DI are standard ways to injecting beans in your application. The selection of constructor or setter methods depends on your application requirements. In this table, we will see the different use cases of constructor and setter injection, and some best practices that will help us decide when to use setter injection over constructor injection, and vice versa:

Constructor injection	Setter injection
Best choice when the dependency is mandatory.	The suitable choice when the dependency is not mandatory.
Constructor injection makes the bean class object immutable.	Setter injection makes the bean class object mutable.
Constructor injection cannot override setter injected values.	Setter injection overrides the constructor injection when we use both constructor and setter injection for the same property.
Partial dependencies are not possible with constructor injection because we must pass all the arguments in the constructor, otherwise, it gives an error.	Partial dependency is possible with setter injection. Suppose we have three dependencies, such as `int`, `string`, and `long`, then with the help of a setter injection, we can inject only the required dependency; other dependencies will be taken as a default value of those primitives.
Creates a circular dependency between objects.	Resolves circular dependency issue in your application. In case of circular dependency, it is better to use a setter instead of constructor injection.

Configuring the DI with Spring

In this section, we will learn different types of processes to configure the DI. The following diagram is a high-level view of how the configuration process works in Spring:

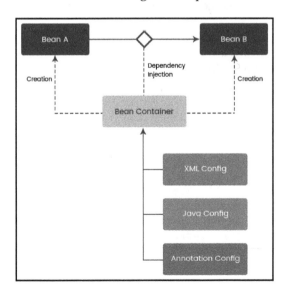

As per the preceding diagram, the Spring container is responsible for creating the bean in your application and building relationships between those beans via the DI pattern; however, as we discussed earlier, it's the developer's responsibility to tell the Spring container, through the metadata, how to create beans and how to wire them together.

The following are three techniques to configure the metadata of your application:

- XML-based configuration: An explicit configuration
- Java-based configuration: An explicit configuration
- Annotation-based configuration: An implicit configuration

In Spring Framework, the preceding three types of configuration mechanisms are available, but you must use one of the configuration processes to wire your bean. In the next section, we will see each of the configuration techniques in detail with examples, and also see which technique in each situation or condition is more suitable than others; however, you can use any technique or approach that suits you best.

Let's now see the DI pattern with an XML-based configuration in detail.

XML-based configuration

The **XML-based configuration** has been the primary configuration technique since Spring started. In this section, we will see the same example as we discussed in the DI pattern, and see how the `CustomerService` object is injected in the `BankingService` class through an XML-based configuration.

For an XML-based configuration, we need to create an `applicationContext.xml` file with a `<beans>` element. The Spring container must be able to manage one or more beans in the application. Beans are described using the `<bean>` element inside a top-level `<beans>` element.

Following is the `applicationContext.xml` file:

```xml
<?xml version="1.0" encoding="UTF-8"?>
<beans xmlns="http://www.springframework.org/schema/beans"
    xmlns:xsi="http://www.w3.org/2001/XMLSchema-instance"
    xmlns:context="http://www.springframework.org/schema/context"
    xsi:schemaLocation="http://www.springframework.org/schema/beans
    http://www.springframework.org/schema/beans/spring-beans.xsd">
    <!-- Bean Configuration definition describe here -->
    <bean class=""/>
</beans>
```

The preceding XML file is the basic structure of XML-based configuration metadata where we need to define our bean configuration. As we learned earlier, our bean configuration pattern may be constructor-based or setter-based, depending on the application requirement. Now, we will see how we can configure a bean using both design patterns, one by one.

The following is the example of a constructor-based DI with an XML-based configuration:

```xml
<!-- CustomerServiceImpl Bean -->
<bean id="customerService"
class="com.packt.springhighperformance.ch2.bankingapp.service.Impl.Cust
omerServiceImpl" />

<!-- Inject customerService via constructor argument -->
<bean id="bankingService"
class="com.packt.springhighperformance.ch2.bankingapp.model.BankingServ
ice">
<constructor-arg ref="customerService" />
</bean>
```

In the previous example, we have injected the CustomerService object in the BankingServices class with a constructor DI pattern. The ref attribute of the </constructor-arg> element is used to pass the reference of the CustomerServiceImpl object.

The following is the example of a setter-based DI with an XML-based configuration:

```xml
<!-- CustomerServiceImpl Bean -->
<bean id="customerService"
class="com.packt.springhighperformance.ch2.bankingapp.service.Impl.Cust
omerServiceImpl" />

<!-- Inject customerService via setter method -->
<bean id="bankingService"
class="com.packt.springhighperformance.ch2.bankingapp.model.BankingServ
ice">
<property name="customerService"
ref="customerService"></property></bean>
```

The `ref` attribute of the `</property>` element is used to pass the reference of the `CustomerServiceImpl` object to the setter method.

The following is the content of the `MainApp.java` file:

```
public class MainApp {

public static void main(String[] args) {
    @SuppressWarnings("resource")
    ApplicationContext context = new
    ClassPathXmlApplicationContext("applicationContext.xml");
    BankingService bankingService =
    context.getBean("bankingService",
    BankingService.class);
    bankingService.showCustomerAccountBalance();
  }
}
```

Java-based configuration

In the previous section, we saw how to configure a bean using XML-based configuration. In this section, we will see the Java-based configuration. The same as XML, Java-based configuration also injects dependency explicitly. The following example defines the Spring bean and its dependencies:

```
@Configuration
public class AppConfig {
  @Bean
  public CustomerService showCustomerAccountBalance() {
    return new CustomerService();
  }
  @Bean
  public BankingService getBankingService() {
    return new BankingService();
  }
}
```

In the Java-based configuration, we must annotate the class with `@Configuration`, and the declaration of the bean can be achieved with the `@Bean` annotation. The previous example of a Java-based configuration is equivalent to an XML-based configuration, as per the following code:

```
<beans>
<bean id="customerService"
class="com.packt.springhighperformance.ch2.bankingapp.service.Impl.Cust
```

```
omerServiceImpl" />

<bean id="bankingService"
class="com.packt.springhighperformance.ch2.bankingapp.model.BankingServ
ice/">
</beans>
```

The previous `AppConfig` class is annotated with the `@Configuration` annotation, which describes that it is a configuration class of the application that contains the details on bean definitions. The method is annotated with the `@Bean` annotation to describe that it is responsible for instantiating, configuring, and initializing a new bean is to be managed by the Spring IoC container. In the Spring container, each bean has a unique ID. Whichever method is annotated with `@Bean` then, by default, that method name will be the bean ID; however, you can also override that default behavior using the `name` attribute of the `@Bean` annotation, as follows:

```
@Bean(name="myBean")
  public CustomerService showCustomerAccountBalance() {
    return new CustomerService();
  }
```

The Spring application context will load the `AppConfig` file and create beans for the application.

The following is the `MainApp.java` file:

```
public class MainApp {

  public static void main(String[] args) {
    AnnotationConfigApplicationContext context = new
    AnnotationConfigApplicationContext(AppConfig.class);
    BankingService bankingService =
    context.getBean(BankingService.class);
    bankingService.showCustomerAccountBalance();
    context.close();
  }
}
```

Annotation-based configuration

In the previous section, we saw the two bean configuration techniques, Java-based and XML-based. Both the techniques inject dependency explicitly. In Java-based, we use the `@Bean` annotated method in the `AppConfig` Java file whereas, in XML-based, we use the `<bean>` element tag in the XML configuration file. **Annotation-based configuration** is another way of creating a bean, where we can move the bean configuration into the component class itself using annotations on the relevant class, method, or field declaration. Here, we will look at how we can configure a bean through annotation, and the different annotations available in Spring Framework.

Annotation-based configuration is turned off by default in Spring, so first, you have to turn it on by entering the `<context:annotation-config/>` element into the Spring XML file shown as follows. After adding it, you are ready to use annotations in your code.

The changes required to be made in `applicationContext.xml` (as we have used it the earlier section) are highlighted as follows:

```
<?xml version="1.0" encoding="UTF-8"?>
<beans xmlns="http://www.springframework.org/schema/beans"
xmlns:xsi="http://www.w3.org/2001/XMLSchema-instance"
xmlns:context="http://www.springframework.org/schema/context"
xsi:schemaLocation="http://www.springframework.org/schema/beans
http://www.springframework.org/schema/beans/spring-beans.xsd
http://www.springframework.org/schema/context
http://www.springframework.org/schema/context/spring-context.xsd">

<!-- Enable Annotation based configuration -->
<context:annotation-config />
<context:component-scan base-
package="com.packt.springhighperformance.ch2.bankingapp.model"/><contex
t:component-scan base-
package="com.packt.springhighperformance.ch2.bankingapp.service"/>
<!-- Bean Configuration definition describe here -->
<bean class=""/>
</beans>
```

 An XML-based configuration will override annotations because an XML-based configuration will be injected after annotations.

The previous XML-based configuration shows that once you configure the
`<context:annotation-config/>` element, it indicates start of annotating your code.
Spring should automatically scan the package defined in `<context:component-scan
base-package=".." />` and identify beans and wire them based on the pattern. Let's
understand a few of the important annotations, and how they work.

The @Autowired annotation

The `@Autowired` annotation injects object dependency implicitly. We can use the
`@Autowired` annotation on a constructor-setter-and-field-based dependency pattern. The
`@Autowired` annotation indicates that auto wiring should be performed for this bean.

Let's look at an example of using the `@Autowired` annotation on a constructor-based
dependency:

```
public class BankingService {

    private CustomerService customerService;
    @Autowired
    public BankingService(CustomerService customerService) {
        this.customerService = customerService;
    }
    ......
}
```

In the previous example, we have `BankingService` that has a dependency
of `CustomerService`. Its constructor is annotated with `@Autowired`, indicating that
Spring instantiates the `BankingService` bean using an annotated constructor and passes
the `CustomerService` bean as a dependency of the `BankingService` bean.

 Since Spring 4.3, the `@Autowired` annotation became optional on classes
with a single constructor. In the preceding example, Spring would still
inject an instance of the `CustomerService` class if you skipped the
`@Autowired` annotation.

Let's look at an example of using the `@Autowired` annotation on a setter-based
dependency:

```
public class BankingService {
    private CustomerService customerService;
    @Autowired
    public void setCustomerService(CustomerService customerService) {
```

```
        this.customerService = customerService;
    }
    . . . . . .
}
```

In the previous example, we saw that the setter method setCustomerService is annotated with the @Autowired annotation. Here, the annotation resolves the dependency by type. The @Autowire annotation can be used on any traditional setter method.

Let's look at an example of using the @Autowired annotation on a field-based dependency:

```
public class BankingService {
    @Autowired
    private CustomerService customerService;

}
```

As per the preceding example, we can see that the @Autowire annotation can be added on public and private properties as well. Spring uses the reflection API to inject the dependencies when added on the property, and that is the reason private properties can also be annotated.

@Autowired with required = false

By default, the @Autowired annotation implies that the dependency is required. This means an exception will be thrown when a dependency is not resolved. You can override that default behavior using the (required=false) option with @Autowired. Let's see the following code:

```
public class BankingService {
    private CustomerService customerService;
    @Autowired (required=false)
    public void setCustomerService(CustomerService customerService) {
        this.customerService = customerService;
    }
    . . . . . .
}
```

In the previous code, if we set the required value as false, then at the time of bean wiring, Spring will leave the bean unwired if the dependency is not resolved. As per Spring's best practices, we should avoid setting required as false until it is absolutely required.

The @Primary annotation

By default, in Spring Framework, DI is done by type, which means that when there are multiple dependencies with the same type, the `NoUniqueBeanDefinitionException` exception will be thrown. It indicates that the Spring container is unable to select a bean for DI because of more than one eligible candidate. In that case, we can use the `@Primary` annotation and take control of the selection process. Let's see the following code:

```
public interface CustomerService {
  public void customerService();
}

@Component
public class AccountService implements CustomerService {
    ....
}
@Component
@Primary
public class BankingService implements CustomerService {
    ....
}
```

In the case of the previous example, there are two customer services available: `BankingService` and `AccountService`. Due to the `@Primary` annotation, components can only use `BankingService` to wire dependencies on `CustomerService`.

The @Qualifier annotation

Handling multiple autowire candidates with `@Primary` is more effective when only one primary candidate can be determined for multiple autowire candidates. The `@Qualifier` annotation gives you more control over the selection process. It allows you to give a reference associated with a specific bean type. That reference can be used to qualify the dependency that needs to be autowired. Let's look at the following code:

```
@Component
public class AccountService implements CustomerService {

}
@Component
@Qualifier("BankingService")
public class BankingService implements CustomerService {

}

@Component
```

```
public class SomeService {
  private CustomerService customerService;

  @Autowired
  @Qualifier("bankingservice")
  public BankingService(CustomerService customerService) {
    this.customerService = customerService;
  }
  .....
}
```

In the previous example, there are two customer services available: `BankingService` and `AccountService`; however, due to `@Qualifier("bankingservice")` being used in the `SomeService` class, `BankingService` will be selected for auto wiring.

Automatic bean detection with stereotype annotations

In the previous section, we learned about the `@Autowired` annotation that handles only wiring. You still have to define the beans themselves so the container is aware of them and can inject them for you. Spring Framework provides us with some special annotations. These annotations are used to create Spring beans automatically in the application context. So, there is no need to configure the bean explicitly either using XML-based or Java-based configuration.

The following are the stereotype annotations in Spring:

- `@Component`
- `@Service`
- `@Repository`
- `@Controller`

Let's look at the following `CustomerService` implementation class. Its implementation is annotated with `@Component`. Please refer to the following code:

```
@Component
public class CustomerServiceImpl implements CustomerService {

  @Override
  public void customerService() {
    System.out.println("This is call customer services");

  }

}
```

In the previous code, the `CustomerServiceImpl` class is annotated with the `@Component` annotation. This means the class that is marked with the `@Component` annotation is considered the bean, and the component-scanning mechanism of Spring scans that class, creates a bean of this class, and pulls it into the application context. So, no need to configure that class explicitly as the bean is either using XML or Java. Spring automatically creates the bean of the `CustomerServiceImpl` class because it is annotated with `@Component`.

In Spring, `@Service`, `@Repository`, and `@Controller` are meta annotations for the `@Component` annotation. Technically, all annotations are the same and provide the same result, such as creating a bean in Spring context; but we should use more specific annotations at different layers of the application because it specifies the intent better, and additional behavior might rely on it in the future.

The following diagram describes the stereotype annotation with an appropriate layer:

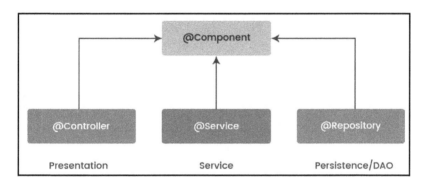

As per the previous example, `@Component` is good enough to create a bean of `CustomerService`. But `CustomerService` is a service layer class, so as per bean configuration best practices, we should use `@Services` instead of the generic annotation `@Component`. Let's look at the following code for the same class annotated with the `@Service` annotation:

```
@Service
public class CustomerServiceImpl implements CustomerService {

  @Override
  public void customerService() {
    System.out.println("This is call customer services");
  }

}
```

Let's see another example of the `@Repository` annotation:

```
@Repository
public class JdbcCustomerRepository implements CustomerRepository {

}
```

In the previous example, the class is annotated with the `@Repository` annotation because the `CustomerRepository` interface is working at the **Data Access Object** (**DAO**) layer of the application. As per bean configuration best practices, we have used the `@Repository` annotation instead of the `@Component` annotation.

 In a real-life scenario, you might face very rare situations where you will need to use the `@Component` annotation. Mostly, you will be using the `@Controller`, `@Service`, and `@Repository` annotations. `@Component` should be used when your class does not fall into either of three categories: service, controller, DAO.

The @ComponentScan annotation

Spring needs to know which packages contain Spring beans, otherwise, you would have to register each bean individually. That's what `@ComponentScan` is used for. In Spring, component scanning is not enabled by default. We need to enable it with the `@ComponentScan` annotation. This annotation is used with the `@Configuration` annotation to allow Spring to know the packages to scan for annotated components and to create beans from them. Let's look at the following simple example of `@ComponentScan`:

```
@Configuration
@ComponentScan(basePackages="com.packt.springhighperformance.ch2.bankin
gapp.model")
public class AppConfig {

}
```

In the `@ComponentScan` annotation, if the `basePackages` attribute is not defined, then scanning will occur from the package of the class that declares this annotation. In the preceding example, Spring will scan all classes of `com.packt.springhighperformance.ch2.bankingapp.model`, and the subpackage of that package. The `basePackages` attribute can accept an array of strings, which means that we can define multiple base packages to scan component classes in the application. Let's look at an example of how we can declare multiple packages in the `basePackage` attribute:

```
@Configuration
```

```
@ComponentScan(basePackages={"com.packt.springhighperformance.ch2.banki
ngapp.model","com.packt.springhighperformance.ch2.bankingapp.service"})
public class AppConfig {
}
```

The @Lazy annotation

By default, all autowired dependencies are created and initialized at startup, meaning the Spring IoC container creates all beans at the time of application startup; however, we can control this pre-initialization of beans at startup by using the `@Lazy` annotation.

The `@Lazy` annotation may be used on any class directly or indirectly annotated with `@Component`, or on methods annotated with `@Bean`. When we use the `@Lazy` annotation, that means the bean will be created and initialized only when it is first requested.

We know that annotation requires less code because we don't need to write the code to inject the dependency explicitly. It helps us reduce the development time, as well. Though annotation offers lots of advantages, it has its drawback, as well.

Disadvantages of annotation are as follows:

- Less documentation than explicit wiring
- If we have a lot of dependency in a program, then it's hard to find it by using the `autowire` attribute of bean
- Annotation makes the process of debugging hard
- It might give unexpected results in case of ambiguity
- Annotation can be overridden by explicit configuration, such as Java or XML

Spring bean scopes

In the previous section, we learned various DI patterns, and saw how to create beans in a Spring container. We also learned various DI configuration such as XML, Java, and annotation. In this section, we will learn more details about bean life and scope available in a Spring container. The Spring container allows us to control the bean at configuration level. This is a very flexible way to define object scope at configuration level, instead of at the Java-class level. In Spring, the bean is controlled through the `scope` attribute that defines what kind of object has to be created and returned. When you describe `<bean>`, you have the option of defining `scope` for that bean. The bean `scope` describes the life cycle and visibility of that bean in the context of where it used. In this section, we will see the different types of bean `scope` in Spring Framework.

Here is an example of defining bean `scope` at XML-based configuration:

```xml
<?xml version="1.0" encoding="UTF-8"?>
<beans xmlns="http://www.springframework.org/schema/beans"
xmlns:xsi="http://www.w3.org/2001/XMLSchema-instance"
xsi:schemaLocation="http://www.springframework.org/schema/beans
http://www.springframework.org/schema/beans/spring-beans.xsd">
<!-- Here scope is not defined, it assume default value 'singleton'.
    It creates only one instance per spring IOC. -->
<bean id="customerService"
class="com.packt.springhighperformance.ch2.bankingapp.service.Impl.Cust
omerServiceImpl" />
<!-- Here scope is prototype, it creates and returns bankingService
object for  every call-->
<bean id="bankingService"
class="com.packt.springhighperformance.ch2.bankingapp.model.BankingServ
ice" scope="prototype">

<bean id="accountService"
class="com.packt.springhighperformance.ch2.bankingapp.model.AccountServ
ice" scope="singleton">
</beans>
```

Here is an example of defining bean `scope` using the `@Scope` annotation:

```java
@Configuration
public class AppConfig {
  @Bean
  @Scope("singleton")
  public CustomerService showCustomerAccountBalance() {
    return new CustomerServiceImpl();

  }
}
```

We can also use a constant instead of the string value in the following manner:

```java
@Scope(value = ConfigurableBeanFactory.SCOPE_SINGLETON)
@Scope(value = ConfigurableBeanFactory.SCOPE_PROTOTYPE)
```

Following are bean scopes available in Spring Framework:

- The `singleton` bean `scope`: As we saw in the previous example of bean configuration in XML-based, if `scope` is not defined in the configuration, then the Spring container considers `scope` as `singleton`. The Spring IoC container creates exactly only one single instance of the object, even if there are multiple references to a bean. Spring stores all `singleton` bean instances in a cache, and all subsequent requests of that named bean return the cached object. This is needed to understand that the Spring bean `singleton scope` is a little different from the typical `singleton` design pattern that we are using in Java. In Spring `singleton`, `scope` creates one object of that bean per one Spring container, meaning if there are multiple Spring containers in single JVM then multiple instances of that bean will be created.
- The `prototype` bean `scope`: When `scope` is set to `prototype`, the Spring IoC container creates a new bean instance of object every time a bean is requested. Prototype-scoped beans are mostly used for stateful beans.

 As a rule, use `prototype` scope for all stateful beans, and the `singleton` scope for stateless beans.

- The `request` bean `scope`: The `request` bean `scope` is only available in a web-aware application context. The `request scope` creates a bean instance for each HTTP request. The bean is discarded as soon as the request processing is done.
- The `session` bean `scope`: The `session` bean `scope` is only available in a web-aware application context. The `session scope` creates a bean instance for every HTTP session.
- The `application` bean `scope`: The `application` bean `scope` is only available in a web-aware application context. The `application scope` creates a bean instance per web application.

Performance assessment with different configurations

In this section, we will learn how different types of bean configuration impact application performance, and also we will see the best practices of bean configuration.

Let's see how the `@ComponentScan` annotation configuration impacts the startup time of a Spring application:

```
@ComponentScan (( {{ "org", "com" }} ))
```

As per the preceding configuration, Spring will scan all the packages of `com` and `org` and, because of that, the startup time of the application will be increased. So, we should scan only those packages that have annotated classes, as non-annotated classes will take time to scan. We should use only one `@ComponentScan` and list all packages, as shown here:

```
@ComponentScan(basePackages={"com.packt.springhighperformance.ch2.banki
ngapp.model","com.packt.springhighperformance.ch2.bankingapp.service"})
```

The preceding configuration is considered as a best practice of defining the `@ComponentScan` annotation. We should specify which of those packages as `basePackage` attribute have annotated classes. It will reduce the startup time of the application.

Lazy loading versus preloading

Lazy loading ensures that beans are loaded on the fly when requested, and **preloading** ensures the beans are loaded before they are used. The Spring IoC container uses preloading by default. So, loading all classes at the start even if they're not used would not be a wise decision because some Java instances would be highly resource-consuming. We should use the required methodology based on the application requirement.

If we need to load our application as fast as possible, then go for lazy loading. If we need our application to run as fast as possible and serve a client request faster, then go for preloading.

Singleton versus prototype bean

In Spring, by default, all beans defined are `singleton`; however, we can change the default behavior and make our bean `prototype`. When the bean `scope` is set to `prototype`, the Spring IoC container creates a new bean instance of an object every time a bean is requested. Prototype beans incur a hit on performance during creation, so when a `prototype` bean uses resources, such as network and database connection, it should be avoided completely; alternatively, design the action carefully.

Spring bean configuration best practices

In this section, we will see some of the best practices for configuring a bean in Spring:

- Use ID as bean identifiers:

```xml
<?xml version="1.0" encoding="UTF-8"?>
<beans xmlns="http://www.springframework.org/schema/beans"
xmlns:xsi="http://www.w3.org/2001/XMLSchema-instance"
xsi:schemaLocation="http://www.springframework.org/schema/beans
http://www.springframework.org/schema/beans/spring-beans.xsd">
    <!-- Bean Configuration definition describe here -->
    <bean id="xxx" name="xxx" class=""/>
</beans>
```

  In the preceding example, we identified the bean using id or name. We should use id to pick the bean instead of name. Usually, it does neither increase readability nor benefit any performance but it's just an industry standard practice which we need to follow.

- Prefer type over index for constructor argument matching. The constructor argument with index attribute is shown as follows:

```xml
<constructor-arg index="0" value="abc"/>
<constructor-arg index="1" value="100"/>
```

- The constructor argument with the type attribute is shown as follows:

```xml
<constructor-arg type="java.lang.String"
value="abc"/>
<constructor-arg type="int" value="100"/>
```

  As per the previous example, we can use index or type as a constructor argument. It is better to use the type attribute instead of index in a constructor argument because it is more readable and less error-prone. But sometimes, type-based arguments might create an ambiguity problem when a constructor has more than one argument of the same type. In that case, we need to use index or a name-based argument.

- Use dependency check at the development phase: In bean definition, we should use the dependency-check attribute. It ensures that the container performs explicit dependency validation. It is useful when all or some of the properties of a bean must be set explicitly, or through auto wiring.

- Do not specify version numbers in Spring schema references: in Spring configuration files, we specify the schema reference for different Spring modules. In schema references, we mention the XML namespace and its version number. Specifying the version number is not mandatory in the configuration file, so you can skip it. In fact, you should skip it all the time. Consider it as a best practice to follow. Spring automatically picks the highest version from the project dependencies (jars). A typical Spring configuration file looks like this:

```xml
<?xml version="1.0" encoding="UTF-8"?>
<beans xmlns="http://www.springframework.org/schema/beans"
xmlns:xsi="http://www.w3.org/2001/XMLSchema-instance"
xsi:schemaLocation="http://www.springframework.org/schema/beans
http://www.springframework.org/schema/beans/spring-beans-3.0.xs
d">
    <!-- Bean Configuration definition describe here -->
    <bean class=""/>
</beans>
```

As per best practices, this can be written like this:

```xml
<?xml version="1.0" encoding="UTF-8"?>
<beans xmlns="http://www.springframework.org/schema/beans"
xmlns:xsi="http://www.w3.org/2001/XMLSchema-instance"
xsi:schemaLocation="http://www.springframework.org/schema/beans
http://www.springframework.org/schema/beans/spring-beans.xsd">
    <!-- Bean Configuration definition describe here -->
    <bean class=""/>
</beans>
```

Add a header comment to each configuration file; it is preferred to add a configuration file header that describes the beans defined in the configuration files. The code of the description tag is as follows:

```xml
<beans>
<description>
This file defines customer service
related beans and it depends on
accountServices.xml, which provides
service bean templates...
</description>
...
</beans>
```

The advantages of the description tag is that some tools may catch up the description from this tag to help you in other places.

DI pitfalls

As we know, there are three DI patterns in the Spring application: constructor-setter-and field-based. Each type has different advantages and disadvantages. Only field-based DI is an incorrect approach and not even recommended by Spring.

Following is an example of a field-based injection:

```
@Autowired
private ABean aBean;
```

As per Spring bean best practices, we should not use field-based dependency in our Spring application. The main reason is that it is impossible to test without Spring context. As we cannot supply the dependency from outside, it will not be possible to instantiate the object independently. As per my opinion, this is the only problem with field-based injections.

As we learned in an earlier section, constructor-based dependency is more suitable for mandatory fields, and we can ensure the immutable nature of the object is obtained; however, the main drawback of a constructor-based dependency is that it creates circular dependency in your application, and as per Spring documentation, *it is generally recommended to not rely on circular dependency between your beans.* So, now we have questions like, *Why not rely on circular dependency?* and *What will happen if we have a circular dependency in our application?* So, the answer to these questions is that it may create two significant and unfortunately silent pitfalls. Let's discuss them.

First pitfall

When you call the `ListableBeanFactory.getBeansOfType()` method, you cannot be sure which beans will be returned. Let's look at the code of the `getBeansOfType()` method in the `DefaultListableBeanFactory.java` class:

```
@Override
@SuppressWarnings("unchecked")
public <T> Map<String, T> getBeansOfType(@Nullable Class<T> type,
boolean includeNonSingletons, boolean allowEagerInit)
    throws BeansException {
    ......
    if (exBeanName != null && isCurrentlyInCreation(exBeanName)) {
      if (this.logger.isDebugEnabled()) {
        this.logger.debug("Ignoring match to currently created bean
        '" +
        exBeanName + "': " +
        ex.getMessage());
```

```
        }
onSuppressedException(ex);
// Ignore: indicates a circular reference when auto wiring
constructors.
// We want to find matches other than the currently created
bean itself.
continue;
      }

      . . . . . .


  }
```

In the preceding code, you can see that the getBeansOfType() method silently skips beans under creation, and only returns those already existing. So, when you have circular dependency between beans, use of the getBeansOfType() method during container startup is not recommended. This is because, as per the preceding code, if you are not using DEBUG or TRACE logging-level, then there will be zero information in your log that Spring skipped a particular bean which is under creation.

Let's see the preceding pitfall with the following example. As per the following diagram, we have three beans, Account, Customer, and Bank, and a circular dependency between them:

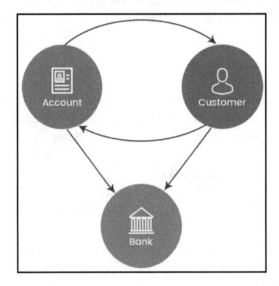

As per the preceding diagram, the following is the `Account`, `Customer`, and `Bank` class:

```
@Component
public class Account {
  private static final Logger LOGGER = Logger.getLogger(Account.class);

  static {
    LOGGER.info("Account | Class loaded");
  }

  @Autowired
  public Account(ListableBeanFactory beanFactory) {
    LOGGER.info("Account | Constructor");
    LOGGER.info("Constructor (Customer?): {}" +
    beanFactory.getBeansOfType(Customer.class).keySet());
    LOGGER.info("Constructor (Bank?): {}" +
    beanFactory.getBeansOfType(Bank.class).keySet());
  }

}

@Component
public class Customer {
  private static final Logger LOGGER =
Logger.getLogger(Customer.class);

  static {
    LOGGER.info("Customer | Class loaded");
  }

  @Autowired
  public Customer(ListableBeanFactory beanFactory) {
    LOGGER.info("Customer | Constructor");
    LOGGER.info("Account (Account?): {}" +
    beanFactory.getBeansOfType(Account.class).keySet());
    LOGGER.info("Constructor (Bank?): {}" +
    beanFactory.getBeansOfType(Bank.class).keySet());
  }

}

@Component
public class Bank {
  private static final Logger LOGGER = Logger.getLogger(Bank.class);

  static {
    LOGGER.info("Bank | Class loaded");
```

```
    }

    public Bank() {
        LOGGER.info("Bank | Constructor");
    }

}
```

Following is the `Main` class:

```
public class MainApp {

    public static void main(String[] args) {
        AnnotationConfigApplicationContext context = new
        AnnotationConfigApplicationContext(AppConfig.class);
        Account account = context.getBean(Account.class);
        context.close();
    }
}
```

Following is the log where we can show how Spring internally loads beans and resolves classes:

```
Account | Class loaded
Account | Constructor
Customer | Class loaded
Customer | Constructor
Account (Account?): {}[]
Bank | Class loaded
Bank | Constructor
Constructor (Bank?): {}[bank]
Constructor (Customer?): {}[customer]
Constructor (Bank?): {}[bank]
```

Spring Framework first loads `Account` and tries to instantiate a bean; however, when running `getBeansOfType(Customer.class)`, it discovers `Customer`, so proceeds with loading and instantiating that one. Inside `Customer`, we can immediately spot the problem: when `Customer` asks for `beanFactory.getBeansOfType(Account.class)`, it gets no results (`[]`). Spring will silently ignore `Account` because it's currently under creation. You can see here that after `Bank` is loaded, everything is as expected.

Here now we can understand that, we cannot predict the output of the `getBeansOfType()` method when we have a circular dependency. However, we can avoid it with using DI properly. In circular dependency, `getBeansOfType()` gives different results, based on factors and we have no any control over it.

Second pitfall (with AOP)

We will learn AOP in detail in the following chapter. Right now, we are not covering this pitfall in detail. I just want you to understand that if you have `Aspect` on a bean, then make sure there is no circular dependency between beans; otherwise, Spring will create two instances of that bean, one without `Aspect` and the other with a proper aspect, without informing you.

Summary

In this chapter, we learned about DI, which is the key feature of Spring Framework. DI helps us to make our code loosely coupled and testable. We learned various DI patterns, including constructor-setter-and field-based. We can use any of the DI patterns in our application based on our requirement, as each type has its own advantages and disadvantages.

We also learned how we can configure DI explicitly and implicitly. We can inject dependency explicitly with the use of XML-based and Java-based configuration. Annotation is used to inject dependency implicitly. Spring provides us with a special type of annotation called **stereotype annotation**. Spring will automatically register the class which annotated with stereotypes annotation. This makes the class available for DI in other classes and this become vital to building out our applications.

In the next chapter, we will be looking at the Spring AOP module. AOP is a powerful programming model that helps us to implement the reusable code.

3
Tuning Aspect-Oriented Programming

In the previous chapter, we took a deep dive into one of Spring's key features: dependency injection (IoC container). DI is an enterprise design pattern, that makes an object loosely-coupled from its required dependencies. We learned about Spring's bean wiring configuration and best practices to follow to achieve optimal results.

Moving further in line with Spring's core features, in this chapter, we will discuss **Aspect-Oriented Programming** (**AOP**). We've already learned that DI promotes programming to the interface and the decoupling of the application's objects, whereas AOP helps to achieve the decoupling of business logic and crosscutting concerns. A **crosscutting concern** is a concern applicable to part of the application or the entire application, for example, security, logging, and caching, which are required in almost every module of the application. AOP and AspectJ help to achieve these crosscutting concerns. In this chapter, we will go through the following topics:

- AOP concepts
- AOP proxies
- Spring AOP method for profiling
- AOP versus AspectJ comparison
- AOP best programming practices

AOP concepts

In this section, we will look at what problems we have to face if we use only the **object-oriented programming** (**OOP**) paradigm. Then we will understand how AOP solves those problems. We will walk through the concepts of AOP and ways to implement AOP concepts.

Limitations of OOP

With the help of OOP fundamentals and design patterns, application development was divided into groups of functionalities. OOP protocols made many things easy and useful, such as introducing an interface with which we can implement loosely-coupled designs, encapsulation with which we can hide object data, and inheritance-extending functionalities, by classes, with which we can reuse work.

These advantages of OOP also add complexity as the system grows. With added complexities, the cost to maintain it and the chances of failure increase. To solve this, modularizing functionalities into simpler and more manageable modules helps reduce complexity.

To modularize a system, we started following a practice of dividing applications into different logical layers, for example, presentation layer, service layer, and data layer. However, even after dividing the functionalities into different layers, there are certain functionalities that are required in all layers, for example, security, logging, caching, and performance monitoring. These functionalities are called crosscutting concerns.

If we implement these crosscutting concerns using inheritance, it will violate the single responsibility of the SOLID principle and increase the object hierarchy. And if we implement them using composition, it will be more complicated. So the implementation of crosscutting concerns using OOP leads to two problems:

- Code tangling
- Code scattering

Let's discuss these problems more.

Code tangling

Code tangling means mixing crosscutting concerns and business logic, which in turn leads to tight coupling. Let's look at the following diagram to understand code tangling:

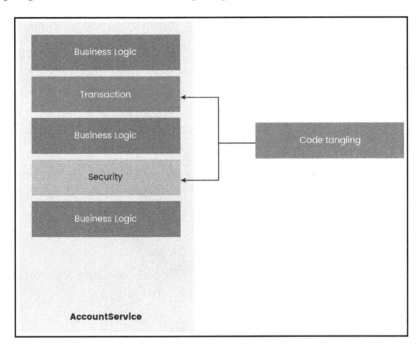

Code tangling

The preceding diagram illustrates how we mix transactions and security code along with our business logic in our service implementation. With such implementation, code reusability is reduced, maintenance is degraded, and the single responsibility principle is violated.

Code scattering

Code scattering means crosscutting concerns are duplicated across all modules of an application. Let's look at the following example to understand code scattering:

```
public class TransferServiceImpl implements TransferService {
    public void transfer(Account source, Account dest, Double amount) {
        //permission check
        if (!hasPermission(user) {
```

```
            throw new AuthorizationException();
        }
    }
}

public class AccountServiceImpl implements AccountService {
    public void withdraw(Account userAccount, Double amount) {
        //Permission check
        if (!hasPermission(user) {
            throw new AuthorizationException();
        }
    }
}
```

As we saw in preceding code sample, the permission check (security) is our crosscutting concern that is duplicated in all services.

These code tangling and code scattering problems are solved by AOP, but how? We will see shortly.

AOP – problem solver

We have seen in the preceding section that with OOP, code tangling and scattering occurs. With AOP, we can achieve the following objectives/benefits:

- Modularizing crosscutting concerns
- Decoupling of modules
- Removing crosscutting concerns regarding module dependency

Spring AOP allows us to keep our crosscutting concerns logic separate from our business logic so we can focus on our application's main logic. To help us perform this separation, Spring provides Aspects, a normal class where we would implement our crosscutting concerns logic. Spring provides ways to inject these Aspects into the right place in our application without mixing them with business logic. We will see more about Aspects, how to implement it, and how to apply it in the following sections.

This diagram illustrates Spring AOP:

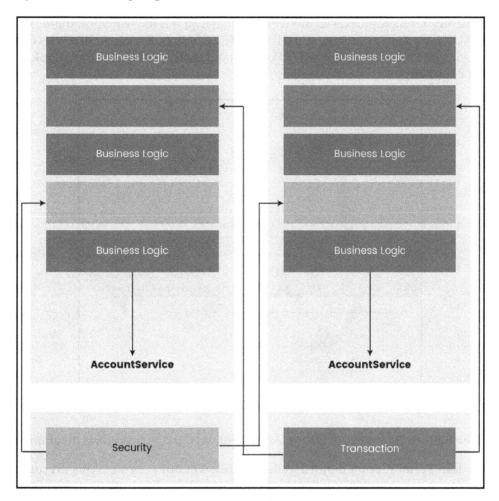

How AOP solves code tangling

Spring AOP terminology and concepts

AOP, like every technology, has its own terminologies. It has its own vocabulary. Spring uses the AOP paradigm in its Spring AOP module. However, Spring AOP has its own terminologies that are Spring-specific. To understand Spring AOP terms, let's look at the following diagram:

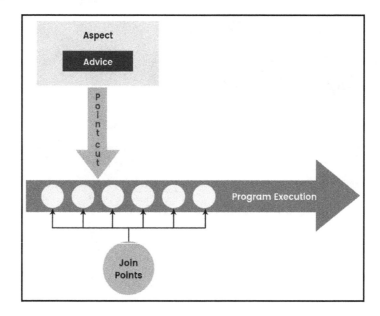

Spring AOP terminologies and concepts

Let's understand each concept of Spring AOP mentioned in the preceding diagram:

- **Join Point:** A point defined in the execution of our program. This execution could be method invocation, exception handling, class initialization, or object instantiation. Spring AOP supports method invocation only. In case we want a join point for anything other than method invocation, we can use Spring and AspectJ together. We will walk through AspectJ later in this chapter.
- **Advice**: A definition of what exactly needs to be done at the join point. Different types of advice are `@Before`, `@After`, `@Around`, `@AfterThrowing`, and `@AfterReturning`. We will see them in action in the *Types of advice* section.

- **Pointcut**: A collection of join point used to define an advice that has to be executed. An advice is not necessarily applied to all join points, so pointcut gives fine-grained control over an advice that is to be executed on components in our application. Pointcuts are defined using an expression and Spring uses the AspectJ pointcut expression language. We will shortly see how this is done.
- **Aspect**: The combination of advice and pointcuts that defines logic in an application and where it should execute. Aspect is implemented using the regular class annotated with the `@Aspect` annotation. This annotation is from Spring AspectJ support.

That's too much theory, isn't it? Now, let's dive into how to apply these Spring AOP concepts in real programming. You might have implemented these AOP concepts in your projects; however, did you know the background of why it was needed? No, so now you know why we need Spring AOP.

 Since Spring 2.0, AOP implementation is made simpler using the AspectJ pointcut language defined either in the schema-based approach (XML) or annotations. We will discuss Spring 2.0 AspectJ support with annotations further in this chapter.

Defining pointcuts

As we learned before, pointcuts define a point where advice should be applied. Spring AOP uses AspectJ's expression language to define a point where advice should be applied. The following are the set of pointcut designators supported in Spring AOP:

Designator	Description
`execution`	It restricts matching to join points by a method execution.
`within`	It restricts matching to join points within certain types only. Example: `within(com.packt.springhighperformance.ch3.TransferService)`.
`args`	It restricts matching to join points where arguments are of the given type. Example: `args(account,..)`.
`this`	It restricts matching to join points where the bean reference or Spring proxy object is an instance of the given type. Example: `this(com.packt.springhighperformance.ch3.TransferService)`.
`target`	It restricts matching to join points where the target object is an instance of the given type. Example: `target(com.packt.springhighperformance.ch3.TransferService)`.
`@within`	It restrict matching to join points where the declared type has the given type of annotation. Example: `@within(org.springframework.transaction.annotation.Transactional)`.
`@target`	It restricts matching to join points where the target object has the given type of annotation. Example: `@target(org.springframework.transaction.annotation.Transactional)`.

`@args`	It restricts matching to join points where the type of the actual arguments passed have annotations of the given type. Example: `@args(com.packt.springhighperformance.ch3.Lockable)`.
`@annotation`	It restricts matching to join points where the executing method has the given annotation. Example: `@annotation(org.springframework.transaction.annotation.Transactional)`.

Let's see how to write the point expression using the `execution` designator:

- Using `execution(<method-pattern>)`: Method matching to the pattern would be advised. The following is the method pattern:

  ```
  [Modifiers] ReturnType [ClassType]
  MethodName ([Arguments]) [throws ExceptionType]
  ```

- To create composite pointcuts by joining other pointcuts, we can use the `&&`, `||`, and `!` operators (these mean AND, OR, and NOT, respectively).

In the preceding method pattern, anything defined in `[ ]` is optional. Values without `[ ]` are mandatory to define.

The following diagram will illustrate point expression using the `execution` designator to apply advice whenever the `findAccountById()` method is executed:

Execution join point pattern

Types of advice

In the preceding section, we learned different terminologies of AOP and how to define the pointcut expression. In this section, we will learn about the different types of advice in Spring AOP:

- `@Before`: This advice is executed before the join point and it is defined in `aspect` using the `@Before` annotation. The declaration is shown in the following code:

  ```
  @Pointcut("execution(*
  ```

```
com.packt.springhighperformance.ch03.bankingapp.service.TransferSer
vice.transfer(..))")
public void transfer() {}

@Before("transfer()")
public void beforeTransfer(JoinPoint joinPoint){
  LOGGGER.info("validate account balance before transferring
amount");
}
```

If the @Before method throws an exception, the transfer target method would not get called. This is a valid use of @Before advice.

- @After: This advice is executed after the join point (method) exits/returns either normally or with any exception. To declare this advice, use the @After annotation. The declaration is shown in the following code:

  ```
  @Pointcut("execution(*
  com.packt.springhighperformance.ch03.bankingapp.service.TransferSer
  vice.transfer(..))")
  public void transfer() {}

  @After("transfer()")
  public void afterTransfer(JoinPoint joinPoint){
    LOGGGER.info("Successfully transferred from source account to
  dest
    account.");
  }
  ```

- @AfterReturning: As we know in @After advice, the advice is executed in any case where the join point exits normally or with an exception. Now, if we want to run an advice only after a matched method returns normally, then what? Then we need @AfterReturning. Sometimes we need to perform some operation based on the value returned by the method. In those cases, we can use the @AfterReturning annotation. The declaration is shown in the following code:

  ```
  @Pointcut("execution(*
  com.packt.springhighperformance.ch03.bankingapp.service.TransferSer
  vice.transfer(..))")
  public void transfer() {}

  @AfterReturning(pointcut="transfer() and args(source, dest,
  amount)", returning="isTransferSuccessful" )
  ```

```
public void afterTransferReturns(JoinPoint joinPoint, Account
source, Account dest, Double amount, boolean isTransferSuccessful){
  if(isTransferSuccessful){
    LOGGGER.info("Amount transferred successfully ");
    //find remaining balance of source account
  }
}
```

- **@AfterThrowing**: This advice is called when an exception is thrown by a matched method in an expression. This is useful when we want to take some action when any particular type of exception is thrown or we want to track method execution to correct errors. It is declared using the @AfterThrowing annotation, as shown in the following code:

```
@Pointcut("execution(*
com.packt.springhighperformance.ch03.bankingapp.service.TransferSer
vice.transfer(..))")
public void transfer() {}

@AfterThrowing(pointcut = "transfer()", throwing =
"minimumAmountException")
public void exceptionFromTransfer(JoinPoint joinPoint,
MinimumAmountException minimumAmountException) {
  LOGGGER.info("Exception thrown from transfer method: " +
  minimumAmountException.getMessage());
}
```

Similar to @AfterThrowing returning attribute, the throwing attribute in the @AfterThrowing advice must match the name of the parameter in the advice method. The throwing attribute restricts matching to those method executions that throws an exception of the specified type.

- **@Around**: The last and final advice that is applied around the matched method. This means that it is a combination of the @Before and @After advice we saw earlier. However, the @Around advice is more powerful than @Before and @After combined. It is powerful because it can decide whether to proceed to the join point method or return its own value or throw an exception. The @Around advice can be used with the @Around annotation. The first parameter of the advice method in @Around advice should be ProceedingJoinPoint. The following is the code sample of how to use the @Around advice:

```
@Pointcut("execution(*
com.packt.springhighperformance.ch03.bankingapp.service.TransferSer
vice.transfer(..))")
public void transfer() {}
```

```
@Around("transfer()")
public boolean aroundTransfer(ProceedingJoinPoint
proceedingJoinPoint){
  LOGGER.info("Inside Around advice, before calling transfer method
");
  boolean isTransferSuccessful = false;
  try {
    isTransferSuccessful = (Boolean)proceedingJoinPoint.proceed();
  } catch (Throwable e) {
    LOGGER.error(e.getMessage(), e);
  }
  LOGGER.info("Inside Around advice, after returning from transfer
method");
  return isTransferSuccessful;
}
```

We can invoke `proceed` once, many times, or not at all within the body of the `@Around` advice.

Aspect instantiation models

By default, the declared `aspect` is `singleton`, so there will be only one instance of our `aspect` per class loader (and not per JVM). The instance of our `aspect` will be destroyed only when the class loader is garbage.

If we need to have our `aspect` with private attributes hold data relative to class instances, the `aspect` needs to be stateful. To do so, Spring with its AspectJ support provides a way using `perthis` and `pertarget` instantiation models. AspectJ is an independent library, and has other instantiation models in addition to `perthis` and `pertarget`, such as `percflow`, `percflowbelow`, and `pertypewithin`, which are not supported in Spring's AspectJ support.

To create a stateful `aspect` using `perthis`, we need to declare `perthis` as follows in our `@Aspect` declaration:

```
@Aspect("perthis(com.packt.springhighperformance.ch03.bankingapp.servic
e.TransferService.transfer())")
public class TransferAspect {
//Add your per instance attributes holding private data
//Define your advice methods
}
```

Once we declare our @Aspect with the perthis clause, one aspect instance will be created for each unique TransferService object executing the transfer method (each unique object that is bound to this at join points matched by the pointcut expression). The instance of aspect goes out of scope when the TransferService object goes out of scope.

pertarget works the same as perthis; however, in pertarget, it creates one aspect instance per unique target object at join points matched by the pointcut expression.

Now you might be wondering how Spring would have applied advice without making calls from the business logic classes to the crosscutting concern class (Aspects). So the answer is, Spring does this using the proxy pattern. It weaves your Aspects to the target objects by creating proxied objects. Let's look at the Spring AOP proxy in detail in the next section.

AOP proxies

It is the proxy pattern that made Spring AOP able to decouple crosscutting concerns from the core application's business logic or functionalities. The proxy pattern is a structural design pattern included in a book by the **Gang of Four** (**GoF**). In practice, the proxy pattern creates different object wrapping out of an original object without changing the behavior of the original object to allow intercepting its method call, and the outside world would feel they are interacting with the original object and not a proxy.

JDK dynamic proxies and CGLIB proxies

The proxy in Spring AOP can be created in two ways:

- JDK proxy (dynamic proxy): The JDK proxy creates a new proxy object by implementing interfaces of the target object and delegating method calls
- CGLIB proxy: The CGLIB proxy creates a new proxy object by extending the target object and delegating method calls

Let's look at these proxy mechanisms and how they differ in the following table:

JDK proxy	CGLIB proxy
It is built in JDK.	It is a custom-developed library.
JDK proxy works on the interface.	CGLIB proxy works on subclassing. This is used when the interface is not present.
It will proxy all interfaces.	It cannot work when the method and class are final.

From Spring 3.2, the CGLIB library is packaged with Spring Core, so there's no need to include this library separately in our application. From Spring 4.0, the constructor of the proxied object will not be called twice, as the CGLIB proxy instance will be created via Objenesis.

By default, Spring will try to use the JDK dynamic proxy if the class of the target object implements the interface; if the class of the target object does not implement any interface then Spring will create a proxy using the CGLIB library.

If the class of the target object implements an interface and it is injected as a concrete class in another bean, then Spring will throw an exception: `NoSuchBeanDefinitionException`. The solution to this problem is either to inject through the interface (which is a best practice) or to annotate the injection with `Scope(proxyMode=ScopedProxyMode.TARGET_CLASS)`. Then Spring will create a proxy object using the CGLIB proxy. This configuration disables Spring's use of JDK proxies. Spring will then always extend concrete classes, even if an interface is injected. The CGLIB proxy uses the decorator pattern to weave advice to the target object by creating a proxy:

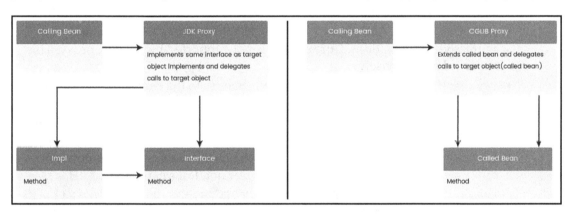

JDK dynamic proxy and CGLIB proxy

Creating a proxy would be able to delegate all calls to a method to interceptors (advice). However, once a method call reaches the target object, any internal method call made within that target object is not going to be intercepted. So, any method call within the object reference would not result in any advice execution. In order to solve this, either refactor the code so that direct self-invocation doesn't happen or use AspectJ weaving. To solve this in Spring, we need to set the expose a proxy property to true and use `AopContext.currentProxy()` to make self-invocation.

Spring recommends using the JDK proxy wherever possible. Hence, try to implement the abstraction layer almost everywhere in your application so that the JDK proxy will be applied when the interface is available and we have not explicitly set it to use the CGLIB proxy only.

ProxyFactoryBean

Spring provides a classic way of creating proxies of objects manually using `ProxyFactoryBean`, which will create an AOP proxy wrapping the target object. `ProxyFactoryBean` provides a way to set advice and advisors that are eventually merged into an AOP proxy. The key properties inherited from the `org.springframework.aop.framework.ProxyConfig` superclass for all AOP proxy factories in Spring are as follows:

- `proxyTargetClass`: If it's true, then the proxy is created using CGLIB only. If it's not set, the proxy will be created using the JDK proxy if the target class implements the interface; otherwise, the proxy will be created using CGLIB.
- `optimize`: For the CGLIB proxy, this instructs the proxy to apply some aggressive optimizations. Currently, it is not supported by the JDK proxy. This needs to be used wisely.
- `frozen`: If a proxy is set as `frozen`, then changes to the configuration are not allowed. This is useful when we don't want callers to modify the proxy after the proxy has been created. This is used for optimization. The default value of this property is `false`.
- `exposeProxy`: Setting this property to true determines whether the current proxy should be exposed to `ThreadLocal` or not. If it's exposed to `ThreadLocal`, then the target can use the `AopContext.currentProxy()` method for self-invocation of the method.

ProxyFactoryBean in action

We will define a regular Spring bean as target bean, say `TransferService`, and then, using `ProxyFactoryBean`, we will create a proxy that will be accessed by our application. To advice the `transfer` method of `TransferService`, we will set the point expression using `AspectJExpressionPointcut` and we will create the interceptor, which we will set into `DefaultPointcutAdvisor` to create the advisor.

The target object or bean is as follows:

```java
public class TransferServiceImpl implements TransferService {
  private static final Logger LOGGER =
  Logger.getLogger(TransferServiceImpl.class);

  @Override
  public boolean transfer(Account source, Account dest, Double amount)
{
    // transfer amount from source account to dest account
    LOGGER.info("Transferring " + amount + " from " +
    source.getAccountName() + "
    to " +   dest.getAccountName());
    ((TransferService)
    (AopContext.currentProxy())).checkBalance(source);
    return true;
  }

  @Override
  public double checkBalance(Account a) {
    return 0;
  }
}
```

The following code is for the method interceptor or advice:

```java
public class TransferInterceptor implements MethodBeforeAdvice{

   private static final Logger LOGGER =
   Logger.getLogger(TransferInterceptor.class);

  @Override
  public void before(Method arg0, Object[] arg1, Object arg2) throws
  Throwable {
     LOGGER.info("transfer intercepted");
  }
}
```

The Spring configuration is as follows:

```java
@Configuration
public class ProxyFactoryBeanConfig {
  @Bean
  public Advisor transferServiceAdvisor() {
      AspectJExpressionPointcut pointcut = new
      AspectJExpressionPointcut();
      pointcut.setExpression("execution(*
      com.packt.springhighperformance.ch03.bankingapp.service
```

```
        .TransferService.checkBalance(..))");
        return new DefaultPointcutAdvisor(pointcut, new
        TransferInterceptor());
    }
    @Bean
    public ProxyFactoryBean transferService(){
      ProxyFactoryBean proxyFactoryBean = new ProxyFactoryBean();
      proxyFactoryBean.setTarget(new TransferServiceImpl());
      proxyFactoryBean.addAdvisor(transferServiceAdvisor());
      proxyFactoryBean.setExposeProxy(true);
      return proxyFactoryBean;
    }
}
```

In the preceding code samples, we have not separately defined TransferService as
Spring bean. We have created an anonymous bean of TransferService and then created
its proxy using ProxyFactoryBean. This has an advantage that there will be only one
object of the TransferService type and no one can obtain an unadvised object. This also
reduces ambiguity if we want to wire this bean to any other bean using the Spring IoC.

With ProxyFactoryBean, we can configure AOP proxies that provide all flexibility of the
programmatic method without needing our application to do AOP configurations.

 It is best to use the declarative method of proxy configuration over the
programmatic method unless we need to perform a manipulative action at
runtime or we want to gain fine-grained control.

Performance JDK dynamic proxy versus CGLIB proxy

We learned what proxies are used for. According to the GoF book, *Design Patterns: Elements
of Reusable Object-Oriented Software*, a proxy is a placeholder for another object to control
access to it. As the proxy lies in between the caller of an object and the real object, it can
decide whether to prevent the invocation of the real (or target) object or perform some
action before the target object is invoked.

Many object-relational mappers use proxy patterns to implement a behavior that prevents
data from being loaded until it is actually needed. Sometimes this is called **lazy loading**.
Spring also uses proxies to develop some of its functionality, such as its transaction
management, security, caching, and the AOP framework.

As proxies objects are an additional object created at runtime, either by JDK proxy or CGLIB library, and sit between the caller object and the target object, it is going to add some overhead to a plain method invocation.

Let's find out how much overhead proxies add to a plain method invocation.

The following snippet shows the Spring Java-based configuration class for the CGLIB proxy:

```
@EnableAspectJAutoProxy
@Configuration
public class CGLIBProxyAppConfig {

  @Bean
  @Scope(proxyMode=ScopedProxyMode.TARGET_CLASS)
  public TransferService transferService(){
    return new TransferServiceImpl();
  }
}
```

The Spring Java-based configuration class for the JDK proxy is as follows:

```
@Configuration
@EnableAspectJAutoProxy
public class JDKProxyAppConfig {

  @Bean
  @Scope(proxyMode=ScopedProxyMode.INTERFACES)
  public TransferService transferService(){
  return new TransferServiceImpl();
  }
}
```

The JUnit class is as follows:

```
public class TestSpringProxyOverhead {
  private static final Logger LOGGER =
  Logger.getLogger(TestSpringProxyOverhead.class);

  @Test
  public void checkProxyPerformance() {
    int countofObjects = 3000;
    TransferServiceImpl[] unproxiedClasses = new
    TransferServiceImpl[countofObjects];
    for (int i = 0; i < countofObjects; i++) {
      unproxiedClasses[i] = new TransferServiceImpl();
    }
```

```
    TransferService[] cglibProxyClasses = new
    TransferService[countofObjects];
    TransferService transferService = null;
    for (int i = 0; i < countofObjects; i++) {
      transferService = new
      AnnotationConfigApplicationContext(CGLIBProxyAppConfig.class)
      .getBean(TransferService.class);
      cglibProxyClasses[i] = transferService;
    }

    TransferService[] jdkProxyClasses = new
    TransferService[countofObjects];
    for (int i = 0; i < countofObjects; i++) {
      transferService = new
      AnnotationConfigApplicationContext(JDKProxyAppConfig.class)
      .getBean(TransferService.class);
      jdkProxyClasses[i] = transferService;
    }

    long timeTookForUnproxiedObjects =
    invokeTargetObjects(countofObjects,
    unproxiedClasses);
    displayResults("Unproxied", timeTookForUnproxiedObjects);

    long timeTookForJdkProxiedObjects =
    invokeTargetObjects(countofObjects,
    jdkProxyClasses);
    displayResults("Proxy", timeTookForJdkProxiedObjects);

    long timeTookForCglibProxiedObjects =
    invokeTargetObjects(countofObjects,
    cglibProxyClasses);
    displayResults("cglib", timeTookForCglibProxiedObjects);

  }

  private void displayResults(String label, long timeTook) {
  LOGGER.info(label + ": " + timeTook + "(ns) " + (timeTook / 1000000)
  + "(ms)");
  }

  private long invokeTargetObjects(int countofObjects,
  TransferService[] classes) {
    long start = System.nanoTime();
    Account source = new Account(123456, "Account1");
    Account dest = new Account(987654, "Account2");
    for (int i = 0; i < countofObjects; i++) {
      classes[i].transfer(source, dest, 100);
```

```
        }
        long end = System.nanoTime();
        long execution = end - start;
        return execution;
    }
}
```

The overhead time varies based on hardware tools, such as CPU and memory. The following is the kind of output we would get:

```
2018-02-06 22:05:01 INFO TestSpringProxyOverhead:52 - Unproxied:
155897(ns) 0(ms)
2018-02-06 22:05:01 INFO TestSpringProxyOverhead:52 - Proxy:
23215161(ns) 23(ms)
2018-02-06 22:05:01 INFO TestSpringProxyOverhead:52 - cglib:
30276077(ns) 30(ms)
```

We can do benchmarking using tools such as Google's Caliper, found at `https://github.com/google/caliper`, or **Java Microbenchmark Harness** (**JMH**), found at `http://openjdk.java.net/projects/code-tools/jmh/`. Many performance tests, using different tools and scenarios, delivered different results. A few tests showed CGLIB is faster than the JDK proxy, and a few got other results. If we test AspectJ, which we'll discuss later in this chapter, performance is still better than the JDK proxy and CGLIB proxy, due to its bytecode-weaving mechanism instead of a proxy object.

The question here is do we really need to worry about the overhead we saw? The answer is both yes and no. We will discuss both these answers.

We don't have to really worry about the overhead because that amount of time the proxy added is negligible and the amount of benefits provided by AOP or the proxy pattern is high. We already saw the benefits of AOP in the preceding sections of this chapter, such as transaction management, security, lazy loading, or anything that is crosscutting but with code simplification, centralized management, or maintenance of code.

Also, we need to worry about the overhead when our application has **Service Level Agreement** (**SLA**) to deliver in milliseconds or our application has a very high volume of concurrent requests or loads. In this case, each millisecond spent is important for our application. However, we still need to use AOP in our application in order to implement crosscutting concerns. So, what we need to take care of here is the right AOP configuration, avoiding the unnecessary scanning of objects for advice, configuring the exact join point to which we want advice, and avoiding the implementation of fine-grained requirements through AOP. For fine-grained requirements user AspectJ (the byte-code-weaving approach).

So the rule of thumb is, use AOP to implement crosscutting concerns and leverage its benefits. However, implement it cautiously, and with the right configurations that do not degrade system performance, by applying advice or proxies to each and every operation.

Caching

In order to improve the performance of an application, caching heavy operations is inevitable. Spring 3.1 added a great abstraction layer called **caching** that helped to abandon all custom-implemented `aspects`, decorators, and code injected into the business logic related to caching.

Spring applies caching to the methods of Spring beans using AOP concepts; we learned about it in the *AOP concepts* section of this chapter. Spring creates proxies of the Spring beans where the methods are annotated to be cached.

In order to leverage the benefits of Spring's caching abstraction layer, just annotate heavy methods with `@Cacheable`. Also, we need to notify our application that methods are cached by annotating our configuration class with `@EnableCaching`. The following is the example of caching a method:

```
@Cacheable("accounts")
public Account findAccountById(int accountId){
```

The `@Cacheable` annotation has the following attributes:

- `value`: Name of cache
- `key`: Caching key for each cached item
- `condition`: Defines whether to apply caching or not based on the evaluation of the **Spring Expression Language (SpEL)** expression
- `unless`: This is another condition written in SpEL, and if it is true, it prevents the return value from being cached

The following are additional annotations provided by Spring related to caching:

- `@CachePut`: It will let the method execute and update the cache
- `@CacheEvict`: It will remove stale data from the cache
- `@Caching`: It allows you to group multiple annotations `@Cacheable`, `@CachePut`, and `@CacheEvict` on the same method
- `@CacheConfig`: It will allow us to annotate our entire class instead of repeating on each method

We can use `@Cacheable` on methods that are retrieving data and use `@CachePut` on a method that performs insertion to update the cache. The code sample is as follows:

```
@Cacheable("accounts" key="#accountId")
public Account findAccountById(int accountId){
@CachePut("accounts" key="#account.accountId")
public Account createAccount(Account account){
```

Annotating methods to cache the data would not store the data; for that, we need to implement or provide `CacheManager`. Spring, by default, provides some cache managers in the `org.springframework.cache` package and one of them is `SimpleCacheManager`. The `CacheManager` code sample is as shown:

```
@Bean
public CacheManager cacheManager() {
   CacheManager cacheManager = new SimpleCacheManager();
   cacheManager.setCaches(Arrays.asList(new
   ConcurrentMapCache("accounts")));
   return cacheManager;
}
```

Spring also provides support to integrate the following third-party cache managers:

- EhCache
- Guava
- Caffeine
- Redis
- Hazelcast
- Your custom cache

AOP method profiling

Applications can have many business methods. Due to some implementation issues, some methods take time and we want to measure how much time is taken by those methods and we may want to analyze method arguments, as well. Spring AOP provides a way to perform method profiling without touching business methods. Let's see how.

PerformanceMonitorInterceptor

Let's see how to perform profiling or monitoring on our method execution. This is done with the help of a simple option provided by Spring AOP using the `PerformanceMonitorInterceptor` class.

As we have learned, Spring AOP allows the defining of crosscutting concerns in applications by intercepting the execution of one or more methods to add extra functionality without touching the core business classes.

The `PerformanceMonitorInterceptor` class from Spring AOP is an interceptor that can be tied to any custom method to be executed at the same time. This class uses a `StopWatch` instance to log the beginning and ending time of the method execution.

Let's monitor the `transfer` method of `TransferService`. The following is the `TransferService` code:

```
public class TransferServiceImpl implements TransferService {

  private static final Logger LOGGER =
  LogManager.getLogger(TransferServiceImpl.class);

  @Override
  public boolean transfer(Account source, Account dest, int amount) {
    // transfer amount from source account to dest account
    LOGGER.info("Transferring " + amount + " from " +
    source.getAccountName() + "
    to " + dest.getAccountName());
    try {
      Thread.sleep(5000);
    } catch (InterruptedException e) {
      LOGGER.error(e);
    }
    return true;
  }
}
```

The following code is `@Pointcut` to monitor the advice method using Spring interceptor:

```
@Aspect
public class TransferMonitoringAspect {
    @Pointcut("execution(*
    com.packt.springhighperformance.ch03.bankingapp.service
    .TransferService.transfer(..))")
    public void transfer() { }
}
```

The following code is the advisor class:

```
public class PerformanceMonitorAdvisor extends DefaultPointcutAdvisor {

private static final long serialVersionUID = -3049371771366224728L;

public PerformanceMonitorAdvisor(PerformanceMonitorInterceptor
performanceMonitorInterceptor) {
AspectJExpressionPointcut pointcut = new AspectJExpressionPointcut();
pointcut.setExpression(
"com.packt.springhighperformance.ch03.bankingapp.aspect.TransferMonito
ringAspect.transfer()");
this.setPointcut(pointcut);
this.setAdvice(performanceMonitorInterceptor);
}
}
```

The following code is the Spring Java configuration class:

```
@EnableAspectJAutoProxy
@Configuration
public class PerformanceInterceptorAppConfig {
  @Bean
  public TransferService transferService() {
    return new TransferServiceImpl();
  }

  @Bean
  public PerformanceMonitorInterceptor performanceMonitorInterceptor()
{
    return new PerformanceMonitorInterceptor(true);
  }
  @Bean
  public TransferMonitoringAspect transferAspect() {
    return new TransferMonitoringAspect();
  }

  @Bean
  public PerformanceMonitorAdvisor performanceMonitorAdvisor() {
    return new
    PerformanceMonitorAdvisor(performanceMonitorInterceptor());
  }
}
```

The expression in pointcut identifies the methods that we want to intercept. We have defined `PerformanceMonitorInterceptor` as a bean and then created `PerformanceMonitorAdvisor` to associate pointcut with the interceptor.

In our `Appconfig`, we have annotated with the `@EnableAspectJAutoProxy` annotation to enable AspectJ support for our beans to create a proxy automatically.

To have `PerformanceMonitorInterceptor` work, we need to set the log level of the target object, `TransferServiceImpl`, to the `TRACE` level as this is the level at which it logs messages.

For every execution of the `transfer` method, we will see the `TRACE` message in the console log:

```
2018-02-07 22:14:53 TRACE TransferServiceImpl:222 - StopWatch
'com.packt.springhighperformance.ch03.bankingapp.service.TransferServic
e.transfer': running time (millis) = 5000
```

Custom monitoring interceptor

`PerformanceMonitorInterceptor` is a very basic and simple way to monitor the execution of our method time. However, most of the time we would need more a controlled way to monitor the method and its parameters. For that, we can implement our custom interceptor, either by extending `AbstractMonitoringInterceptor` or writing around advice or a custom annotation. Here we will write a custom interceptor extending `AbstractMonitoringInterceptor`.

Let's extend the `AbstractMonitoringInterceptor` class and override the `invokeUnderTrace` method to log the `start`, `end`, and duration of a method. We can also log a warning if the method execution lasts more than 5 milliseconds. The following is the code sample for the custom monitoring interceptor:

```
public class CustomPerformanceMonitorInterceptor extends
AbstractMonitoringInterceptor {
    private static final long serialVersionUID = -4060921270422590121L;
    public CustomPerformanceMonitorInterceptor() {
    }

    public CustomPerformanceMonitorInterceptor(boolean
useDynamicLogger) {
        setUseDynamicLogger(useDynamicLogger);
    }
```

```
@Override
protected Object invokeUnderTrace(MethodInvocation invocation, Log
log)
    throws Throwable {
        String name = createInvocationTraceName(invocation);
        long start = System.currentTimeMillis();
        log.info("Method " + name + " execution started at:" + new
        Date());
        try {
            return invocation.proceed();
        }
        finally {
            long end = System.currentTimeMillis();
            long time = end - start;
            log.info("Method "+name+" execution lasted:"+time+" ms");
            log.info("Method "+name+" execution ended at:"+new Date());
            if (time > 5){
                log.warn("Method execution took longer than 5 ms!");
            }
        }
    }
}
```

Every other step we saw in the basic PerformanceMonitorInterceptor would be same,
just replace PerformanceMonitorInterceptor with
CustomPerformanceMonitorInterceptor.

The following output is generated:

```
2018-02-07 22:23:44 INFO TransferServiceImpl:32 - Method
com.packt.springhighperformance.ch03.bankingapp.service.TransferService
.transfer execution lasted:5001 ms
2018-02-07 22:23:44 INFO TransferServiceImpl:33 - Method
com.packt.springhighperformance.ch03.bankingapp.service.TransferService
.transfer execution ended at:Wed Feb 07 22:23:44 EST 2018
2018-02-07 22:23:44 WARN TransferServiceImpl:36 - Method execution took
longer than 5 ms!
```

Spring AOP versus AspectJ

So far, we have seen AOP using proxy patterns and runtime weaving. Now let's look at
AOP at compile time and load time weaving.

What is AspectJ?

As we know from the start of this chapter, AOP is a programming paradigm that helps to decouple our code by separating the implementation of crosscutting concerns. AspectJ is the original implementation of AOP, which implements both concerns and the weaving of crosscutting concerns using extensions of Java programming language.

To enable AspectJ in our project, we need AspectJ libraries and AspectJ provides different libraries based on its usage. One can find all its libraries, at `https://mvnrepository.com/artifact/org.aspectj`.

In AspectJ, `Aspects` will be created in a file with the extension `.aj`. The following is the sample `TransferAspect.aj` file:

```
public aspect TransferAspect {
    pointcut callTransfer(Account acc1, Account acc2, int amount) :
     call(public * TransferService.transfer(..));

    boolean around(Account acc1, Account acc2, int amount) :
      callTransfer(acc1, acc2,amount) {
        if (acc1.balance < amount) {
            return false;
        }
        return proceed(acc1, acc2,amount);
    }
}
```

To enable compile-time weaving, when we have both `aspect` code and code to which we want to weave `aspects`, use the Maven plugin as follows:

```
<plugin>
    <groupId>org.codehaus.mojo</groupId>
    <artifactId>aspectj-maven-plugin</artifactId>
    <version>1.11</version>
    <configuration>
        <complianceLevel>1.8</complianceLevel>
        <source>1.8</source>
        <target>1.8</target>
        <showWeaveInfo>true</showWeaveInfo>
        <verbose>true</verbose>
        <Xlint>ignore</Xlint>
        <encoding>UTF-8 </encoding>
    </configuration>
    <executions>
        <execution>
            <goals>
```

```
            <!-- use this goal to weave all your main classes -->
            <goal>compile</goal>
            <!-- use this goal to weave all your test classes -->
            <goal>test-compile</goal>
        </goals>
    </execution>
  </executions>
</plugin>
```

To perform post-compile time weaving, when we want to weave existing class files and JAR files, use Mojo's AspectJ Maven plugin as follows. The artifact or JAR files we reference to weave must be listed as `<dependencies/>` in the Maven project and listed as `<weaveDependencies/>` in the `<configuration>` of the AspectJ Maven plugin. The following is the Maven sample for how to define weaving dependencies:

```
<configuration>
    <weaveDependencies>
        <weaveDependency>
            <groupId>org.agroup</groupId>
            <artifactId>to-weave</artifactId>
        </weaveDependency>
        <weaveDependency>
            <groupId>org.anothergroup</groupId>
            <artifactId>gen</artifactId>
        </weaveDependency>
    </weaveDependencies>
</configuration>
```

To perform **Load-time weaving (LTW)**, when we want to defer our weaving until the class loader loads a class file, we would need a weaving agent; use the Maven plugin as follows:

```
<plugin>
    <groupId>org.apache.maven.plugins</groupId>
    <artifactId>maven-surefire-plugin</artifactId>
    <version>2.20.1</version>
    <configuration>
        <argLine>
            -javaagent:"${settings.localRepository}"/org/aspectj/
            aspectjweaver/${aspectj.version}/
            aspectjweaver-${aspectj.version}.jar
        </argLine>
        <useSystemClassLoader>true</useSystemClassLoader>
        <forkMode>always</forkMode>
    </configuration>
</plugin>
```

For LTW, it looks for `aop.xml` in the classpath under the `META-INF` folder. The file contains the `aspect` and `weaver` tags as follows:

```
<aspectj>
    <aspects>
        <aspect name="com.packt.springhighperformance.ch3.bankingapp.
        aspectj.TransferAspect"/>
        <weaver options="-verbose -showWeaveInfo">
            <include
            within="com.packt.springhighperformance.ch3.bankingapp
            .service.impl.TransferServiceImpl"/>
        </weaver>
    </aspects>
</aspectj>
```

So this was just an introduction for how to enable AspectJ in our project.

Differences between Spring AOP and AspectJ

Let's look at the differences between Spring AOP (runtime weaving) and AspectJ (compile-time and LTW).

Capabilities and goals

Spring AOP provides a simple AOP implementation to implement crosscutting concerns using the proxy pattern and decorator pattern. It is not considered a complete AOP solution, Spring can be applied to the beans that are managed by a Spring container.

AspectJ is the original AOP technology, aiming to provide a complete AOP solution. It is more robust, however, and more complicated than Spring AOP. The benefit of AspectJ is that it can be applied across all domain objects.

Weaving

Both Spring AOP and AspectJ use the different types of weaving and, based on their weaving mechanism, their behavior regarding performance and ease of use are different.

To perform runtime weaving of our `aspects` during the execution of the application, Spring creates proxies of the targeted object using either the JDK dynamic proxy or CGLIB proxy, which we discussed earlier.

As opposed to Spring AOP's runtime weaving, AspectJ performs weaving at compile-time or classload-time. We already saw different types of AspectJ weaving in the preceding section.

Join points

As Spring AOP creates proxies of target classes or objects to apply crosscutting concerns (Aspects), it needs to perform subclassing of the targeted class or object. As we already know, with subclassing, Spring AOP cannot apply crosscutting concerns on classes or methods that are final or static.

On the other hand, AspectJ weaves crosscutting concerns into the actual code using byte-code weaving and hence it doesn't need to subclass the targeted class or object.

Simplicity

In Spring AOP, the runtime weaving of Aspects will be performed by the container at startup and hence it integrates seamlessly with our building process.

On the other hand, in AspectJ, we have to perform this using an extra compiler (ajc) unless we are doing this post-compilation or in LTW. For this reason, Spring is simpler and more manageable than AspectJ.

With Spring AOP, we cannot use or apply the full power of AOP because Spring AOP is proxy-based and can only be applied to Spring-managed beans.

AspectJ is based on byte-code weaving, meaning it modifies our code and hence it enables us to use the full power of AOP on any bean of our application.

Performance

From a performance point of view, compile-time weaving would be faster than run-time weaving. Spring AOP is a proxy-based framework, so it creates additional objects for proxies at runtime and there are more method invocations per aspect, which affects performance negatively.

On the other hand, AspectJ weaves aspects into the main code before the application starts and hence there's no additional runtime overhead. There are benchmarks available on the internet that say AspectJ is much faster than Spring AOP.

It is not like one framework is better than another. A choice would be made based on the requirements and many different factors, such as overhead, simplicity, manageability/maintainability, complexity, and learning curve. If we are using fewer `aspects` and there is no need to apply `aspect` apart from a Spring bean or method executions, then the performance difference between Spring AOP and AspectJ is trivial. We can use AspectJ and Spring AOP together to achieve our requirements as well.

AspectJ with Spring

Spring provides small libraries to enable AspectJ `aspects` into Spring projects. This library is named `spring-aspects.jar`. As we know from our earlier discussion, Spring allows dependency injection or AOP advice only on Spring bean. With Spring's AspectJ support using this small library, we can enable any object created outside the container for Spring-driven configuration. Just annotate the outside object with `@Configurable`. Annotating a non-Spring bean with `@Configurable` would require `AnnotationBeanConfigurerAspect` in `spring-aspects.jar`. The `AnnotationBeanConfigurerAspect` configuration needed by Spring can be done by annotating our configuration Java configuration class with `@EnableSpringConfigured`.

Spring provides a finer way to enable **Load-time weaving** (LTW) by enabling a per-class loader basis. This gives much more fine-grained control, especially when we are deploying large or multiple applications into a single JVM environment.

To use LTW with Spring, we need to implement our `aspect` or advice as we had implemented earlier in the *AOP concepts* sections and, as per the AspectJ concepts, we need to create `aop.xml` in the `META-INF` folder, as follows:

```
<!DOCTYPE aspectj PUBLIC "-//AspectJ//DTD//EN"
"http://www.eclipse.org/aspectj/dtd/aspectj.dtd">
<aspectj>
    <weaver>
        <!-- only weave classes in our application-specific packages --
>
        <include within="com.packt.springhighperformance.ch3.bankingapp
        .service.impl.TransferServiceImpl"/>
        <include within="com.packt.springhighperformance.ch3.bankingapp
        .aspects.TransferServiceAspect"/>
    </weaver>
    <aspects>
        <!-- weave in just this aspect -->
        <aspect name="com.packt.springhighperformance.ch3.bankingapp
        .aspects.TransferServiceAspect"/>
```

```
    </aspects>
</aspectj>
```

The last thing we need to do is annotate our Java-based Spring configuration with `@EnableLoadTimeWeaving`. We need to add `-javaagent:path/to/org.springframework.instrument-{version}.jar` in our server launch script.

AOP best programming practices

We have learned about why AOP is needed in our application. We learned about its concepts and how to use it in detail. Let's see what best practices should be followed when using AOP in our application.

Pointcut expressions

We learned about pointcut in terms of AOP. Now let's see what we should take care of when using pointcut:

- Spring with AspectJ processes the pointcuts during compilation and tries to match and optimize matching performance. However, examining code and matching (statically or dynamically) would be a costly process. So, for optimal performance, think twice about what we want to achieve and narrow down our search or matching criteria as much as possible.
- All the designators we learned earlier in this chapter are divided into three categories:
  - Method signature pattern: `execution`, `get`, `set`, `call`, `handler`
  - Type signature pattern: `within`, `withincode`
  - Contextual signature pattern: `this`, `target`, `@annotation`
- In order to achieve good performance, write pointcut that includes the method at least and type signature pattern. It is not like matching would not work if we use only the method or type pattern; however, it is always recommended to join the method and type signature together. The type signature is very fast as it narrows down the search space by quickly opting out join points that could not be further processed.
- Declare pointcuts on empty methods and refer to those pointcuts by their empty method name (named pointcut), so in case of any change to an expression, we have to change only at one place.

- It is also recommended to declare small-named pointcuts and combine them by name to build complex pointcuts. Referring to pointcuts by name would follow the default Java method visibility rules. The following is the code sample of defining small pointcuts and joining them:

```
@Pointcut("execution(public * *(..))")
private void anyPublicMethod() {}

@Pointcut("within(com.packt.springhighperformance.ch3.bankingapp.Tr
ansferService..*)")
private void transfer() {}

@Pointcut("anyPublicMethod() && transfer()")
private void transferOperation() {}
```

- Try to create anonymous beans for pointcuts when they are not shared to avoid direct access by an application.
- Try to use static pointcuts where arguments need not be matched. These are faster and cached by Spring when the method is invoked first. Dynamic pointcuts are costly because they are evaluated on every method invocation because caching cannot be done as the argument would differ.

Advice ordering

Now we know how to write advice and how to create `Aspect`. Let's see how advice ordering can help us to prioritize our advice when we have multiple advice on the same join point:

- Let's say we wrote two before or after advice in different aspects and both want to run at the same join point. In this case, the order of execution of the advice would be based on the which aspect comes first in the execution of classes. To avoid this and apply our advice one after the other, Spring provides a way to specify the order of execution by either implementing the `Ordered` interface by an aspect or applying the `@Order` annotation. The lower the value of the order, the higher the precedence.
- While declaring an advice, always use the least powerful form of advice; for example, if a simple before advice would achieve our requirement, we should not use the around advice.

Best practices of AOP proxies

We learned about AOP proxies and how AOP proxies work. We learned about different types of proxies in Spring AOP. The following are best practices to be followed while implementing AOP proxies in Spring:

- Unless we need to perform a manipulative action at runtime or we want to gain fine-grained control of our proxies, use the declarative method of proxy configuration over the programmatic method.
- Spring recommends JDK dynamic proxy over the CGLIB proxy wherever possible. If we are building our application from scratch and there is no requirement to create proxies of third-party APIs, implement the abstraction layer to loosely-couple the implementation using the interface and let Spring use the JDK dynamic proxy mechanism to create proxies.
- In case of CGLIB proxies, make sure the methods are not `final`, as `final` methods cannot be overridden and hence they cannot be advised.
- According to Spring, it is not possible to have `aspects` themselves be the target of advice from other `aspects`. There are workarounds for this situation; move the `aspect` method to a new Spring bean annotated with `@Component`, `@Autowire` this new Spring bean to `aspect`, and just call the advised method. `MethodProfilingAspect` is `aspect` defining a pointcut on all join points under `com.packt.springhighperformance.ch3.bankingapp`:

```
@Aspect
public class MethodProfilingAspect {
  @Around("execution(*
  com.packt.springhighperformance.ch3.bankingapp.*.*(..))")
  public Object log(ProceedingJoinPoint joinPoint){
    System.out.println("Before
    Around"+joinPoint.getTarget().getClass().getName());
    Object retVal = null;
    try {
       retVal = joinPoint.proceed();
    } catch (Throwable e) {
      e.printStackTrace();
    }
    System.out.println("After
    Around"+joinPoint.getTarget().getClass().getName());
    return retVal;
  }
```

- The following `ValidatingAspect` is aspect defined under the
  `com.packt.springhighperformance.ch3.bankapp` package, however a call
  to the `validate` method would not be advised by `MethodProfilingAspect`:

```
@Aspect
public class ValidatingAspect {

 @Autowired
 private ValidateService validateService;

 @Before("execution(*
com.packt.springhighperformance.ch3.bankingapp.TransferService.tran
 sfe  r(..))")
 public void validate(JoinPoint jp){
 validateService.validateAccountNumber();
 }
}
```

- The following is the solution by creating a separate class with the `@Component`
  annotation and implementing the `validate` method. This class will be a Spring-
  managed bean and it will be advised:

```
@Component
public class ValidateDefault{

  @Autowired
  private ValidateService validateService;
  public void validate(JoinPoint jp){
        validateService.validateAccountNumber();
    }
}
```

- The following code of `ValidatingAspect` injects the `ValidateDefault` Spring
  bean and calls the `validate` method:

```
@Aspect
public class ValidatingAspect {

 @Autowired
 private ValidateDefault validateDefault;

 @Before("execution(*
com.packt.springhighperformance.ch3.bankingapp.TransferService.tran
 sfer(..))")
 public void validate(JoinPoint jp){
```

```
        validateDefault.validate(jp);
    }
}
```

Never implement fine-grained requirements through AOP or use AspectJ for such requirements. Do not use @Configurable on Spring-managed bean classes, otherwise it would do double initialization, once through the container and once through the aspect.

Caching

We have seen how to improve our application's performance with the use of caching. The following are the best practices to be followed when implementing caching in Spring:

- Spring cache annotations should be used on concrete classes and not on interfaces. If we choose to use proxy-target-class="true", caching will not work because the Java annotation from the interfaces cannot be inherited.
- Try not use @Cacheable and @CachePut together on the same method.
- Do not cache very low-level methods close, such as CPU-intensive and in-memory computations. Spring's caching might be overkill in those scenarios.

Summary

In this chapter, we looked at the Spring AOP module. AOP is a powerful programming paradigm that complements object-oriented programming. AOP helps to decouple crosscutting concerns from business logic and helps us to focus only on business logic when working on business requirements. Decoupled crosscutting concerns help to implement the reusable code.

We learned about AOP concepts, its terminologies, and how to implement advice. We learned about proxies and how Spring AOP is implemented using the proxy pattern. We learned best practices to be followed while working on Spring AOP to achieve better quality and performance.

In the next chapter, we will learn about Spring MVC. Spring Web MVC provides a web framework that is based on MVC. Using Spring Web MVC as a web framework enables us to develop loosely-coupled web applications with the benefit of writing test cases without using request and response objects. We will see how can we optimize the Spring MVC implementation to achieve better results using async method features, multithreading, and authentication caching.

Spring MVC Optimization

4

In the previous chapter, we learned about the Spring **Aspect-Oriented Programming** (**AOP**) module, AOP concepts, its various terminologies, and how to implement advice. We also saw the proxy concept and its implementation using the proxy pattern. We went through the best practices to follow to achieve quality and performance with the Spring AOP.

Spring MVC is the most popular Java web application framework nowadays. It is provided by Spring itself. Spring Web MVC helps to develop a flexible and loosely coupled web-based application. Spring MVC follows the **Model-View-Controller** (**MVC**) pattern, which separates the input logic, business logic, and presentation logic while providing loose coupling between components. The Spring MVC module allows us to write a test case without using the request and response object in the web application. So, it removes the overhead of testing the web components in the enterprise application. Spring MVC also supports multiple new view technologies and allows for extending. Spring MVC provides a clear definition of roles for controllers, view resolvers, handler mappings, and POJO beans, which makes it simple to create Java web applications.

In this chapter, we will learn about the following topics:

- Spring MVC configuration
- Spring asynchronous processing, `@Async` annotation
- `CompletableFuture` with Spring Async
- Spring Security configuration

- Authentication cache
- Fast and stateless API authentication with Spring Security
- Monitoring and managing Tomcat with JMX
- Spring MVC performance improvements

Spring MVC configuration

The Spring MVC architecture is designed along with a front controller servlet, the `DispatcherServlet`, which is a front controller pattern implementation and acts as an entry point for all of the HTTP requests and responses. The `DispatcherServlet` can be configured and mapped using Java configuration or in the deployment descriptor file, `web.xml`. Before moving on to the configuration part, let's understand the flow of Spring MVC architecture.

Spring MVC architecture

In the Spring MVC framework, there are multiple core components that maintain the flow of request and response execution. These components are clearly separated and have different interfaces and implementation classes, so they can be used according to requirements. These core components are as follows:

Component	Summary
`DispatcherServlet`	It acts as a front controller of the Spring MVC framework through the life cycle of HTTP requests and responses.
`HandlerMapping`	When a request comes, this component is responsible for deciding which controller will handle the URL.
`Controller`	It executes the business logic and maps the resultant data in `ModelAndView`.
`ModelAndView`	It holds the model data object in terms of the execution result and the view object to render.
`ViewResolver`	It decides the view to be rendered.
`View`	It shows the result data from a model object.

The following diagram illustrates the flow of the preceding components in the Spring MVC architecture:

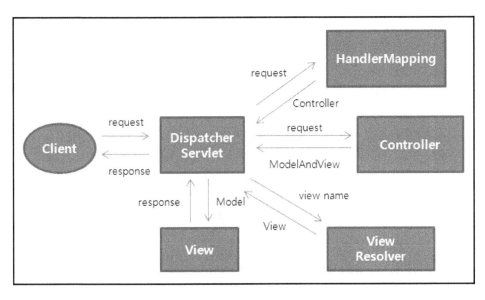

Spring MVC architecture

Let's understand the basic flow of the architecture:

1. When the incoming **request** comes, it is intercepted by the front controller, DispatcherServlet. After intercepting the **request**, the front controller finds the appropriate HandlerMapping.

2. The HandlerMapping maps the client **request** call to the appropriate Controller, based on the configuration file or from the annotation Controller list, and returns the Controller information to the front controller.

3. The DispatcherServlet dispatches the **request** to the appropriate Controller.

4. The Controller executes the business logic defined under the Controller method and returns the resultant data, in the form of ModelAndView, back to the front controller.

5. The front controller gets the **view name** based on the values in the ModelAndView and passes it to the ViewResolver to resolve the actual view, based on the configured view resolver.

6. The **view** uses the **Model** object to render the screen. The output is generated in the form of HttpServletResponse and passed to the front controller.

7. The front controller sends the **response** back to the servlet container to send the output back to the user.

Now, let's understand the Spring MVC configuration methods. Spring MVC configuration can be set up in the following ways:

- XML-based configuration
- Java-based configuration

Before we start with the configuration using the preceding methods, let's define the steps that are involved in setting up the Spring MVC application:

1. Configuring front controller
2. Creating Spring application context
3. Configuring ViewResolver

XML-based configuration

In an XML-based configuration, we will do the Spring MVC configuration externally, using the XML files. Let's move forward with the configuration, following the preceding steps.

Configuring front controller

To configure the front controller servlet, DispatcherServlet, in an XML-based configuration, we need to add the following XML code in the web.xml file:

```xml
<servlet>
  <servlet-name>spring-mvc</servlet-name>
  <servlet-class>
    org.springframework.web.servlet.DispatcherServlet
  </servlet-class>
  <init-param>
    <param-name>contextConfigLocation</param-name>
    <param-value>/WEB-INF/spring-mvc-context.xml</param-value>
  </init-param>
  <load-on-startup>1</load-on-startup>
</servlet>

<servlet-mapping>
  <servlet-name>spring-mvc</servlet-name>
  <url-pattern>/</url-pattern>
</servlet-mapping>
```

In the preceding XML code, at first, we configured the `DispatcherServlet`. Then, we mentioned the context configuration location, `/WEB-INF/spring-mvc-context.xml`. We set the `load-on-startup` value as `1`, so the servlet container will load this servlet upon startup. In the second part, we defined the `servlet-mapping` tag to map a URL `/` to `DispatcherServlet`. Now, we will define the Spring application context in the next step.

It is good to configure the `load-on-startup` element under the `DispatcherServlet` configuration to load it at the highest priority. This is because, in a cluster environment, you might face timeout issues if Spring is not up and you get a large number of calls hitting your web app once it's deployed.

Creating a Spring application context

After configuring the `DispatcherServlet` in `web.xml`, let's move ahead to create a Spring application context. For that, we need to add the following XML code in the `spring-mvc-context.xml` file:

```xml
<beans>
<!-- Schema definitions are skipped. -->
<context:component-scan base-
package="com.packt.springhighperformance.ch4.controller" />
<mvc:annotation-driven />
</beans>
```

In the preceding XML code, we first defined a component scan tag, `<context:component-scan />`, for the `com.packt.springhighperformance.ch4.controller` package, so that all of the beans and controllers get created and autowired.

Then, we have used `<mvc:annotation-driven />` to register automatically different beans and components that includes request mapping, data binding, validation, and auto conversion feature with `@ResponseBody`.

Configuring ViewResolver

To configure `ViewResolver`, we need to specify a bean for the class `InternalResourceViewResolver` in the `spring-mvc-context.xml` file, after `<mvc:annotation-driven />`. Let's do that:

```
<beans>
<!-- Schema definitions are skipped. -->
<context:component-scan base-
package="com.packt.springhighperformance.ch4.controller" />
<mvc:annotation-driven />

<bean
 class="org.springframework.web.servlet.view.InternalResourceViewResolv
er">
    <property name="prefix">
      <value>/WEB-INF/views/</value>
    </property>
    <property name="suffix">
      <value>.jsp</value>
    </property>
  </bean>
</beans>
```

After configuring `ViewResolver`, we will create a `Controller` to test the configuration. But, before moving on to that, let's see the Java-based configuration.

Java-based configuration

For the Java-based Spring MVC configuration, we will follow the same steps that we did with the XML-based configuration. In a Java-based configuration, all of the configurations will be done under the Java class. Let's follow the sequence.

Configuring front controller

With Spring 5.0, there are three ways to configure `DispatcherServlet` programmatically, by implementing or extending any of the following three classes:

- `WebAppInitializer` interface
- `AbstractDispatcherServletInitializer` abstract class
- `AbstractAnnotationConfigDispatcherServletInitializer` abstract class

We will use the `AbstractDispatcherServletInitializer` class, as it is the preferred approach for applications that use Java-based Spring configuration. It is preferred because it allows us to start a servlet application context, as well as a root application context.

We need to create the following class to configure `DispatcherServlet`:

```
import
org.springframework.web.servlet.support.AbstractAnnotationConfigDispatc
herServletInitializer;

public class SpringMvcWebInitializer extends
AbstractAnnotationConfigDispatcherServletInitializer {

  @Override
  protected Class<?>[] getRootConfigClasses() {
    return null;
  }

  @Override
  protected Class<?>[] getServletConfigClasses() {
    return new Class[] { SpringMvcWebConfig.class };
  }

  @Override
  protected String[] getServletMappings() {
    return new String[] { "/" };
  }
}
```

The previous class code is equivalent to the `web.xml` file configuration that we created in the *XML-based configuration* section. In the preceding class, the `getRootConfigClasses()` method is used to specify the root application context configuration classes (or `null`, if not required). `getServletConfigClasses()` is used to specify the web application configuration classes (or `null`, if not required). The `getServletMappings()` method is used to specify the servlet mappings for the `DispatcherServlet`. Root config classes will be loaded first, then servlet config classes will be loaded. Root config classes will create an `ApplicationContext`, which will act as a parent context, whereas servlet config classes will create a `WebApplicationContext`, and it will act as a child context of the parent context.

Creating a Spring application context and configuring a ViewResolver

In Spring 5.0, to create a Spring application context and to configure a `ViewResolver` using Java configuration, we need to add the following code in the class:

```
@Configuration
@EnableWebMvc
@ComponentScan({
"com.packt.springhighperformance.ch4.bankingapp.controller"})
public class SpringMvcWebConfig implements WebMvcConfigurer {

  @Bean
  public InternalResourceViewResolver resolver() {
    InternalResourceViewResolver resolver = new
    InternalResourceViewResolver();
    resolver.setPrefix("/WEB-INF/views/");
    resolver.setSuffix(".jsp");
    return resolver;
  }

}
```

In the preceding code, we created a class, `SpringMvcWebConfig`, implementing a `WebMvcConfigurer` interface, which provides options for customizing Spring MVC configuration. The `@EnableWebMvc` object enables the default configuration for Spring MVC. The `@ComponentScan` object specifies the base packages to scan for controllers. The two annotations `@EnableWebMvc` and `@ComponentScan` are equivalent to the `<context:component-scan />` and `<mvc:annotation-driven />` that we created in `spring-mvc-context.xml` in the *XML-based configuration* section. The `resolve()` method returns `InternalResourceViewResolver`, which helps in mapping logical view names from a preconfigured directory.

Creating a controller

Now, let's create a controller class to map the /home request, as follows:

```
package com.packt.springhighperformance.ch4.controller;

import org.springframework.stereotype.Controller;
import org.springframework.web.bind.annotation.RequestMapping;

@Controller
```

```
public class BankController {

  @RequestMapping(value = "/home")
  public String home() {
    return "home";
  }
}
```

In the preceding code, @Controller defines a Spring MVC controller that contains request mappings. The @RequestMapping(value = "home") object defines a mapping URL, /home, to a method, home(). So, when the browser hits a /home request, it executes the home() method.

Creating a view

Now, let's create a view, home.jsp, in the src/main/webapp/WEB-INF/views/home.jsp folder, with the following HTML content:

```
<html>
<head>
<meta http-equiv="Content-Type" content="text/html;
charset=ISO-8859-1">
<title>Spring MVC</title>
</head>
<body>
  <h2>Welcome to Bank</h2>
</body>
</html>
```

Now, when we run this application, it will show the following output:

In the next section, we will learn about Spring asynchronous processing.

Spring asynchronous processing, @Async annotation

Spring provides support for asynchronous method execution. This can also be achieved using threads, but it makes the code more complex and sometimes results in more bugs and errors. When we need to execute a simple action in an asynchronous manner, it is a cumbersome process to handle it using threads. There are cases in which it is necessary to perform the operation asynchronously, like sending a message from one machine to another machine. The main advantage of asynchronous processing is that the caller will not have to wait for the completion of the called method. In order to execute a method in a separate thread, you need to annotate the method with the @Async annotation.

Asynchronous processing support can be enabled by using the @EnableAsync annotation to run the @Async methods in the background thread pool. The following is an example of Java configuration to enable asynchronous processing:

```
@Configuration
@EnableAsync
public class SpringAppAsyncConfig { ... }
```

Asynchronous processing can also be enabled by using XML configuration, as follows:

```
<task:executor id="myappexecutor" pool-size="10" />
<task:annotation-driven executor="myappexecutor"/>
```

@Async annotation modes

There are two modes of @Async annotation processing methods:

- Fire and forget mode
- Result retrieval mode

Fire and forget mode

In this mode, a method will be configured as a `void` type, to be run asynchronously:

```
@Async
public void syncCustomerAccounts() {
    logger.info("Customer accounts synced successfully.");
}
```

Result retrieval mode

In this mode, a method will be configured with a return type by wrapping the result with the `Future` type:

```
@Service
public class BankAsyncService {
  private static final Logger LOGGER =
  Logger.getLogger(BankAsyncService.class);
  @Async
    public Future<String> syncCustomerAccount() throws
    InterruptedException {
    LOGGER.info("Sync Account Processing Started - Thread id: " +
    Thread.currentThread().getId());
    Thread.sleep(2000);
    String processInfo = String.format("Sync Account Processing
    Completed - Thread Name= %d, Thread Name= %s",
    Thread.currentThread().getId(),
    Thread.currentThread().getName());
    LOGGER.info(processInfo);
    return new AsyncResult<String>(processInfo);
    }
}
```

Spring also provides support for the `AsyncResult` class, which implements the `Future` interface. It can be used to track the result of asynchronous method invocation.

Limitations of @Async annotation

The `@Async` annotation has the following limitations:

- The method needs to be `public` so that it can be proxied
- Self-invocation of the asynchronous method would not work, because it bypasses the proxy and calls the underlying method directly

Thread pool executor

You might wonder how we declare the thread pools that asynchronous methods will use. By default, for the thread pool, Spring will try to find either a unique `TaskExecutor` bean defined in the context or an `Executor` bean, named `TaskExecutor`. If neither of the preceding two options is resolvable, Spring will use `SimpleAsyncTaskExecutor` to process asynchronous method processing.

However, sometimes we do not want to use the same thread pool for all of the application's tasks. We can have different thread pools, with different configurations for each method. For that, we just need to pass the executor name to the `@Async` annotation for each method.

To enable asynchronous support, the `@Async` annotation is not enough; we need to use the `@EnableAsync` annotation in our configuration classes.

In Spring MVC, when we configure `DispatcherServlet` using the `AbstractAnnotationConfigDispatcherServletInitializer` initializer class, which extends `AbstractDispatcherServletInitializer`, it has the `isAsyncSupported` flag enabled by default.

Now, we need to declare a thread pool definition for asynchronous method invocation. In Spring MVC Java-based configuration, this can be done by overriding the `configureAsyncSupport()` method of the `WebMvcConfigurer` interface in the Spring Web MVC configuration class. Let's override this method, as follows:

```
@Override
public void configureAsyncSupport(AsyncSupportConfigurer configurer) {
    ThreadPoolTaskExecutor t = new ThreadPoolTaskExecutor();
        t.setCorePoolSize(10);
        t.setMaxPoolSize(100);
        t.setThreadNamePrefix("BankAccountSync");
        t.initialize();
        configurer.setTaskExecutor(t);
}
```

In the preceding method, we have configured the thread pool executor by overriding the `configureAsyncSupport()` method. Now, let's call the asynchronous method created in the service class `BankAsyncService` by using a controller class, as follows:

```
@Controller
public class BankController {
   private static final Logger LOGGER =
Logger.getLogger(BankAsyncService.class);
```

```
@Autowired
BankAsyncService syncService;

@RequestMapping(value = "/syncacct")
@ResponseBody
public Callable<String> syncAccount() {
  LOGGER.info("Entering in controller");

  Callable<String> asyncTask = new Callable<String>() {

    @Override
    public String call() throws Exception {
      Future<String> processSync = syncService.syncCustomerAccount();
      return processSync.get();
    }
  };

  LOGGER.info("Leaving from controller");
  return asyncTask;
}
}
```

In the preceding example, when we request /syncacct, it will invoke syncAccount()
and return the result of the asynchronous method in a separate thread.

CompletableFuture with Spring Async

The CompletableFuture class was introduced in Java 8, and it provides a simple way to
write asynchronous, multithreaded, non-blocking code. With Spring MVC, it is also
possible to use CompletableFuture with controllers, services, and repositories from
public methods annotated with @Async. CompletableFuture implements the Future
interface, which provides the result of an asynchronous computation.

We can create CompletableFuture in the following simple way:

```
CompletableFuture<String> completableFuture = new
CompletableFuture<String>();
```

To get the result of this CompletableFuture, we can call the CompletableFuture.get()
method. This method will be blocked until Future is completed. For that, we can manually
call the CompletableFuture.complete() method to complete Future:

```
completableFuture.complete("Future is completed")
```

runAsync() – running a task asynchronously

When we want to execute a background activity task asynchronously and do not want to return anything from that task, we can use the `CompletableFuture.runAsync()` method. It takes a parameter as a `Runnable` object and returns the `CompletableFuture<Void>` type.

Let's try to use the `runAsync()` method by creating another controller method in our `BankController` class, with the following example:

```java
@RequestMapping(value = "/synccust")
  @ResponseBody
  public CompletableFuture<String> syncCustomerDetails() {
    LOGGER.info("Entering in controller");

    CompletableFuture<String> completableFuture = new
    CompletableFuture<>();
    CompletableFuture.runAsync(new Runnable() {
      @Override
      public void run() {
        try {
          completableFuture.complete(syncService.syncCustomerAccount()
          .get());
        } catch (InterruptedException | ExecutionException e) {
          completableFuture.completeExceptionally(e);
        }
      }
    });
      LOGGER.info("Leaving from controller");
      return completableFuture;
  }
```

In the preceding example, when a request comes with the `/synccust` path, it will run `syncCustomerAccount()` in a separate thread and will complete the task without returning any value.

supplyAsync() – running a task asynchronously, with a return value

When we want to return a result after finishing a task asynchronously, we can use `CompletableFuture.supplyAsync()`. It takes `Supplier<T>` as a parameter and returns `CompletableFuture<T>`.

Let's check the `supplyAsync()` method by creating another controller method in our `BankController` class, with the following example:

```
@RequestMapping(value = "/synccustbal")
  @ResponseBody
  public CompletableFuture<String> syncCustomerBalance() {
    LOGGER.info("Entering in controller");

    CompletableFuture<String> completableFuture =
    CompletableFuture.supplyAsync(new Supplier<String>() {
      @Override
      public String get() {
        try {
          return syncService.syncCustomerBalance().get();
        } catch (InterruptedException | ExecutionException e) {
          LOGGER.error(e);
        }
        return "No balance found";
      }
    });
      LOGGER.info("Leaving from controller");
      return completableFuture;
  }
```

The `CompletableFuture` object uses the global thread pool, `ForkJoinPool.commonPool()`, to execute tasks in a separate thread. We can create a thread pool and pass it to `runAsync()` and `supplyAsync()` methods.

The following are two variants of the `runAsync()` and `supplyAsync()` methods:

```
CompletableFuture<Void> runAsync(Runnable runnable)
CompletableFuture<Void> runAsync(Runnable runnable, Executor executor)
CompletableFuture<U> supplyAsync(Supplier<U> supplier)
CompletableFuture<U> supplyAsync(Supplier<U> supplier, Executor
executor)
```

Attaching a callback to the CompletableFuture

`CompletableFuture.get()` blocks the object and waits until the `Future` task is completed and the result is returned. To build an asynchronous system, there should be a callback, automatically called when the `Future` task has completed. We can attach a callback to `CompletableFuture` by using the `thenApply()`, `thenAccept()`, and `thenRun()` methods.

Spring Security configuration

Spring Security is a widely used security service framework for Java EE-based enterprise applications. At the authentication level, Spring Security provides different kinds of authentication models. Some of these models are provided by third parties, and some sets of authentication features are provided by Spring Security itself. Some of the following authentication mechanisms are provided by Spring Security:

- Form-based authentication
- OpenID authentication
- LDAP specifically used in large environments
- Container-managed authentication
- Custom authentication systems
- JAAS

Let's look at an example to activate Spring Security in a web application. We will use an in-memory configuration.

Configuring Spring Security dependencies

To configure Spring Security in a web application, we need to add the following Maven dependencies to our **Project Object Model (POM)** file:

```xml
<!-- spring security -->
<dependency>
    <groupId>org.springframework.security</groupId>
    <artifactId>spring-security-web</artifactId>
    <version>${spring.framework.version}</version>
</dependency>
<dependency>
    <groupId>org.springframework.security</groupId>
    <artifactId>spring-security-config</artifactId>
    <version>${spring.framework.version}</version>
</dependency>
```

Configuring a security filter for incoming requests

When implementing security in a web application, it is better to validate all of the incoming requests. In Spring Security, the framework itself looks at the incoming request and authenticates the user to perform an action, based on the provided access. To intercept all of the incoming requests to a web application, we need to configure `filter`, `DelegatingFilterProxy`, which will delegate the requests to a Spring-managed bean, `FilterChainProxy`:

```
<filter>
    <filter-name>springSecurityFilterChain</filter-name>
    <filter-class>
        org.springframework.web.filter.DelegatingFilterProxy
    </filter-class>
</filter>
<filter-mapping>
    <filter-name>springSecurityFilterChain</filter-name>
    <url-pattern>/*</url-pattern>
</filter-mapping>
```

Based on the `filter` configuration, all of the requests will go through this `filter`. Now, let's configure security-related stuff, like authentication, URL security, and role access.

Configuring Spring Security

Now, we will configure Spring Security authentication and authorization by creating a Spring Security configuration class as follows:

```
@EnableWebSecurity
public class SpringMvcSecurityConfig extends
WebSecurityConfigurerAdapter {
  @Autowired
  PasswordEncoder passwordEncoder;
  @Override
  protected void configure(AuthenticationManagerBuilder auth)
  throws
  Exception {
    auth
    .inMemoryAuthentication()
    .passwordEncoder(passwordEncoder)
    .withUser("user").password(passwordEncoder.encode("user@123"))
    .roles("USER")
```

```
        .and()
        .withUser("admin").password(passwordEncoder.
        encode("admin@123")
        ).roles("USER", "ADMIN");
    }
    @Bean
    public PasswordEncoder passwordEncoder() {
        return new BCryptPasswordEncoder();
    }
    @Override
    protected void configure(HttpSecurity http) throws Exception {
        http.authorizeRequests()
        .antMatchers("/login").permitAll()
        .antMatchers("/admin/**").hasRole("ADMIN")
        .antMatchers("/**").hasAnyRole("ADMIN","USER")
        .and().formLogin()
        .and().logout().logoutSuccessUrl("/login").permitAll()
        .and()
        .csrf().disable();
    }
}
```

Let's understand the preceding configuration:

- `@EnableWebSecurity`: It enables Spring Security's web security support, and also provides the Spring MVC integration.
- `WebSecurityConfigurerAdapter`: It provides a set of methods that are used to enable specific web security configuration.
- `protected void configure(AuthenticationManagerBuilder auth)`: We have used in-memory authentication in this example. It can be used to connect to the database using `auth.jdbcAuthentication()`, or to a **Lightweight Directory Access Protocol (LDAP)** using `auth.ldapAuthentication()`.
- `.passwordEncoder(passwordEncoder)`: We have used the password encoder `BCryptPasswordEncoder`.
- `.withUser("user").password(passwordEncoder.encode("user@123"))`: It sets the user ID and encoded password for authentication.
- `.roles("USER")`: It assigns roles to the user.
- `protected void configure(HttpSecurity http)`: It is used to secure different URLs that need security.
- `.antMatchers("/login").permitAll()`: It permits all of the users to access the login page.

- `.antMatchers("/admin/**").hasRole("ADMIN")`: It permits access to the admin panel to the users who have the ADMIN role.
- `.antMatchers("/**").anyRequest().hasAnyRole("ADMIN", "USER")`: It means that to make any request with "/", you must be logged in with the ADMIN or USER role.
- `.and().formLogin()`: It will provide a default login page, with username and password fields.
- `.and().logout().logoutSuccessUrl("/login").permitAll()`: It sets the logout success page when a user logs out.
- `.csrf().disable()`: By default, the **Cross Site Request Forgery** (CSRF) flag is enabled. Here, we have disabled it from configuration.

Adding a controller

We will use the following `BankController` class for URL mapping:

```
@Controller
public class BankController {
  @GetMapping("/")
  public ModelAndView home(Principal principal) {
    ModelAndView model = new ModelAndView();
    model.addObject("title", "Welcome to Bank");
    model.addObject("message", "Hi " + principal.getName());
    model.setViewName("index");
    return model;
  }
  @GetMapping("/admin**")
  public ModelAndView adminPage() {
    ModelAndView model = new ModelAndView();
    model.addObject("title", "Welcome to Admin Panel");
    model.addObject("message", "This is secured page - Admin
    Panel");
    model.setViewName("admin");
    return model;
  }
  @PostMapping("/logout")
  public String logout(HttpServletRequest request,
  HttpServletResponse
  response) {
    Authentication auth =
    SecurityContextHolder.getContext().getAuthentication();
    if (auth != null) {
      new SecurityContextLogoutHandler().logout(request, response,
```

```
      auth);
      request.getSession().invalidate();
   }
   return "redirect:/login";
  }
}
```

Now, when we run this example, it will first show the login authentication form provided by the Spring Framework, before we try to access any URL of the web application. If a user logs in with the USER role and tries to access the admin panel, they will be restricted from accessing it. If a user logs in with the ADMIN role, they will be able to access both the user panel and the admin panel.

Authentication cache

Spring Security performance becomes one of the major concerns when there is a maximum number of calls hit on the application. By default, Spring Security creates a new session for each new request and prepares a new security context every single time. This becomes an overhead when maintaining user authentication, and due to that, performance is lowered.

For example, we have an API that requires authentication on each request. If there are multiple calls made to this API, it will impact the performance of the application which uses this API. So, let's understand this problem without a caching implementation. Take a look at the following logs, where we call an API using the curl command, without a caching implementation:

```
curl -sL --connect-timeout 1 -i
http://localhost:8080/authentication-cache/secure/login -H
"Authorization: Basic Y3VzdDAwMTpUZXN0QDEyMw=="
```

Take a look at the following log:

```
21:53:46.302 RDS DEBUG JdbcTemplate - Executing prepared SQL query
21:53:46.302 RDS DEBUG JdbcTemplate - Executing prepared SQL statement
[select username,password,enabled from users where username = ?]
21:53:46.302 RDS DEBUG DataSourceUtils - Fetching JDBC Connection from
DataSource
21:53:46.302 RDS DEBUG SimpleDriverDataSource - Creating new JDBC
Driver Connection to
[jdbc:h2:mem:testdb;DB_CLOSE_DELAY=-1;DB_CLOSE_ON_EXIT=false]
21:53:46.307 RDS DEBUG DataSourceUtils - Returning JDBC Connection to
DataSource
21:53:46.307 RDS DEBUG JdbcTemplate - Executing prepared SQL query
21:53:46.307 RDS DEBUG JdbcTemplate - Executing prepared SQL statement
```

```
[select username,authority from authorities where username = ?]
21:53:46.307 RDS DEBUG DataSourceUtils - Fetching JDBC Connection from
DataSource
21:53:46.307 RDS DEBUG SimpleDriverDataSource - Creating new JDBC
Driver Connection to
[jdbc:h2:mem:testdb;DB_CLOSE_DELAY=-1;DB_CLOSE_ON_EXIT=false]
21:53:46.307 RDS DEBUG DataSourceUtils - Returning JDBC Connection to
DataSource
```

Each time we call this API, it will authenticate the username and password with the database value. This affects the application performance and can lead to an unnecessary load if users are making frequent calls.

One of the dignified solutions to overcome this issue is caching the user authentication for a specific time limit. We will use the implementation of `UserCache` with a properly configured `AuthenticationProvider`, and pass it to `AuthenticationManagerBuilder`. We will use `EhCache` to play with the cached object. We can employ this solution through the following steps:

1. Implementing the caching configuration class
2. Providing `UserCache` to `AuthenticationProvider`
3. Providing `AuthenticationProvider` to `AuthenticationManagerBuilder`

Implementing the caching configuration class

We have created the following class, which will provide the `UserCache` bean that will provide it to `AuthenticationProvider`:

```
@Configuration
@EnableCaching
public class SpringMvcCacheConfig {

  @Bean
  public EhCacheFactoryBean ehCacheFactoryBean() {
    EhCacheFactoryBean ehCacheFactory = new EhCacheFactoryBean();
    ehCacheFactory.setCacheManager(cacheManagerFactoryBean()
    .getObject());
    return ehCacheFactory;
  }

  @Bean
  public CacheManager cacheManager() {
    return new
    EhCacheCacheManager(cacheManagerFactoryBean().getObject());
```

```
  }

  @Bean
  public EhCacheManagerFactoryBean cacheManagerFactoryBean() {
    EhCacheManagerFactoryBean cacheManager = new
    EhCacheManagerFactoryBean();
    return cacheManager;
  }

  @Bean
  public UserCache userCache() {
    EhCacheBasedUserCache userCache = new EhCacheBasedUserCache();
    userCache.setCache(ehCacheFactoryBean().getObject());
    return userCache;
  }
}
```

In the preceding class, `@EnableCaching` enables cache management.

Providing UserCache to AuthenticationProvider

Now, we will provide the created `UserCache` bean to `AuthenticationProvider`:

```
@Bean
public AuthenticationProvider authenticationProviderBean() {
    DaoAuthenticationProvider authenticationProvider = new
    DaoAuthenticationProvider();
    authenticationProvider.setPasswordEncoder(passwordEncoder);
    authenticationProvider.setUserCache(userCache);
    authenticationProvider.
    setUserDetailsService(userDetailsService());
    return authenticationProvider;
}
```

Providing AuthenticationProvider to AuthenticationManagerBuilder

Now, let's provide `AuthenticationProvider` to `AuthenticationManagerBuilder` in the Spring Security configuration class:

```
@Autowired
    @Override
    protected void configure(AuthenticationManagerBuilder auth) throws
```

```
Exception {
    auth
       .eraseCredentials(false)
       //Providing AuthenticationProvider to
        AuthenticationManagerBuilder.
       .authenticationProvider(authenticationProviderBean())
       .jdbcAuthentication()
       .dataSource(dataSource);
}
```

Now, let's call that API and check the performance of authentication. If we call the API four times, the following log will be generated:

```
22:46:55.314 RDS DEBUG EhCacheBasedUserCache - Cache hit: false;
username: cust001
22:46:55.447 RDS DEBUG JdbcTemplate - Executing prepared SQL query
22:46:55.447 RDS DEBUG JdbcTemplate - Executing prepared SQL statement
[select username,password,enabled from users where username = ?]
22:46:55.447 RDS DEBUG DataSourceUtils - Fetching JDBC Connection from
DataSource
22:46:55.447 RDS DEBUG SimpleDriverDataSource - Creating new JDBC
Driver Connection to
[jdbc:h2:mem:testdb;DB_CLOSE_DELAY=-1;DB_CLOSE_ON_EXIT=false]
22:46:55.463 RDS DEBUG DataSourceUtils - Returning JDBC Connection to
DataSource
22:46:55.463 RDS DEBUG JdbcTemplate - Executing prepared SQL query
22:46:55.463 RDS DEBUG JdbcTemplate - Executing prepared SQL statement
[select username,authority from authorities where username = ?]
22:46:55.463 RDS DEBUG DataSourceUtils - Fetching JDBC Connection from
DataSource
22:46:55.463 RDS DEBUG SimpleDriverDataSource - Creating new JDBC
Driver Connection to
[jdbc:h2:mem:testdb;DB_CLOSE_DELAY=-1;DB_CLOSE_ON_EXIT=false]
22:46:55.479 RDS DEBUG DataSourceUtils - Returning JDBC Connection to
DataSource
22:46:55.603 RDS DEBUG EhCacheBasedUserCache - Cache put: cust001
22:47:10.118 RDS DEBUG EhCacheBasedUserCache - Cache hit: true;
username: cust001
22:47:12.619 RDS DEBUG EhCacheBasedUserCache - Cache hit: true;
username: cust001
22:47:14.851 RDS DEBUG EhCacheBasedUserCache - Cache hit: true;
username: cust001
```

As you can see in the preceding log, initially, `AuthenticationProvider` searches the `UserDetails` object from the cache; if it fails to get it from the cache, `AuthenticationProvider` will query the database for `UserDetails` and will put the updated object into the cache and for all the later calls, it will retrieve the `UserDetails` object from the cache.

 If you update the password for a user and try to authenticate the user with the new password, and it fails to match the value in the cache, then it will query the `UserDetails` from the database.

Fast and stateless API authentication with Spring Security

Spring Security also provides stateless APIs for securing non-browser clients, such as mobile applications or other apps. We will learn how to configure Spring Security for securing stateless APIs. Also, we will figure out the important points that need to be considered when designing security solutions and improving the performance of user authentication.

API authentication with the JSESSIONID cookie

It's not a good practice for API clients to use form-based authentication, due to the essential need for providing a `JSESSIONID` cookie with the chain of requests. Spring Security also provides an option to use HTTP basic authentication, which is an older approach but works fine. In the HTTP basic authentication approach, user/password details need to be sent with a request header. Let's take a look at the following example of an HTTP basic authentication configuration:

```
@Override
protected void configure(HttpSecurity http) throws Exception {
    http
        .authorizeRequests()
        .anyRequest().authenticated()
        .and()
        .httpBasic();
}
```

In the preceding example, the `configure()` method is from the `WebSecurityConfigurerAdapter` abstract class, which provides a default implementation of this method. The subclasses should invoke this method by calling `super`, as it may override their configuration. This configuration approach has one disadvantage; whenever we call the secured endpoint, it creates a new session. Let's check this by using the `curl` command to call the endpoint:

```
C:\>curl -sL --connect-timeout 1 -i
http://localhost:8080/fast-api-spring-security/secure/login/ -H
"Authorization: Basic Y3VzdDAwMTpDdXN0QDEyMw=="
HTTP/1.1 200 OK
Server: Apache-Coyote/1.1
Set-Cookie: JSESSIONID=B85E9773E6C1E71CE0EC1AD11D897529; Path=/fast-
api-spring-security; HttpOnly
X-Content-Type-Options: nosniff
X-XSS-Protection: 1; mode=block
Cache-Control: no-cache, no-store, max-age=0, must-revalidate
Pragma: no-cache
Expires: 0
X-Frame-Options: DENY
Content-Type: text/plain;charset=ISO-8859-1
Content-Length: 19
Date: Tue, 27 Mar 2018 18:07:43 GMT

Welcome to the Bank
```

We have one session ID cookie; let's call it again:

```
C:\>curl -sL --connect-timeout 1 -i
http://localhost:8080/fast-api-spring-security/secure/login/ -H
"Authorization: Basic Y3VzdDAwMTpDdXN0QDEyMw=="
HTTP/1.1 200 OK
Server: Apache-Coyote/1.1
Set-Cookie: JSESSIONID=14FEB3708295324482BE1DD600D015CC; Path=/fast-
api-spring-security; HttpOnly
X-Content-Type-Options: nosniff
X-XSS-Protection: 1; mode=block
Cache-Control: no-cache, no-store, max-age=0, must-revalidate
Pragma: no-cache
Expires: 0
X-Frame-Options: DENY
Content-Type: text/plain;charset=ISO-8859-1
Content-Length: 19
Date: Tue, 27 Mar 2018 18:07:47 GMT

Welcome to the Bank
```

As you can see, we have two different session IDs in each response. In the preceding example, for testing purposes, we sent the `Authorization` header with an encoded username and password. You can get the `Basic Y3VzdDAwMTpDdXN0QDEyMw==` header value from the browser when you hit the URL, by providing a username and password for authentication.

API authentication without the JSESSIONID cookie

As there is no need for sessions for API client authentication, we can easily get rid of the session ID with the following configuration:

```
@Override
protected void configure(HttpSecurity http) throws Exception {
        http
         .sessionManagement()
           .sessionCreationPolicy(SessionCreationPolicy.STATELESS)
           .and()
           .authorizeRequests()
           .anyRequest().authenticated()
           .and()
           .httpBasic();
}
```

As you can see, in the preceding configuration, we have used `SessionCreationPolicy.STATELESS`. With this option, there will not be a session cookie added in the response header. Let's see what happens after this change:

```
C:\>curl -sL --connect-timeout 1 -i
http://localhost:8080/fast-api-spring-security/secure/login/ -H
"Authorization: Basic Y3VzdDAwMTpDdXN0QDEyMw=="
HTTP/1.1 200 OK
Server: Apache-Coyote/1.1
X-Content-Type-Options: nosniff
X-XSS-Protection: 1; mode=block
Cache-Control: no-cache, no-store, max-age=0, must-revalidate
Pragma: no-cache
Expires: 0
X-Frame-Options: DENY
Content-Type: text/plain;charset=ISO-8859-1
Content-Length: 19
Date: Tue, 27 Mar 2018 18:24:32 GMT

Welcome to the Bank
```

In the preceding example, there is no session cookie found in the response header. So, in this way, we can manage stateless authentication for APIs using Spring Security.

Monitoring and managing Tomcat with JMX

Java Management Extension (JMX) provides a powerful mechanism to monitor and manage Java applications. It can be enabled in Tomcat to monitor threads, CPU usage, and heap memory, and to configure **MBeans**. Spring provides JMX support out of the box, and we can use it to easily integrate our Spring application into JMX architecture.

JMX support provides the following core features:

- Easy and flexible support for controlling the management interface of beans
- Declarative support for exposing MBeans over remote connectors
- Automatic registration of Spring beans as JMX MBean
- Simplified support to proxy both local and remote MBean resources

JMX functionality has three levels:

- **Instrumentation level**: This level contains the components and resources that are represented by one or more Java beans, which are known as **managed beans,** or MBean.
- **Agent level**: This is known as an intermediate agent, called the **MBean server**. It gets the request from the remote management level and passes it to the appropriate MBean. It can also receive notifications related to state changes from MBeans and forward them back to the remote management level.
- **Remote management level:** This layer is made of connectors, adapters, or client programs. It sends requests to the agent level and receives the responses to the requests. Users can connect to the MBean server using either a connector or a client program, such as JConsole, with a protocol such as **Remote Method Invocation** (**RMI**) or **Internet Inter-ORB Protocol** (**IIOP**), and use an adapter.

In short, a user at the remote management level sends a request to the agent level, which finds the appropriate MBean at the instrumentation level, and sends the response back to the user.

Connecting JMX to monitor Tomcat

To configure JMX on Tomcat, we need to set the relevant system properties upon JVM startup. We can use the following methods.

We can update the `catalina.sh` or `catalina.bat` file in `{tomcat-folder}\bin\`, adding the following values:

```
-Dcom.sun.management.jmxremote
-Dcom.sun.management.jmxremote.port={port to access}
-Dcom.sun.management.jmxremote.authenticate=false
-Dcom.sun.management.jmxremote.ssl=false
```

For example, we can add the following values at `{tomcat-folder}\bin\catalina.bat`:

```
set JAVA_OPTS="-Dcom.sun.management.jmxremote
-Dcom.sun.management.jmxremote.port=8990
-Dcom.sun.management.jmxremote.authenticate=false
-Dcom.sun.management.jmxremote.ssl=false"
```

If you want to configure JMX for your Tomcat in Eclipse, you need to do the following:

1. Go to **Window** | **Show View** | **Server**.
2. Open the Tomcat **Overview** configuration window by double-clicking on **Tomcat v8.0 Server at localhost**.
3. Under **General Information,** click on **Open launch configuration**.
4. Select the **Arguments** tab of **Edit launch configuration properties**.
5. In **VM arguments,** add the following properties, and then click **OK**:

```
-Dcom.sun.management.jmxremote
-Dcom.sun.management.jmxremote.port=8990
-Dcom.sun.management.jmxremote.authenticate=false
-Dcom.sun.management.jmxremote.ssl=false
```

After making this change, we need to restart the Tomcat server. After that, we need to test the connection with JConsole. After opening JConsole, we need to provide **Remote Process** with a hostname and port number, as follows:

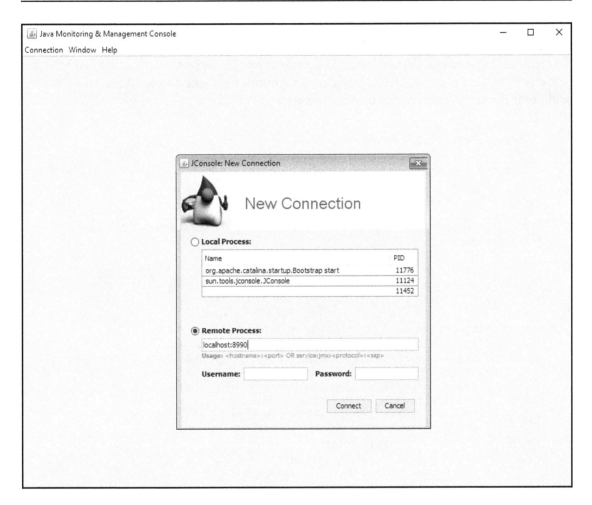

In the preceding screenshot, we have provided the hostname as `localhost` and the port number as `8990`. When you click on **Connect**, you will get a dialog box where you need to click on **Insecure connection,** and then you will be connected to JConsole.

Creating an MBean

To create an MBean, we can use @Managed annotations to convert any class into an MBean. The class BankTransferService transfers an amount from one account to another. We will use this example for further understanding:

```
@Component
@ManagedResource(objectName =
"com.packt.springhighperformance.ch4.mbeans :
name=BankMoneyTransferService", description = "Transfers money from one
account to another")
public class BankMoneyTransferService {

  private Map<String, Integer> accountMap = new HashMap<String,
  Integer>();
   {
    accountMap.put("12345", 20000);
    accountMap.put("54321", 10000);
   };

  @ManagedOperation(description = "Amount transfer")
  @ManagedOperationParameters({
      @ManagedOperationParameter(name = "sourceAccount", description =
       "Transfer from account"),
      @ManagedOperationParameter(name = "destinationAccount",
        description = "Transfer to account"),
      @ManagedOperationParameter(name = "transferAmount",
      description =
        "Amount to be transfer") })
  public void transfer(String sourceAccount, String
  destinationAccount, int transferAmount) {
    if (transferAmount == 0) {
      throw new IllegalArgumentException("Invalid amount");
    }
    int sourceAcctBalance = accountMap.get(sourceAccount);
    int destinationAcctBalance = accountMap.get(destinationAccount);

    if ((sourceAcctBalance - transferAmount) < 0) {
      throw new IllegalArgumentException("Not enough balance.");
    }
    sourceAcctBalance = sourceAcctBalance - transferAmount;
    destinationAcctBalance = destinationAcctBalance + transferAmount;

    accountMap.put(sourceAccount, sourceAcctBalance);
    accountMap.put(destinationAccount, destinationAcctBalance);
  }
```

```
@ManagedOperation(description = "Check Balance")
public int checkBalance(String accountNumber) {
    if (StringUtils.isEmpty(accountNumber)) {
        throw new IllegalArgumentException("Enter account no.");
    }
    if (!accountMap.containsKey(accountNumber)) {
        throw new IllegalArgumentException("Account not found.");
    }
    return accountMap.get(accountNumber);
}

}
```

In the preceding class, the @ManagedResource annotation will mark the class as MBean, and the @ManagedAttribute and @ManagedOperation annotations can be used to expose any attributes or methods. The @Component annotation will make sure that all classes annotated with @Component, @Service, or @Repository will be added to the Spring context.

Exporting an MBean in a Spring context

Now, we need to create an MBeanExporter in a Spring application context. We just need to add the following tag in the Spring context XML configuration:

```
<context:mbean-export/>
```

We need to add the component-scan element before the <context:mbean-export/> element; otherwise, the JMX server will not be able to find any beans.

So, our Spring context configuration will look like the following:

```
<?xml version="1.0" encoding="UTF-8"?>
<beans><!-- Skipped schema definitions -->

    <context:component-scan base-
    package="com.packt.springhighperformance.ch4.mbeans" />
<context:mbean-export/>

</beans>
```

Now, we just need to start our Tomcat server and open the JConsole to see our MBean. After connecting to JConsole, go to the **MBeans** tab, where you can see our package folder, which contains our `BankMoneyTransferService` MBean, listed in the sidebar:

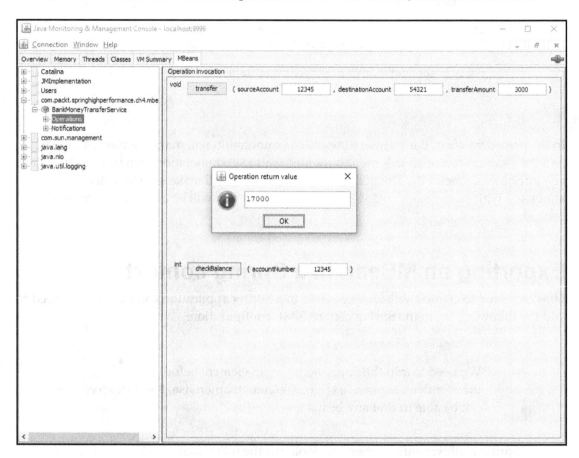

As you can see in the earlier example, our MBean is generated and listed in the JConsole. Now, we can transfer an amount from one account to another by clicking on the **Transfer** button, invoking the method `transfer()`, which we created in our MBean. When we click on the **checkBalance** button, it will show the current balance in a pop up based on the entered account number. In the background, it will invoke the `checkBalance()` method of the `BankMoneyTransferService` class.

Spring MVC performance improvements

Spring MVC application performance can be improved through multiple strategies and tips. Here, we have listed some of the strategies that can improve the performance enormously:

- High performance using connection pooling
- Hibernate improvements
- Testing improvements
- Proper server maintenance
- Using the authentication cache with Spring Security
- Implementing the Executor service framework

High performance using connection pooling

A standout amongst the most important features to enhance performance in Spring MVC is **connection pooling**. In this mechanism, N number of database connections are created and managed in a pool to increase the application's performance. When an application needs to utilize a connection, it just requests a connection, uses it, and then returns it to the pool. The main advantage of this procedure is that there are connections promptly available in the connection pool, so they can be utilized right away. The pool itself deals with the life cycle of the connection, so the developer doesn't have to wait for the connection to get established.

Hibernate improvements

Another major point to enhance performance is regarding Hibernate. Dirty checking is one of the features provided by Hibernate. In dirty checking, Hibernate automatically distinguishes whether an object is modified and needs to be updated. Hibernate does the dirty work to keep a mind on the performance cost, whenever required. At the point when a specific entity has a corresponding table with a large number of columns, the cost increases. To minimize the dirty checking cost, we can set the transaction to readOnly, which will increase the performance and eliminate the need for any dirty checks:

```
@Transactional(readOnly=true)
public void performanceTestMethod() {
    ....
}
```

Another improvement related to Hibernate can be taken care is by flushing and clearing the Hibernate session intermittently. At the point when data is inserted/modified in the database, Hibernate stores a version of the entities already persisted in its session, just in case they are updated again before the session is closed. We can restrict Hibernate from storing the entities in its session longer than really required. Once data is inserted, we do not need to store the entities in the persistent state anymore. We can therefore safely flush and clear the `entityManager` to synchronize the state of entities with the database and delete the entities from the cache. This will keep the application away from memory constraints, and is sure to positively impact performance:

```
entityManager.flush();
entityManager.clear();
```

One more improvement can be made by using **lazy initialization**. If we are using Hibernate, we should make sure that the lazy initialization feature is used properly. We should only use lazy load for the entities if it is required. For example, if we have a custom entity collection like `Set<Employee>` which is configured for lazy initialization, then each entity of that collection will be loaded separately using individual queries. So, if there are multiple entities lazy initialized in a set, then there will a large number of queries executed in sequence, which can majorly impact the performance.

Testing improvements

For testing improvements, we can build a test environment where an application can be executed, and get the result inside of it. We can write repeatable performance testing scripts and focus on both the absolute performance (like the page rendering time) and the performance on a scale (like the performance degrade on load). We can use a profiler in our test environment.

Proper server maintenance

One major performance aspect is related to proper server maintenance (if performance is the main concern). The following are some important points that should be considered to improve performance:

- Cleaning the temporary files periodically by creating a scheduled automated script.
- Using a load balancer when multiple server instances are running.
- Optimizing the configuration based on the application needs. For example, in the case of Tomcat, we can refer to Tomcat configuration recommendations.

Using the authentication cache with Spring Security

There can be a significant point of view to enhance performance, which can be identified when using Spring Security. Spring Security should be properly configured to improve performance when the request handling time is measured to be on the undesirable side. There might be a case where the actual request handling time is measured around 100 ms and Spring Security authentication adds 400-500 extra milliseconds. We can eliminate this performance cost using an authentication cache with Spring Security.

Implementing Executor service framework

With all possible improvements, if concurrency is maintained in terms of request handling, performance can be improved. There might be a case when load testing is performed with multiple concurrent hits to our application, and it may affect our application's performance. In such cases, we should tune up the thread defaults on the Tomcat server. In the event that there is high concurrency, the HTTP requests will be put on hold until a thread becomes available to process them.

The default server thread implementation can be extended by using the Executor framework within our business logic, to make concurrent asynchronous calls from within a method in a single thread execution flow.

Summary

In this chapter, we got a clear idea of the Spring MVC module and learned about different configuration methods. We also learned about the Spring asynchronous processing concept, with `CompletableFeature` implementation. After that, we went through the Spring Security module and learned about configuration. We also understood the authentication part of Spring Security with the stateless API. Then, we went through the monitoring part of Tomcat with JMX. At the end, we looked at Spring MVC performance improvements.

In the next chapter, we will learn about Spring database interaction. We will start with Spring JDBC configuration with optimal database design and configuration. Then, we will go through the optimal connection pooling configuration. We will also cover the concept of `@Transactional` for performance improvement. Finally, we will go through database design best practices.

5
Understanding Spring Database Interactions

In previous chapters, we learned about Spring core features, such as **dependency injection** (DI) and its configuration. We also saw how we can implement reusable code with the help of Spring **Aspect-Oriented Programming** (**AOP**). We learned how we can develop loosely coupled web applications with the help of Spring **Model-View-Controller** (**MVC**), and how we can optimize Spring MVC implementation to achieve better results using asynchronous features, multithreading, and authentication caching.

In this chapter, we will learn about database interaction with Spring Framework. Database interaction is the biggest bottleneck in application performance. Spring Framework supports all major data access technologies, such as **Java Database Connectivity** (**JDBC**) directly, any **object-relational mapping** (**ORM**) framework (such as Hibernate), the **Java Persistence API** (**JPA**), and others. We can choose any of the data access technologies to persist our application data. Here, we will explore database interaction with Spring JDBC. We will also learn about common performance traps with Spring JDBC and the best practices of database design. We will then take a look at Spring transaction management and optimal connection pooling configuration.

The following topics will be covered in this chapter:

- Spring JDBC configuration
- Database design for optimal performance
- Transaction management
- Declarative ACID using `@Transactional`
- Optimal isolation levels
- Optimal fetch size
- Optimal connection pooling configuration

- Tomcat JDBC connection pool versus HikariCP
- Database design best practices

Spring JDBC configuration

Without using JDBC, we cannot connect to a database using Java only. JDBC will be involved, either directly or indirectly, in connecting a database. But there are problems faced by Java programmers if they are working directly with core JDBC. Let's see what those problems are.

Problems with core JDBC

The following illustrates the problems that we have to face when we work with the core JDBC API:

```
String query = "SELECT COUNT(*) FROM ACCOUNT";
try (Connection conn = dataSource.getConnection();
    Statement statement = conn.createStatement();
    ResultSet rsltSet = statement.executeQuery(query))
    {
    if(rsltSet.next()){
        int count = rsltSet.getInt(1);
        System.out.println("count : " + count);
    }
    } catch (SQLException e) {
    // TODO Auto-generated catch block
        e.printStackTrace();
    }
}
```

In the preceding example, I have highlighted some code. Only the code in bold format is important; the rest is plumbing code. So, we have to write that redundant code every time, to perform a database operation.

Let's see some other problems with core JDBC:

- JDBC API exceptions are checked that forces the developers to handle errors, which increases the code, as well as the complexity, of the application
- In JDBC, we have to close the database connection; if the developer forgets to close the connection, then we get some connection issues in our application

Solving problems with Spring JDBC

To overcome the preceding problems with core JDBC, Spring Framework provides excellent database integration with the Spring JDBC module. Spring JDBC provides the `JdbcTemplate` class, which helps us to remove the plumbing code, and also helps the developer to concentrate only on the SQL query and parameters. We just need to configure the `JdbcTemplate` with a `dataSource` and write code like this:

```
jdbcTemplate = new JdbcTemplate(dataSource);
int count = jdbcTemplate.queryForObject("SELECT COUNT(*) FROM
CUSTOMER", Integer.class);
```

As we saw in the previous example, Spring provides a simplification for handling database access by using the JDBC template. The JDBC template uses core JDBC code internally and provides a new and efficient way to deal with the database. The Spring JDBC template has the following advantages, as compared to core JDBC:

- The JDBC template cleans up the resources automatically, by releasing database connections
- It converts the core JDBC `SQLException` into `RuntimeExceptions`, which provides a better error detection mechanism
- The JDBC template provides various methods to write the SQL queries directly, so it saves a lot of work and time

The following diagram shows a high-level overview of the Spring JDBC template:

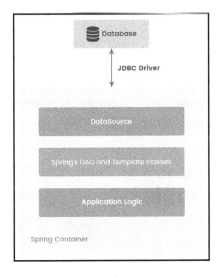

The various approaches provided by the Spring JDBC for accessing the database are as follows:

- JdbcTemplate
- NamedParameterJdbcTemplate
- SimpleJdbcTemplate
- SimpleJdbcInsert
- SimpleJdbcCall

Spring JDBC dependencies

The following are the Spring JDBC dependencies available in the pom.xml file:

- The following code is for the Spring JDBC dependency:

```
<dependency>
  <groupId>org.springframework</groupId>
  <artifactId>spring-jdbc</artifactId>
  <version>${spring.framework.version}</version>
</dependency>
```

- The following code is for the PostgreSQL dependency:

```
<dependency>
  <groupId>org.postgresql</groupId>
  <artifactId>postgresql</artifactId>
  <version>42.2.1</version>
</dependency>
```

In the preceding code, we have specified the dependency for Spring JDBC and PostgreSQL, respectively. The rest of the dependencies will be automatically resolved by Maven. Here, I am using the PostgreSQL database for our testing purposes, so I have added a PostgreSQL dependency. If you are using some other RDBMS, then you should make changes in the dependencies accordingly.

Spring JDBC example

In this example, we are using the PostgreSQL database. The table schema is as follows:

```
CREATE TABLE account
(
   accountNumber numeric(10,0) NOT NULL,
```

```
    accountName character varying(60) NOT NULL,
    CONSTRAINT accountNumber_key PRIMARY KEY (accountNumber)
)
WITH (
    OIDS=FALSE
);
```

We will use the DAO pattern for JDBC operations, so let's create a Java bean that will model our `Account` table:

```java
package com.packt.springhighperformance.ch5.bankingapp.model;

public class Account {
    private String accountName;
    private Integer accountNumber;

    public String getAccountName() {
        return accountName;
    }

    public void setAccountName(String accountName) {
        this.accountName = accountName;
    }

    public Integer getAccountNumber() {
        return accountNumber;
    }

    public void setAccountNumber(Integer accountNumber) {
        this.accountNumber = accountNumber;
    }
    @Override
    public String toString(){
        return "{accountNumber="+accountNumber+",accountName
        ="+accountName+"}";
    }
}
```

The following `AccountDao` interface declares the operation that we want to implement:

```java
public interface AccountDao {
    public void insertAccountWithJdbcTemplate(Account account);
    public Account getAccountdetails();
}
```

The Spring bean configuration class is as follows. For bean configuration, simply annotate a method with the `@Bean` annotation. When `JavaConfig` finds such a method, it will execute that method and register the return value as a bean within `BeanFactory`. Here, we have registered `JdbcTemplate`, `dataSource`, and `AccountDao` beans:

```
@Configuration
public class AppConfig{
  @Bean
  public DataSource dataSource() {
    DriverManagerDataSource dataSource = new DriverManagerDataSource();
    // PostgreSQL database we are using...
    dataSource.setDriverClassName("org.postgresql.Driver");
    dataSource.setUrl("jdbc:postgresql://localhost:5432/TestDB");
    dataSource.setUsername("test");
    dataSource.setPassword("test");
    return dataSource;
  }

  @Bean
  public JdbcTemplate jdbcTemplate() {
    JdbcTemplate jdbcTemplate = new JdbcTemplate();
    jdbcTemplate.setDataSource(dataSource());
    return jdbcTemplate;
  }

  @Bean
  public AccountDao accountDao() {
    AccountDaoImpl accountDao = new AccountDaoImpl();
    accountDao.setJdbcTemplate(jdbcTemplate());
    return accountDao;
  }

}
```

In the previous configuration file, we created a `DataSource` object of the class `DriverManagerDataSource`. This class provides a basic implementation of `DataSource` that we can use. We have also passed the PostgreSQL database URL, username, and password as properties to the `dataSource` bean. Also, the `dataSource` bean is set to the `AccountDaoImpl` bean, and we are ready with our Spring JDBC implementation. The implementation is loosely coupled, and if we want to switch to some other implementation or move to another database server, then we need to make changes only in the bean configuration. This is one of the major advantages provided by the Spring JDBC framework.

Here is the implementation of AccountDAO where we use the Spring JdbcTemplate class to insert data into the table:

```
@Repository
public class AccountDaoImpl implements AccountDao {
  private static final Logger LOGGER =
  Logger.getLogger(AccountDaoImpl.class);
  private JdbcTemplate jdbcTemplate;

  public void setJdbcTemplate(JdbcTemplate jdbcTemplate) {
    this.jdbcTemplate = jdbcTemplate;
  }

  @Override
  public void insertAccountWithJdbcTemplate(Account account) {
    String query = "INSERT INTO ACCOUNT (accountNumber,accountName)
    VALUES (?,?)";
    Object[] inputs = new Object[] { account.getAccountNumber(),
    account.getAccountName() };
    jdbcTemplate.update(query, inputs);
    LOGGER.info("Inserted into Account Table Successfully");
  }

  @Override
  public Account getAccountdetails() {
    String query = "SELECT accountNumber, accountName FROM ACCOUNT
    ";
    Account account = jdbcTemplate.queryForObject(query, new
    RowMapper<Account>(){
      public Account mapRow(ResultSet rs, int rowNum)
        throws SQLException {
          Account account = new Account();
          account.setAccountNumber(rs.getInt("accountNumber"));
          account.setAccountName(rs.getString("accountName"));
          return account;
      }});
    LOGGER.info("Account Details : "+account);
    return account;
  }
}
```

In the previous example, we used the org.springframework.jdbc.core.JdbcTemplate class to access a persistence resource. The Spring JdbcTemplate is the central class in the Spring JDBC core package and provides a lot of methods to execute queries and automatically parse ResultSet to get the object or list of objects.

The following is the test class for the preceding implementation:

```
public class MainApp {

    public static void main(String[] args) throws SQLException {
        AnnotationConfigApplicationContext applicationContext = new
        AnnotationConfigApplicationContext(
        AppConfig.class);
        AccountDao accountDao =
        applicationContext.getBean(AccountDao.class);
        Account account = new Account();
        account.setAccountNumber(101);
        account.setAccountName("abc");
        accountDao.insertAccountWithJdbcTemplate(account);
        accountDao.getAccountdetails();
        applicationContext.close();
    }
}
```

When we run the previous program, we get the following output:

```
May 15, 2018 7:34:33 PM
org.springframework.context.support.AbstractApplicationContext
prepareRefresh
INFO: Refreshing
org.springframework.context.annotation.AnnotationConfigApplicationConte
xt@6d5380c2: startup date [Tue May 15 19:34:33 IST 2018]; root of
context hierarchy
May 15, 2018 7:34:33 PM
org.springframework.jdbc.datasource.DriverManagerDataSource
setDriverClassName
INFO: Loaded JDBC driver: org.postgresql.Driver
2018-05-15 19:34:34 INFO AccountDaoImpl:36 - Inserted into Account
Table Successfully
2018-05-15 19:34:34 INFO AccountDaoImpl:52 - Account Details :
{accountNumber=101,accountName=abc}
May 15, 2018 7:34:34 PM
org.springframework.context.support.AbstractApplicationContext doClose
INFO: Closing
org.springframework.context.annotation.AnnotationConfigApplicationConte
xt@6d5380c2: startup date [Tue May 15 19:34:33 IST 2018]; root of
context hierarchy
```

Database design for optimal performance

Nowadays, it is very easy to design a database with the help of modern tools and processes, but we must know that it is a very crucial part of our application and it directly impacts the application performance. Once an application has been implemented with an inaccurate database design, it's too late to fix it. We have no other option but to buy expensive hardware to cope with the problem. So, we should be aware of some of the basic concepts and best practices of database table design, database partitioning, and good indexing, which improve our application's performance. Let's see the fundamental rules and best practices for developing high-performance database applications.

Table design

The table design type can be normalized or denormalized, but each type has its own benefits. If the table design is normalized, it means that redundant data is eliminated, and data is logically stored with the primary key/foreign key relationship, which improves data integrity. If the table design is denormalized, it means increased data redundancy and creates inconsistent dependencies between tables. In the denormalized type, all of the data for a query is usually stored in a single row in the table; that's why it is faster to retrieve data and improves query performance. In the normalized type, we have to use joins in our queries to fetch the data from the database and, due to the joins, the performance of the query is impacted. Whether we should use normalization or denormalization totally depends on our application's nature and the business requirements. Normally, databases planned for **online transaction processing (OLTP)** are typically more normalized than databases planned for **online analytical processing (OLAP)**. From a performance point of view, normalization is generally used where more INSERT/UPDATE/DELETE operations are required, while denormalization is used where more READ operations are required.

Vertical partitioning of a table

In the use of vertical partitioning, we split a table with many columns into multiple tables with particular columns. For example, we must not define very wide text or **binary large object (BLOB)** data columns infrequently queried tables because of performance issues. This data must be placed in a separate table structure, and a pointer can be used in queried tables.

What follows is a simple example of how we can use vertical partitioning on a `customer` table and move a binary data type column, `customer_Image`, into a separate table:

```
CREATE TABLE customer
(
  customer_ID numeric(10,0) NOT NULL,
  accountName character varying(60) NOT NULL,
  accountNumber numeric(10,0) NOT NULL,
  customer_Image bytea
);
```

Partition data vertically, as follows:

```
CREATE TABLE customer
(
  customer_Id numeric(10,0) NOT NULL,
  accountName character varying(60) NOT NULL,
  accountNumber numeric(10,0) NOT NULL
);

CREATE TABLE customer_Image
(
  customer_Image_ID numeric(10,0) NOT NULL,
  customer_Id numeric(10,0) NOT NULL,
  customer_Image bytea
);
```

In JPA/Hibernate, we can easily map the previous example with a lazy one-to-many relationship between the tables. The data usages of the `customer_Image` table are not frequent, so we can set it as lazily loaded. Its data is retrieved when a client requests the specific columns of the relationship.

Use indexing

We should use indexes for frequently used queries on big tables because index functionality is one of the best ways to improve the read performance of a database schema. Index entries are stored in a sorted order, which helps when processing the GROUP BY and ORDER BY clauses. Without an index, a database has to perform sort operations at the time of query executions. Through indexes, we can minimize the query execution time and improve query performance, but we should take care when creating indexes on a table; there are certain drawbacks, as well.

We should not create too many indexes on tables that update frequently because, at the time of any data modification on the table, indexing is also changed. We should use a maximum of four to five indexes on a table. If the table is read-only, then we can add more indexes without worrying.

Here are the guidelines to build the most effective indexes for your application, which are valid for every database:

- In order to achieve the maximum benefits of indexes, we should use indexes on appropriate columns. Indexes should be used on those columns that are frequently used in WHERE, ORDER BY, or GROUP BY clauses in queries.
- Always choose integer data type columns for indexing because they provide better performance than other data type columns. Keep indexes small because short indexes are processed faster in terms of I/O.
- Clustered indexes are usually better for queries retrieving a range of rows. Non-clustered indexes are usually better for point queries.

Using the correct data type

A data type determines the type of data that can be stored in a database table column. When we create a table, we should define the proper data type for each column, as per its storage requirement. For example, a SMALLINT occupies 2 bytes of space, while an INT occupies 4 bytes of space. When we define the INT data type, it means that we must store all 4 bytes into that column every time. If we are storing a number like 10 or 20, then it's a waste of bytes. This will eventually make your reads slower because the database must read over multiple sectors of the disk. Also, choosing the right data type helps us store the right data into the column. For example, if we use the date data type for a column, then the database does not allow any string and numeric data in a column that does not represent a date.

Defining column constraints

Column constraints enforce limits on the data or types of data that can be inserted/updated/deleted from a table. The whole purpose of constraints is to maintain the data integrity during an UPDATE/DELETE/INSERT into a table. However, we should only define constraints where appropriate; otherwise, we will create a negative impact on performance. For example, defining NOT NULL constraints does not impose noticeable overhead during query processing, but defining CHECK constraints might create a negative effect on performance.

Using stored procedures

Data access performance can be tuned by using stored procedures to process data in the database server to reduce the network overhead, and also by caching data within your application to reduce the number of accesses.

Transaction management

A database transaction is a critical part of any application. A database transaction is a sequence of actions that are treated as a single unit of work. These actions should either be completed entirely or take no effect at all. The management of the sequence of actions is known as **transaction management**. Transaction management is an important part of any RDBMS-oriented enterprise applications, to ensure data integrity and consistency. The concept of transactions can be described with four key properties: **atomicity**, **consistency**, **isolation**, **and durability** (**ACID**).

Transactions are described as ACID, which stands for the following:

- Atomicity: A transaction should be treated as a single unit of operation, which means that either the entire sequence of operations is completed, or it takes no effect at all
- Consistency: Once a transaction is completed and committed, then your data and resources will be in a consistent state that conforms to business rules
- Isolation: If many transactions are being processed with the same dataset at the same time, then each transaction should be isolated from others to prevent data corruption
- Durability: Once a transaction has completed, the results of the transaction are written to persistent storage and cannot be erased from the database due to system failure

Choosing a transaction manager in Spring

Spring provides different transaction managers, based on different platforms. Here, a different platform means a different persistence framework, such as JDBC, MyBatis, Hibernate, and **Java Transaction API** (**JTA**). So, we have to choose the transaction manager provided by Spring accordingly.

The following diagram describes platform-specific transaction management provided by Spring:

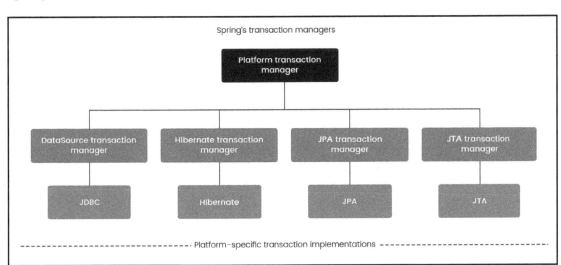

Spring supports two types of transaction management:

- Programmatic: This means that we can write our transactions using Java source code directly. This gives us extreme flexibility, but it is difficult to maintain.
- Declarative: This means that we can manage transactions in either a centralized way, by using XML, or in a distributed way, by using annotations.

Declarative ACID using @Transactional

Declarative transactions are highly recommended because they keep transaction management out of business logic and are easy to configure. Let's see an example of annotation-based declarative transaction management.

Let's use the same example that was used in the Spring JDBC section. In our example, we are using `JdbcTemplate` for database interaction. So, we need to add `DataSourceTransactionManager` in our Spring configuration file.

The following is the Spring bean configuration class:

```
@Configuration
@EnableTransactionManagement
public class AppConfig {
```

```
@Bean
public DataSource dataSource() {
    DriverManagerDataSource dataSource = new
    DriverManagerDataSource();
    dataSource.setDriverClassName("org.postgresql.Driver");
    dataSource.setUrl("jdbc:postgresql:
    //localhost:5432/TestDB");
    dataSource.setUsername("test");
    dataSource.setPassword("test");
    return dataSource;
}

@Bean
public JdbcTemplate jdbcTemplate() {
    JdbcTemplate jdbcTemplate = new JdbcTemplate();
    jdbcTemplate.setDataSource(dataSource());
    return jdbcTemplate;
}

@Bean
public AccountDao accountDao(){
  AccountDaoImpl accountDao = new AccountDaoImpl();
  accountDao.setJdbcTemplate(jdbcTemplate());
  return accountDao;
}
@Bean
public PlatformTransactionManager transactionManager() {
    DataSourceTransactionManager transactionManager = new
    DataSourceTransactionManager();
    transactionManager.setDataSource(dataSource());
    return transactionManager;
}

}
```

In the previous code, we created a dataSource bean. It is used to create the DataSource object. Here, we need to provide the database configuration properties, such as DriverClassName, Url, Username, and Password. You can change these values based on your local settings.

We are using JDBC to interact with the database; that is why we have created a transactionManager bean of the type org.springframework.jdbc.datasource.DataSourceTransactionManager.

The @EnableTransactionManagement annotation is used to turn on transaction support in our Spring application.

The following is an `AccountDao` implementation class to create a record in an `Account` table:

```
@Repository
public class AccountDaoImpl implements AccountDao {
  private static final Logger LOGGER =
  Logger.getLogger(AccountDaoImpl.class);
  private JdbcTemplate jdbcTemplate;

  public void setJdbcTemplate(JdbcTemplate jdbcTemplate) {
    this.jdbcTemplate = jdbcTemplate;
  }

  @Override
  @Transactional
  public void insertAccountWithJdbcTemplate(Account account) {
    String query = "INSERT INTO ACCOUNT (accountNumber,accountName)
    VALUES (?,?)";
    Object[] inputs = new Object[] { account.getAccountNumber(),
    account.getAccountName() };
    jdbcTemplate.update(query, inputs);
    LOGGER.info("Inserted into Account Table Successfully");
    throw new RuntimeException("simulate Error condition");
  }
}
```

In the previous code, we provided declarative transaction management through annotating the `insertAccountWithJdbcTemplate()` method with the `@Transactional` annotation. The `@Transactional` annotation can be used with a method, as well as at the class level. In the previous code, I threw the `RuntimeException` exception after inserting `Account`, to check how the transaction will be rolled back after an exception is generated.

The following is the `main` class to check our transaction management implementation:

```
public class MainApp {
  private static final Logger LOGGER = Logger.getLogger(MainApp.class);

  public static void main(String[] args) throws SQLException {
    AnnotationConfigApplicationContext applicationContext = new
    AnnotationConfigApplicationContext(
    AppConfig.class);

    AccountDao accountDao =
    applicationContext.getBean(AccountDao.class);
    Account account = new Account();
    account.setAccountNumber(202);
    account.setAccountName("xyz");
```

```
        accountDao.insertAccountWithJdbcTemplate(account);
        applicationContext.close();
    }
}
```

Now, when we run the preceding code, we get the following output:

```
INFO: Loaded JDBC driver: org.postgresql.Driver
2018-04-09 23:24:09 INFO AccountDaoImpl:36 - Inserted into Account
Table Successfully
Exception in thread "main" java.lang.RuntimeException: simulate Error
condition at
com.packt.springhighperformance.ch5.bankingapp.dao.Impl.AccountDaoImpl.
insertAccountWithJdbcTemplate(AccountDaoImpl.java:37)
```

In the previous log, data is inserted into the `Account` table successfully. But, if you check the `Account` table, you won't find a row there, which means that the transaction is rolled back completely after `RuntimeException`. Spring Framework is committing the transaction only if the method returns successfully. If there is an exception, it rolls back the whole transaction.

Optimal isolation levels

As we learned in the previous section, the concept of a transaction is described with ACID. Transaction isolation level is a concept that is not limited to Spring Framework but is applicable to any application that interacts with a database. The isolation level defines how the changes made to some data repository by one transaction affect other concurrent transactions, and also how and when that changed data becomes available to other transactions. In Spring Framework, we define the isolation level of a transaction along with the `@Transaction` annotation.

The following snippet is an example of how we can define the `isolation` level in a transactional method:

```
@Autowired
private AccountDao accountDao;

@Transactional(isolation=Isolation.READ_UNCOMMITTED)
public void someTransactionalMethod(User user) {

    // Interact with accountDao

}
```

In the preceding code, we defined a method with a transaction `isolation` level of `READ_UNCOMMITTED`. This means that the transaction in this method is executed with that `isolation` level.

Let's see each `isolation` level in detail in the following sections.

Read uncommitted

Read uncommitted is the lowest isolation level. This isolation level defines that a transaction may read data that is still uncommitted by other transactions, which means that the data is not consistent with other parts of the table or the query. This isolation level ensures the quickest performance because data is read from a table block directly, and there is no need for further processing, validation, or other verification; but it may lead to some issues, such as dirty reads.

Let's see the following diagram:

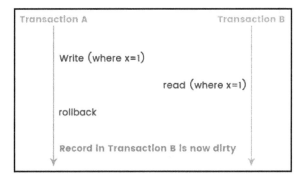

In the preceding diagram, **Transaction A** writes data; meanwhile, **Transaction B** reads that same data before **Transaction A** commits it. Later, **Transaction A** decides to **rollback**, due to some exception. Now, the data in **Transaction B** is inconsistent. Here, **Transaction B** was running in a `READ_UNCOMMITTED` isolation level, so it was able to read data from **Transaction A** before a commit occurred.

Note that `READ_UNCOMMITTED` can also create issues like **non-repeatable reads** and **phantom reads**. A non-repeatable read occurs when a transaction isolation selected as `READ_COMMITTED`.

Let's see the `READ_COMMITTED` isolation level in detail.

Read committed

The read committed isolation level defines that a transaction can't read data that is not committed by other transactions. This means that the dirty read is no longer an issue, but other issues may occur.

Let's see the following diagram:

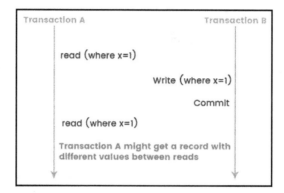

In this example, **Transaction A** reads some data. Then, **Transaction B** writes that same data and commits. Later, **Transaction A** reads that same data again and may get different values, because **Transaction B** already made changes to that data and committed. This is a non-repeatable read.

Note that READ_COMMITTED can also create issues like **phantom reads**. A phantom reads occurs when a transaction isolation is selected as REPEATABLE_READ.

Let's see the REPEATABLE_READ isolation level in detail.

Repeatable read

The REPEATABLE_READ isolation level defines that if a transaction reads one record from the database multiple times, the results of all of those reading operations must be the same. This isolation helps us to prevent issues like dirty reads and non-repeatable reads, but it may create another issue.

Let's see the following diagram:

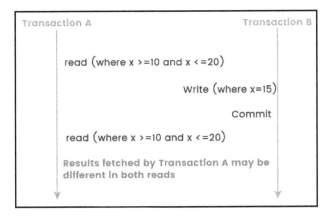

In this example, **Transaction A** reads a range of data. Simultaneously, **Transaction B** inserts new data in the same range that **Transaction A** initially fetched and commits. Later, **Transaction A** reads the same range again and will also get the record that **Transaction B** just inserted. This is a phantom read. Here, **Transaction A** fetched a range of records from the database multiple times and got different result sets.

Serializable

The serializable isolation level is the highest and more restrictive of all isolation levels. It protects against dirty, non-repeatable reads and phantom reads. Transactions are executed with locking at all levels (**read**, **range**, and **write** locking), so they appear as if they were executed in a serialized way. In serializable isolation, we will ensure that no issues will happen, but concurrently executing transactions occurs to be serially executing that degrade the performance of the application.

The following is a summary of the relationships between isolation levels and read phenomena:

Levels	Dirty reads	Non-repeatable reads	Phantom reads
READ_UNCOMMITTED	Yes	Yes	Yes
READ_COMMITTED	No	Yes	Yes
REPEATABLE_READ	No	No	Yes
SERIALIZABLE	No	No	No

If the isolation level is not explicitly set, then the transaction uses a default isolation level, as per the related database.

Optimal fetch size

The network traffic between the application and the database server is one of the key factors of your application performance. If we can reduce the traffic, it will help us improve the performance of the application. The fetch size is the number of rows retrieved from the database at one time. It depends on the JDBC driver. The default fetch size of most of the JDBC drivers is 10. In normal JDBC programming, if you want to retrieve 1,000 rows, then you will need 100 network round-trips between the application and database server to retrieve all of the rows. It will increase the network traffic, and also impact performance. But if we set the fetch size to 100, then the number of network round-trips will be 10. This will greatly improve the performance of your application.

Many frameworks, such as Spring or Hibernate, give you very convenient APIs to do this. If we do not set the fetch size, then it will take the default value and provide poor performance.

The following sets the `FetchSize`, with standard JDBC calls:

```
PreparedStatement stmt = null;
ResultSet rs = null;

try
{
  stmt = conn. prepareStatement("SELECT a, b, c FROM TABLE");
  stmt.setFetchSize(200);

  rs = stmt.executeQuery();
  while (rs.next()) {
    ...
  }
}
```

In the previous code, we can set the fetch size on each `Statement` or `PreparedStatement`, or even on `ResultSet`. By default, `ResultSet` uses the fetch size of `Statement`; `Statement` and `PreparedStatement` use the fetch size of a specific JDBC driver.

We can also set the `FetchSize` in the Spring `JdbcTemplate`:

```
JdbcTemplate jdbc = new JdbcTemplate(dataSource);
jdbc.setFetchSize(200);
```

The following points should be considered when setting the fetch size:

- Make sure that your JDBC driver supports configuring the fetch size
- The fetch size should not be hardcoded; keep it configurable because it depends on JVM heap memory size, which varies with different environments
- If the fetch size is large, the application might encounter an out of memory issue

Optimal connection pooling configuration

JDBC uses a connection pool when accessing a database. **Connection pooling** is similar to any other form of object pooling. Connection pooling usually involves little or no code modification, but it can provide significant benefits in terms of application performance. Database connection performs the various task while creating, such as initializing a session in the database, performing user authentication and establishing transaction contexts. Creating a connection is not a zero cost process; therefore, we should create connections in an optimal way and reduce impacts on performance. A connection pool allows for the reuse of physical connections and minimizes expensive operations in the creation and closure of sessions. Also, maintaining many idle connections is expensive for a database management system, and the pool can optimize the usage of idle connections or disconnect those no longer used.

Why is pooling useful? Here are a few reasons:

- Frequently opening and closing connections can be expensive; it is better to cache and reuse.
- We can limit the number of connections to the database. This will stop from accessing a connection until it is available. This is especially helpful in distributed environments.
- We can use multiple connection pools for common operations, based on our requirements. We can design one connection pool for OLAP and another for OLAP, each with different configurations.

In this section, we will see what the optimal connection pooling configuration is, to help improve the performance.

The following is a simple connection pool configuration for PostgreSQL:

```
<Resource type="javax.sql.DataSource"
          name="jdbc/TestDB"
          factory="org.apache.tomcat.jdbc.pool.DataSourceFactory"
          driverClassName="org.postgresql.Driver"
          url="jdbc:postgresql://localhost:5432/TestDB"
          username="test"
          password="test"
/>
```

Sizing the connection pool

We need to work with the following attributes to size the connection pool:

- `initialSize`: The `initialSize` attribute defines the number of connections that will be established when the connection pool is started.
- `maxActive`: The `maxActive` attribute can be used to limit the maximum number of established connections to the database.
- `maxIdle`: The `maxIdeal` attribute is used to maintain the maximum number of idle connections in the pool at all times.
- `minIdle`: The `minIdeal` attribute is used to maintain the minimum number of idle connections in the pool at all times.
- `timeBetweenEvictionRunsMillis`: The validation/cleaner thread runs every `timeBetweenEvictionRunsMillis` milliseconds. It's a background thread that can test idle, abandoned connections, and resize the pool while the pool is active. The thread is also responsible for connection leak detection. This value should not be set below 1 second.
- `minEvictableIdleTimeMillis`: The minimum amount of time an object may sit idle in the pool before it is eligible for eviction.

Validate connections

The advantage of setting this configuration is that an invalid connection will never be used, and it helps us to prevent client errors. The disadvantage of this configuration is a small performance penalty because to validate the connection, one round-trip to the database is required to check whether the session is still active. The validation is accomplished via sending a small query to the server, but the cost of this query could be lower.

The configuration parameters for validating connections are as follows:

- `testOnBorrow`: When the `testOnBorrow` attribute is defined as true, the connection object is validated before use. If it fails to validate, it will be dropped into the pool, and another connection object will be chosen. Here, we need to make sure that the `validationQuery` attribute is not null; otherwise, there is no effect on configuration.
- `validationInterval`: The `validationInterval` attribute defines the frequency of the validating connection. It should not be more than 34 seconds. If we set a larger value, it will improve the application performance, but will also increase the chances of a stale connection being present in our application.
- `validationQuery`: The `SELECT 1` PostgreSQL query is used to validate connections from the pool before sending them to serve a request.

Connection leaks

The following configuration settings can help us to detect connection leaks:

- `removeAbandoned`: This flag should be true. It means that abandoned connections are removed if they exceed `removeAbandonedTimeout`.
- `removeAbandonedTimeout`: This is in seconds. A connection is considered abandoned if it's running more than `removeAbandonedTimeout`. The value depends on the longest running query in your applications.

So, in order to get optimal pool sizing, we need to modify our configuration to meet one of following conditions:

```
<Resource type="javax.sql.DataSource"
        name="jdbc/TestDB"
        factory="org.apache.tomcat.jdbc.pool.DataSourceFactory"
        driverClassName="org.postgresql.Driver"
        url="jdbc:postgresql://localhost:5432/TestDB"
        username="test"
        password="test"
        initialSize="10"
        maxActive="100"
        maxIdle="50"
        minIdle="10"
        suspectTimeout="60"
        timeBetweenEvictionRunsMillis="30000"
        minEvictableIdleTimeMillis="60000"
        testOnBorrow="true"
```

```
                          validationInterval="34000"
                          validationQuery="SELECT 1"
                          removeAbandoned="true"
                          removeAbandonedTimeout="60"
                          logAbandoned="true"
              />
```

Tomcat JDBC connection pool versus HikariCP

There are many open source connection pool libraries available, such as C3P0, Apache Commons DBCP, BoneCP, Tomcat, Vibur, and Hikari. But which one to use depends on certain criteria. The following criteria will help to decide which connection pool to go with.

Reliability

Performance is always good, but the reliability of a library is always more important than performance. We should not go with a library that gives a higher performance but is not reliable. The following things should be considered when selecting a library:

- How widely it is used?
- How is the code maintained?
- The number of outstanding bugs open in the library.
- It's community of developers and users.
- How active is the library development?

Performance

Performance is also considered important criteria. The performance of the library depends on how it is configured, and the environment in which it is tested. We need to make sure that the library that we choose will have good performance in our own environment, with our own configurations.

Features

It is also important to look at the features provided by the library. We should check all parameters, and also check the default value of the parameters if we don't provide them. Also, we need to look at some of the connection strategies, such as auto-commit, isolation level, and statement caching.

Ease of use

It is important how easily we can configure the connection pool with the use of a library. Also, it should be well documented and frequently updated.

The following table lists the differences between a Tomcat JDBC connection pool and HikariCP:

Tomcat JDBC	HikariCP
Does not test connections on `getConnection()` by default.	Tests connections on `getConnection()`.
Does not close abandoned open statements.	Tracks and closes abandoned connections.
Does not by default reset auto-commit and transaction levels for connections in the pool; users must configure custom interceptors to do this.	Resets auto-commit, transaction isolation, and read-only status.
Pool prepared statement properties are not used.	We can use pool prepared statement properties.
Does not, by default, execute a `rollback()` on connections returned to the pool.	By default, executes a `rollback()` on connections returned to the pool.

Database interaction best practices

This section lists some basic rules that developers should be aware of when developing any applications. A failure to follow the rules will result in a poorly performing application.

Using Statement versus PreparedStatement versus CallableStatement

Choose between the `Statement`, `PreparedStatement`, and `CallableStatement` interfaces; it depends on how you plan to use the interface. The `Statement` interface is optimized for a single execution of an SQL statement, while the `PreparedStatement` object is optimized for SQL statements that will be executed multiple times, and `CallableStatement` is generally preferred for executing stored procedures:

- `Statement`: The `PreparedStatement` is used to execute normal SQL queries. It is preferred when a particular SQL query is to be executed only once. The performance of this interface is very low.

- `PreparedStatement`: The `PreparedStatement` interface is used to execute parametrized or dynamic SQL queries. It is preferred when a particular query is to be executed multiple times. The performance of this interface is better than the `Statement` interface (when used for multiple executions of the same query).
- `CallableStatement`: The `CallableStatement` interface is preferred when the stored procedures are to be executed. The performance of this interface is high.

Using Batch instead of PreparedStatement

Inserting a large amount of data into a database is typically done by preparing an `INSERT` statement and executing that statement multiple times. This increases the number of JDBC calls and impacts the performance. To reduce the number of JDBC calls and improve the performance, you can send multiple queries to the database at a time by using the `addBatch` method of the `PreparedStatement` object.

Let's look at the following example:

```
PreparedStatement ps = conn.prepareStatement(
"INSERT INTO ACCOUNT VALUES (?, ?)");
for (n = 0; n < 100; n++) {
    ps.setInt(accountNumber[n]);
    ps.setString(accountName[n]);
    ps.executeUpdate();
}
```

In the preceding example, `PreparedStatement` is used to execute an `INSERT` statement multiple times. For executing the preceding `INSERT` operation, 101 network round-trips are required: one to prepare the statement, and the remaining 100 to execute the `INSERT` SQL statement. So, inserting and updating a large amount of data actually increases network traffic and, due to that, impacts performance.

Let's see how we can reduce the network traffic and improve performance with the use of `Batch`:

```
PreparedStatement ps = conn.prepareStatement(
"INSERT INTO ACCOUNT VALUES (?, ?)");
for (n = 0; n < 100; n++) {
    ps.setInt(accountNumber[n]);
    ps.setString(accountName[n]);
    ps.addBatch();
}
ps.executeBatch();
```

In the previous example, I used the `addBatch()` method. It consolidates all 100 `INSERT` SQLs and executes the entire operation with only two network round-trips: one for preparing the statement and another for executing the batch of consolidated SQLs.

Minimizing the use of database metadata methods

Although almost no JDBC application can be written without database metadata methods, compared to other JDBC methods, database metadata methods are slow. When we use a metadata method, a `SELECT` statement makes two round-trips to the database: one for metadata, and the second for the data. This is very performance expensive. We can improve the performance by minimizing the use of metadata methods.

> An application should cache all metadata, as they will not change, so multiple executions are not needed.

Using get methods effectively

JDBC provides different types of methods to retrieve data from a result set, such as `getInt`, `getString`, and `getObject`; the `getObject` method is the generic one, and you can use it for all data types. But, we should always avoid the use of `getObject` because it gives worse performance than others. When we get data with the use of `getObject`, the JDBC driver must perform extra processing to determine the type of value being fetched and generate the appropriate mapping. We should always use the specific method for the data type; this provides better performance than using a generic one like `getObject`.

We can also improve the performance by using a column number instead of a column name; for example, `getInt(1)`, `getString(2)`, and `getLong(3)`. If we are using a column name instead of a column number (for example, `getString("accountName")`), then the database driver first converts the column name to uppercase (if required), then compares `accountName` with all columns available in the result set. This processing time directly impacts performance. We should reduce that processing time with the use of column numbers.

When to avoid connection pooling

The use of connection pooling on certain kinds of applications can definitely degrade the performance. If your application has any of the following characteristics, it is not a suitable candidate for connection pooling:

- If an application restarts many times daily, we should avoid connection pooling because, based on the configuration of the connection pool, it may be populated with connections each time the application is started, which would cause a performance penalty up front.
- If you have single-user applications, such as applications only generating reports (in this type of application, the user only uses the application three to four times daily, for generating reports), then avoid connection pooling. The memory utilization for establishing a database connection three to four times daily is low, compared to the database connection associated with a connection pool. In such cases, configuring a connection pool degrades the overall performance of the application.
- If an application runs only batch jobs, there is no advantage to using connection pooling. Normally, a batch job is run at the end of the day or month or year, during the off hours, when performance is not as much of a concern.

Choose commit mode carefully

When we commit a transaction, the database server must write the changes made by the transaction to the database. This involves expensive disk input/output and the driver need to send requests over the socket.

In most standard APIs, the default commit mode is auto-commit. In the auto-commit mode, the database performs a commit for each SQL statement, such as INSERT, UPDATE, DELETE, and SELECT statements. The database driver sends a commit request to the database after each SQL statement operation. This request requires one network round-trip. The round-trip to the database occurs even though the SQL statement execution made no changes to the database. For example, the driver makes a network round-trip even when a SELECT statement is executed. The auto-commit mode usually impacts performance because of the significant amount of disk input/output needed to commit every operation.

So, we set the auto-commit mode to off to improve the performance of the application, but leaving the transaction active is also not advisable. Leaving transactions active can reduce throughput by holding locks on rows for longer than necessary and preventing other users from accessing the rows. Commit transactions in intervals that allow maximum concurrency.

Setting the auto-commit mode to off and doing a manual commit is also not advisable for certain applications. For example, consider a banking application that allows users to transfer money from one account to another. To protect the data integrity of that work, it is required to commit the transaction after both accounts are updated with the new amounts.

Summary

In this chapter, we got a clear idea of the Spring JDBC module and learned how Spring JDBC helps to remove the boilerplate code that we use in core JDBC. We also learned how to design our database for optimal performance. We saw the various benefits of transaction management in Spring. We learned about various configuration techniques, such as isolation level, fetch size, and connection pooling, which improves the performance of our application. At the end, we looked at the best practices for database interaction, which can help us to improve our application's performance.

In the next chapter, we will see database interaction using ORM frameworks (such as Hibernate), and we will learn about Hibernate configurations in Spring, common Hibernate traps, and Hibernate performance tuning.

6
Hibernate Performance Tuning and Caching

In the previous chapter, we learned how to access a database in our application using JDBC. We learned how to optimally design our database, transaction management, and connection pooling, to get the best performance from our application. We also learned how to prevent SQL injection by using a prepared statement in JDBC. We saw how we can remove traditional boilerplate code for managing transactions, exceptions, and commits by using JDBC templates.

In this chapter, we will move toward some advanced ways of accessing the database using **object-relational mapping (ORM)** frameworks, such as Hibernate. We will learn how we can improve database access in an optimal way by using ORM. With Spring Data, we can further remove the boilerplate code of implementing the **Data Access Object (DAO)** interface.

The following are the topics we will go through in this chapter:

- Introduction to Spring Hibernate and Spring Data
- Spring Hibernate configuration
- Common Hibernate traps
- Hibernate performance tuning

Introduction to Spring Hibernate and Spring Data

As we saw in previous chapters, **Java Database Connectivity (JDBC)** exposes an API that hides the database vendor-specific communication. However, it suffers from the following limitations:

- JDBC development is very much verbose, even for trivial tasks
- JDBC batching requires a specific API and is not transparent
- JDBC does not provide built-in support for explicit locking and optimistic concurrency control
- There is a need to handle transactions explicitly, with lots of duplicate code
- Joined queries require additional processing to transform the `ResultSet` into domain models, or **data transfer objects (DTO)**

Almost all limitations of JDBC are covered by ORM frameworks. ORM frameworks provide for object mapping, lazy loading, eager loading, managing resources, cascading, error handling, and other services at the data access layer. One of the ORM frameworks is Hibernate. **Spring Data** is a layer implemented by the Spring Framework to provide boilerplate code and ease the access to different kinds of persistence stores used in applications. Let's see an overview of Spring Hibernate and Spring Data in the following sections.

Spring Hibernate

Hibernate evolved from the frustration of EJB's complexities and performance issues. Hibernate provided a way to abstract SQL and allowed developers to focus on persisting objects. Hibernate, as an ORM framework, helps to map objects to tables in relational databases. Hibernate had its own standards when introduced, and code became tightly coupled with its standard implementation. So, to make persistence generic and vendors agnostic, **Java Community Process (JCP)** developed a standardized API specification, known as the **Java Persistence API (JPA)**. All ORM frameworks started following this standard, and so does Hibernate.

Spring doesn't implement its own ORM; however, it supports any ORM framework, such as Hibernate, iBatis, JDO, and so on. With the ORM solution, we can easily persist and access data in the form of **Plain Old Java Object** (**POJO**) objects from relational databases. The Spring ORM module is an extension of the Spring JDBC DAO module. Spring also provides ORM templates, such as the JDBC-based templates we saw in `Chapter 5`, *Understanding Spring Database Interactions*.

Spring Data

As we know, in the last couple of years, unstructured and non-relational databases (known as NoSQL) have become popular. With the Spring JPA, talking to relational databases became easy; so, how can we talk to non-relational databases? Spring developed a module called Spring Data to provide a common approach to talk to a wide variety of data stores.

As each persistence store has different ways to connect and retrieve/update data, Spring Data provides a common approach to accessing data from each different store.

The following are the features of Spring Data:

- Easy integration with multiple data stores, through various repositories. Spring Data provides generic interfaces for each data store in the form of repositories.
- The ability to parse and form queries based on repository method names provided the convention is followed. This reduces the amount of code to be written to fetch data.
- Basic auditing support, such as created by and updated by a user.
- Fully integrated with the Spring core module.
- Integrated with the Spring MVC to expose **REpresentational State Transfer** (**REST**) controllers through the Spring Data REST module.

The following is a small sample of the Spring Data repository. We don't need to implement this method to write a query and fetch an account by ID; it will be done by Spring Data internally:

```
public interface AccountRepository extends CrudRepository<Account,
Long> {
    Account findByAccountId(Long accountId);
}
```

Spring Hibernate configuration

We know that Hibernate is a persistence framework that provides relationship mapping between objects and database tables and that it has rich features to improve performance and the optimal use of resources such as caching, eager and lazy loading, event listeners, and so on.

The Spring Framework provides full support to integrate many persistence ORM frameworks, and so does Hibernate. Here, we will see Spring with JPA, using Hibernate as a persistence provider. Also, we will see Spring Data with the JPA repository using Hibernate.

Spring with JPA using Hibernate

As we know, JPA is not an implementation; it is the specification for persistence. The Hibernate framework follows all of the specifications, and it also has its own additional features. Using the JPA specification in an application enables us to easily switch the persistence provider later if needed.

To use Hibernate on its own requires `SessionFactory`, and to use Hibernate with JPA requires `EntityManager`. We are going to use JPA, and the following is the Spring Java-based Hibernate JPA configuration:

```
@Configuration
@EnableTransactionManagement
@PropertySource({ "classpath:persistence-hibernate.properties" })
@ComponentScan({ "com.packt.springhighperformance.ch6.bankingapp" })
public class PersistenceJPAConfig {

  @Autowired
  private Environment env;

  @Bean
  public LocalContainerEntityManagerFactoryBean entityManagerFactory()
{
    LocalContainerEntityManagerFactoryBean em = new
    LocalContainerEntityManagerFactoryBean();
    em.setDataSource(dataSource());
    em.setPackagesToScan(new String[] {
    "com.packt.springhighperformance
    .ch6.bankingapp.model" });

    JpaVendorAdapter vendorAdapter = new HibernateJpaVendorAdapter();
```

```
   em.setJpaVendorAdapter(vendorAdapter);
   em.setJpaProperties(additionalProperties());

   return em;
}

@Bean
public BeanPostProcessor persistenceTranslation() {
   return new PersistenceExceptionTranslationPostProcessor();
}

@Bean
public DataSource dataSource() {
   DriverManagerDataSource dataSource = new DriverManagerDataSource();
   dataSource.setDriverClassName(this.env.get
   Property("jdbc.driverClassName"));
   dataSource.setUrl(this.env.getProperty("jdbc.url"));
   dataSource.setUsername(this.env.getProperty("jdbc.user"));
   dataSource.setPassword(this.env.getProperty("jdbc.password"));
   return dataSource;
}

@Bean
public PlatformTransactionManager
transactionManager(EntityManagerFactory emf) {
    JpaTransactionManager transactionManager = new
    JpaTransactionManager();
    transactionManager.setEntityManagerFactory(emf);
    return transactionManager;
}

@Bean
public PersistenceExceptionTranslationPostProcessor
  exceptionTranslation() {
   return new PersistenceExceptionTranslationPostProcessor();
}

private Properties additionalProperties() {
  Properties properties = new Properties();
  properties.setProperty("hibernate.hbm2ddl.auto",
  this.env.getProperty("hibernate.hbm2ddl.auto"));
  properties.setProperty("hibernate.dialect",
  this.env.getProperty("hibernate.dialect"));
  properties.setProperty("hibernate.generate_statistics",
  this.env.getProperty("hibernate.generate_statistics"));
  properties.setProperty("hibernate.show_sql",
  this.env.getProperty("hibernate.show_sql"));
  properties.setProperty("hibernate.cache.use_second_level_cache",
```

```
        this.env.getProperty("hibernate.cache.use_second_level_cache"));
        properties.setProperty("hibernate.cache.use_query_cache",
        this.env.getProperty("hibernate.cache.use_query_cache"));
        properties.setProperty("hibernate.cache.region.factory_class",
        this.env.getProperty("hibernate.cache.region.factory_class"));
        return properties;
    }
}
```

In the preceding configuration, we configured `EntityManager` using the `LocalContainerEntityManagerFactoryBean` class. We set `DataSource` to provide information on where to find our database. As we are using JPA, which is the specification followed by a different vendor, we specified which vendor we are using in our application by setting `HibernateJpaVendorAdapter` and setting vendor-specific additional properties.

Now that we have configured the JPA-based ORM framework in our application, let's see how to create a DAO in our application when using ORM.

The following is the `AbstractJpaDAO` class, having the basic common method required for all of our DAOs:

```
public abstract class AbstractJpaDAO<T extends Serializable> {

    private Class<T> clazz;

    @PersistenceContext
    private EntityManager entityManager;

    public final void setClazz(final Class<T> clazzToSet) {
        this.clazz = clazzToSet;
    }

    public T findOne(final Integer id) {
        return entityManager.find(clazz, id);
    }

    @SuppressWarnings("unchecked")
    public List<T> findAll() {
        return entityManager.createQuery("from " +
        clazz.getName()).getResultList();
    }

    public void create(final T entity) {
        entityManager.persist(entity);
    }
```

```
    public T update(final T entity) {
        return entityManager.merge(entity);
    }

    public void delete(final T entity) {
        entityManager.remove(entity);
    }

    public void deleteById(final Long entityId) {
        final T entity = findOne(entityId);
        delete(entity);
    }
}
```

The following is the `AccountDAO` class, which manages the `Account` entity-related method:

```
@Repository
public class AccountDAO extends AbstractJpaDAO<Account> implements
IAccountDAO {

  public AccountDAO() {
    super();
    setClazz(Account.class);
  }
}
```

The preceding examples of DAO implementation are pretty basic, and is what we generally do in our applications. In case DAO throws an exception such as `PersistenceException`, and instead of showing an exception to the user, we would want to show the right, human-readable message to the end users. To provide a readable message when an exception occurs, Spring provides a translator which we need to define in our configuration class as follows:

```
@Bean
    public BeanPostProcessor persistenceTranslation() {
        return new PersistenceExceptionTranslationPostProcessor();
    }
```

The `BeanPostProcessor` command works when we annotate our DAOs with the `@Repository` annotation. The `PersistenceExceptionTranslationPostProcessor` bean will act as an advisor for the beans, which are annotated with the `@Repository` annotation. Remember that we learned about advises in `Chapter 3`, *Tuning Aspect-Oriented Programming*. When advised, it will re-throw Spring-specific unchecked data access exceptions caught in the code.

So, this was the basic configuration of Spring JPA using Hibernate. Now, let's see the Spring Data configuration.

Spring Data configuration

As we learned in the introduction, Spring Data provides a common approach to connect different data stores. Spring Data provides basic abstraction through the `Repository` interface. The `Repository` interface is the core interface of Spring Data. Basic repositories provided by Spring Data are as follows:

- `CrudRepository` provides basic CRUD operations
- `PagingAndSortingRepository` provides methods to do the pagination and sorting of records
- `JpaRepository` provides JPA-related methods, such as flush and insert/update/delete in a batch, and so on

`Repository`, in Spring Data, eliminates the implementation of DAOs and templates such as `HibernateTemplate` or `JdbcTemplate`. Spring Data is so abstract that we don't even need to write any method implementation for basic CRUD operations; we just need to define interfaces based on `Repository` and define proper naming conventions for methods. Spring Data will take care of creating a query based on a method name, and execute it to a database.

The Java configuration for Spring Data remains the same as what we saw for the Spring JPA, using Hibernate, except for the addition of defining repositories. The following is a snippet of declaring repositories to the configuration:

```
@Configuration
@EnableTransactionManagement
@PropertySource({ "classpath:persistence-hibernate.properties" })
@ComponentScan({ "com.packt.springhighperformance.ch6.bankingapp" })
    @EnableJpaRepositories(basePackages =
"com.packt.springhighperformance.ch6.bankingapp.repository")
public class PersistenceJPAConfig {

}
```

In this chapter, we are not going to dive too deeply into Hibernate and Spring Data-specific development. However, we will dive into the problems faced when not using Hibernate or JPA optimally and with the right configuration in our application, and solutions to the problems, with the best practices to achieve high performance. Let's look at the common Hibernate problems we face when using it in our applications.

Common Hibernate traps

The JPA and Hibernate ORM are the most popular frameworks used in most Java applications to interact with a relational database. Their popularity increased because they use the mapping between the object-oriented domain and underlying relational database to abstract the database interactions and make it very easy to implement simple CRUD operations.

Under this abstraction, Hibernate uses a lot of optimizations and hides all database interactions behind its API. Oftentimes, don't even know when Hibernate will execute an SQL statement. Because of this abstraction, it becomes hard to find inefficiencies and potential performance problems. Let's see the common Hibernate problems that we face in our applications.

Hibernate n + 1 problem

When using JPA and Hibernate, the fetch type adds a good amount of impact to an application's performance. We should always fetch as much data as we need to fulfill a given business requirement. To do so, we set the associated entities FetchType as LAZY. When we set these associated entities fetch type as LAZY, we implement a nested select in our applications, because we are not aware how these associations are fetched under the abstraction provided by ORM frameworks. Nested selects are nothing but two queries, where one is the outer, or main, query (which fetches the result from a table) and the other is executed for each row as a result of the main query (to fetch the corresponding or related data from other table/s).

The following example shows how we unintentionally implement something that does nested select:

```
Account account = this.em.find(Account.class, accountNumber);
List<Transaction> lAccountTransactions = account.getTransaction();
for(Transaction transaction : lAccountTransactions){
  //.....
}
```

Mostly, a developer tends to write code like the preceding example, and won't realize how an ORM framework like Hibernate could be fetching data internally. Here, ORM frameworks like Hibernate execute one query to get the `account`, and a second query to get transactions for that `account`. Two queries are fine, and won't impact the performance much. These two queries are for one association in an entity.

Let's suppose that we have five associations in the `Account` entity: `Transactions`, `UserProfile`, `Payee`, and so on. When we try to fetch each association from the `Account` entity, the framework executes one query for each association, resulting in 1 + 5 = 6 queries. Six queries won't impact much, right? These queries are for one user, so what if the number of concurrent users of our application is 100? Then we will have 100 * (1 + 5) = 600 queries. Now, that is something that would impact the performance. This 1 + 5 queries while fetching `Account` is called the **n + 1** problem in Hibernate. We will see some approaches to avoiding this problem in the *Hibernate performance tuning* section of this chapter.

The open session in view anti-pattern

We saw in the preceding section that in order to defer fetching until the associated entity is needed, we set the fetch type of the associated entities as `LAZY`. When we try to access these associated entities in our presentation layer (if they are not initialized in our business (service) layer), an exception is thrown by Hibernate, called `LazyInitializationException`. When the service layer method completes its execution, Hibernate commits the transaction and closes the session. So, by the time the view is rendered, the active session is not available to fetch the associated entities.

To avoid `LazyInitializationException`, one of the solutions is an open session in view. This means that we keep the Hibernate session open in view so that the presentation layer can fetch the required associated entities, and then close the session.

In order to enable this solution, we need to add a web filter to our application. If we are using Hibernate on its own, we need to add `filter`, `OpenSessionInViewFilter`; if we are using JPA, then we need to add `filter OpenEntityManagerInViewFilter`. As we are using JPA with Hibernate in this chapter, the following is the snippet to add `filter`:

```
<filter>
    <filter-name>OpenEntityManagerInViewFilter</filter-name>
    <filter-
class>org.springframework.orm.jpa.support.OpenEntityManagerInViewFilter
</filter-class>
    ....
</filter>
```

```
...
<filter-mapping>
    <filter-name>OpenEntityManagerInViewFilter</filter-name>
    <url-pattern>/*</url-pattern>
</filter-mapping>
```

The solution provided by the **Open Session in View** (**OSIV**) pattern to avoid the exception might not look terrible at first glance; however, there are problems with using the OSIV solution. Let's go over some issues with the OSIV solution:

1. The service layer opens the transaction when its method is invoked and closes it when the method execution completes. Afterward, there is no explicit open transaction. Every additional query executed from the view layer will be executed in auto-commit mode. Auto-commit mode could be dangerous from a security and database point of view. Due to the auto-commit mode, the database needs to flush all of the transaction logs to disk immediately, causing high I/O operations.

2. It will violate the single responsibility of SOLID principles, or separation of concern because database statements are executed by both the service layer and the presentation layer.

3. It will lead to the n + 1 problem that we saw in the preceding *Hibernate n + 1 problem* section, though Hibernate offers some solutions that can cope with this scenario: @BatchSize and FetchMode.SUBSELECT, however, would apply to all of the business requirements, whether we want to or not.

4. The database connection is held until the presentation layer completes rendering. This increases the overall database connection time and impacts transaction throughput.

5. If an exception occurs in the fetching session or executing queries in the database, it will occur while rendering the view, so it will not be feasible to render a clean error page to the user.

Unknown Id.generator exception

Most of the time, we will want to use database sequencing for our table primary key. In order to do so, we know that we need to add the generator attribute in the @GeneratedValue annotation on our entity. The @GeneratedValue annotation allows us to define a strategy for our primary key.

The following is the code snippet that we add in our entity to set database sequencing for our primary key:

```
@Id
@GeneratedValue(strategy = GenerationType.SEQUENCE, generator =
"accountSequence")
private Integer id;
```

Here, we thought that `accountSequence` was the database sequence name provided to the `generator`; however, when the application runs, it gives an exception. To solve this exception, we annotate our entity with `@SequenceGenerator` and give the name as `accountSequence`, and the database sequence name that Hibernate needs to use. The following shows how to set the `@SequenceGenerator` annotation:

```
@Id
@GeneratedValue(strategy = GenerationType.SEQUENCE, generator =
"accountSequence")
@SequenceGenerator(name = "accountSequence", sequenceName =
"account_seq", initialValue = 100000)
private Long accountId;
```

We saw common problems faced during implementation. Now, let's see how to tune Hibernate to achieve high performance.

Hibernate performance tuning

In the preceding section, we saw common Hibernate traps or issues. These issues don't necessarily mean faults in Hibernate; sometimes, they are from incorrect usage of the framework, and in some cases, limitations of the ORM framework itself. In the following sections, we will see how to improve performance in Hibernate.

Approaches to avoid the n + 1 problem

We already saw the n + 1 problem in the *Hibernate n + 1 problem* section. Too many queries will slow down our application's overall performance. So, in order to avoid these additional queries with lazy loading, let's see what options are available.

Fetch join using JPQL

Normally, we call the `findById` method of DAO to fetch the outer or parent entity and then call the getter methods of associations. Doing so leads to n + 1 queries because the framework will execute additional queries for each association. Instead, we can write a JPQL query using the `createQuery` method of `EntityManager`. In this query, we can join our associated entity, which we want to fetch along with the outer entity by using `JOIN FETCH`. The following is an example of how to get `JOIN FETCH` entities:

```
Query query = getEntityManager().createQuery("SELECT a FROM Account AS
a JOIN FETCH a.transactions WHERE a.accountId=:accountId",
Account.class);
query.setParameter("accountId", accountId);
return (Account)query.getSingleResult();
```

The following is the log that states that only one query is executed:

```
2018-03-14 22:19:29 DEBUG ConcurrentStatisticsImpl:394 - HHH000117:
HQL: SELECT a FROM Account AS a JOIN FETCH a.transactions WHERE
a.accountId=:accountId, time: 72ms, rows: 3
Transactions:::3
2018-03-14 22:19:29 INFO StatisticalLoggingSessionEventListener:258 -
Session Metrics {
    26342110 nanoseconds spent acquiring 1 JDBC connections;
    0 nanoseconds spent releasing 0 JDBC connections;
    520204 nanoseconds spent preparing 1 JDBC statements;
    4487788 nanoseconds spent executing 1 JDBC statements;
    0 nanoseconds spent executing 0 JDBC batches;
    0 nanoseconds spent performing 0 L2C puts;
    0 nanoseconds spent performing 0 L2C hits;
    0 nanoseconds spent performing 0 L2C misses;
    13503978 nanoseconds spent executing 1 flushes (flushing a total of
    4 entities and 1 collections);
    56615 nanoseconds spent executing 1 partial-flushes (flushing a
    total of 0 entities and 0 collections)
}
```

`JOIN FETCH` tells `entityManager` to load the selected entity, as well as the associated entity, in the same query.

The advantage of this approach is that Hibernate fetches everything within one query. From a performance point of view, this option is good, because everything is fetched in a single query instead of multiple queries. This reduces the round-trips to the database for each separate query.

The disadvantage of this approach is that we need to write additional code to execute the query. It's not an issue until we have a few associations or relations to fetch. But, it gets worse if the entity has many associations and we need to fetch different associations for each different use case. So, in order to fulfill each different use case, we need to write different queries with required associations. Too many different queries for each use case would be quite messy, and also difficult to maintain.

This option would be a good approach if the number of queries requiring different join fetch combinations was low.

Join fetch in Criteria API

This approach is the same as JOIN FETCH in JPQL; however, this time, we are using the Criteria API of Hibernate. The following is an example of how to use JOIN FETCH in the Criteria API:

```
CriteriaBuilder criteriaBuilder =
    getEntityManager().getCriteriaBuilder();
    CriteriaQuery<?> query =
    criteriaBuilder.createQuery(Account.class);
    Root root = query.from(Account.class);
    root.fetch("transactions", JoinType.INNER);
    query.select(root);
    query.where(criteriaBuilder.equal(root.get("accountId"),
    accountId));

    return (Account)this.getEntityManager().createQuery(query)
    .getSingleResult();
```

This option has the same advantages and disadvantages as JPQL. Most of the time, when we write a query using the Criteria API, it is use case-specific. So, this option might not be a huge problem in those cases, and it would be a good approach to reduce the amount of queries performed.

Named entity graph

Then named entity graph is a new feature, introduced in JPA 2.1. In this approach, we can define a graph of entities that need to be queried from the database. We can define the entity graph on our entity class by using the @NamedEntityGraph annotation.

The following is an example of how to define a graph using `@NamedEntityGraph` on the entity class:

```
@Entity
@NamedEntityGraph(name="graph.transactions", attributeNodes=
@NamedAttributeNode("transactions"))
public class Account implements Serializable {

    private static final long serialVersionUID = 1232821417960547743L;

    @Id
    @GeneratedValue(strategy = GenerationType.AUTO)
    @Column(name = "account_id", updatable = false, nullable = false)
    private Long accountId;
    private String name;
    @OneToMany(mappedBy = "account", fetch=FetchType.LAZY)
    private List<Transaction> transactions = new ArrayList<Transaction>
    ();
    .....
}
```

An entity graph definition is independent of the query and defines which attributes to be fetched from the database. An entity graph can be used as a load or a fetch graph. If a load graph is used, all attributes that are not specified in the entity graph definition will keep following their default `FetchType`. If a fetch graph is used, only the attributes specified by the entity graph definition will be treated as `FetchType.EAGER`, and all other attributes will be treated as `LAZY`. The following is an example of how to use a named entity graph as a `fetchgraph`:

```
EntityGraph<?> entityGraph =
getEntityManager().createEntityGraph("graph.transactions");
Query query = getEntityManager().createQuery("SELECT a FROM Account AS
a WHERE a.accountId=:accountId", Account.class);

query.setHint("javax.persistence.fetchgraph", entityGraph);
query.setParameter("accountId", accountId);
return (Account)query.getSingleResult();
```

We are not going to go into detail on named entity graphs in this book. This is one of the best approaches to resolve the n + 1 issue with Hibernate. This is an improved version of `JOIN FETCH`. An advantage on top of `JOIN FETCH` is that it will be reused for different use cases. The only disadvantage of this approach is that we must annotate the named entity graph for each combination of associations that we want to fetch in a single query. So, this can get quite messy if we have too many different combinations to set.

Dynamic entity graph

A dynamic entity graph is similar to a named entity graph, with the difference that we can define it dynamically through the Java API. The following is an example of how to define an entity graph using the Java API:

```
EntityGraph<?> entityGraph =
getEntityManager().createEntityGraph(Account.class);
entityGraph.addSubgraph("transactions");
Map<String, Object> hints = new HashMap<String, Object>();
hints.put("javax.persistence.fetchgraph", entityGraph);

return this.getEntityManager().find(Account.class, accountId, hints);
```

So, if we have lots of use case-specific entity graphs, this approach will be an advantage over named entity graph where adding an annotation on our entity for each use case makes code unreadable. We can keep all use case-specific entity graphs in our business logic. With this approach, the disadvantage is that we need write more code and in order to make code reusable, we need to write more of the methods for each related business logic.

Finding performance issues with Hibernate statistics

Most of the time, we face slow responses on the production system, while our local or test system works just fine. Most of these cases are because of slow database queries. In a local instance, we don't know the exact volume of requests and volume of data that we have in production. So, how do we find out which query is causing the problem, without adding logs to our application code? The answer is the Hibernate `generate_statistics` configuration.

We need to set the Hibernate property `generate_statistics` to true, as this property is false by default. This property impacts the overall performance, as it logs all database activities. So, enable this property only when you want to analyze slow queries. This property will generate summarized multiline logs, showing how much overall time is spent on database interaction.

If we want to log the execution of each query, we need to enable `org.hibernate.stat` to the DEBUG level in log configuration; similarly, if we want to log SQL queries (with times), we need to enable `org.hibernate.SQL` to the DEBUG level.

The following is an example of a printed log:

```
2018-03-13 23:05:16 DEBUG ConcurrentStatisticsImpl:394 - HHH000117:HQL:SELECT a FROM Account a WHERE account_id=:accountId,time: 5ms, rows: 1
2018-03-13 23:05:16 INFO  StatisticalLoggingSessionEventListener:258 - Session Metrics |
    28914003 nanoseconds spent acquiring 1 JDBC connections;
    0 nanoseconds spent releasing 0 JDBC connections;
    309332 nanoseconds spent performing 2 JDBC statements;
    4733531 nanoseconds spent executing 2 JDBC statements;
    0 nanoseconds spent executing 0 JDBC bacehos;
    0 nanoseconds spent performing 0 L2C puts;
    0 nanoseconds spent performing 0 L2C hits;
    0 nanoseconds spent performing 0 L2C misses;
    16616588 nanoseconds spent executing 1 flushes (flushing a total of 4 entities and 1 collections);
    73846 nanoseconds spent executing 1 partial-flushes (flushing a total of 0 entities and 0 collections)
}
```

Total SQL queries executed

Query executed

Number of rows returned

Time taken to execute all SQL queries

Hibernate generate_statistics logs

An overall statistics information log shows the number of JDBC connections used, statements, caches, and performed flushes. We always need to check the number of statements first to see if there is an n + 1 issue.

Using query-specific fetching

It is always recommended to select only those columns which are required for our use case. If you are using the `CriteriaQuery`, use projections to select required columns. Fetching the entire entity would degrade the application's performance when the table has too many columns, so the database needs to go through each block of the stored page to retrieve them, and we might not even need all of those columns in our use case. Also, if we are using an entity instead of the DTO class, persistence context has to manage the entities and also fetches associated/child entities when required. This adds an overhead. Instead of fetching the entire entity, fetch only the required columns:

```
SELECT a FROM Account a WHERE a.accountId= 123456;
```

Fetch a specific column as follows:

```
SELECT a.accountId, a.name FROM Account a WHERE a.accountId = 123456;
```

The better way to use query-specific fetching is to use DTO projection. Our entities are managed by a persistence context. So, it would be easier to fetch `ResultSet` to the entity, in case we want to update it. We set the new values to the setter methods, and Hibernate will take care of the SQL statements to update it. This easiness comes with the price of performance since Hibernate needs to do dirty checks on all managed entities to find out if it needs to save any changes to the database. DTO are the POJO classes which are the same as our entities, however, it's not managed by persistence.

We can fetch specific columns in JPQL by using the constructor expression, as follows:

```
entityManager.createQuery("SELECT new
com.packt.springhighperformance.ch6.bankingapp.dto.AccountDto(a.id,
a.name) FROM Account a").getResultList();
```

Similarly, we can do the same thing by using `CriteriaQuery` and `JPAMetamodel`, as follows:

```
CriteriaBuilder cb = em.getCriteriaBuilder();
CriteriaQuery q = cb.createQuery(AccountDTO.class);
Root root = q.from(Account.class);
q.select(cb.construct(AccountDTO.class,
root.get(Account_.accountNumber), root.get(Account_.name)));

List authors = em.createQuery(q).getResultList();
```

Caching and its best practices

We already saw how caching works in Spring in `Chapter 3`, *Tuning Aspect-Oriented Programming*. Here, we will see how caching works in Hibernate, and what different types of caching are available in Hibernate. In Hibernate, there are three different types of caching, as follows:

- First level cache
- Second level cache
- Query cache

Let's understand how each cache mechanism works in Hibernate.

First level cache

In the first level cache, Hibernate caches entities in session objects. The Hibernate first level cache is enabled by default, and we cannot disable it. Still, Hibernate provides methods through which we can delete particular objects from the cache, or completely clear the cache from a session object.

As Hibernate does a first level cache in a session object, any object cached will not be visible to another session. When the session is closed, the cache is cleared. We are not going to go into detail on this caching mechanism, as it is available by default, and there is no way to tune or disable it. There are certain methods to know for this level of cache, as follows:

- Use the session's `evict()` method to delete a single object from the Hibernate first level cache
- Use the session's `clear()` method to clear the cache completely
- Use the session's `contains()` method to check whether an object is present in the Hibernate cache

Second level cache

One benefit of database abstraction layers, such as ORM frameworks, is their ability to transparently cache data:

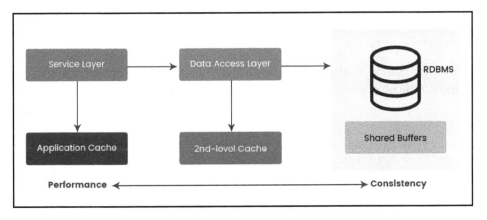

Caching at the database and application level

The application cache is not an option for many large enterprise applications. With the application cache, we help to reduce many round-trips to get required data from the database cache. The application-level cache stores entire objects, which are retrieved based on hash table keys. Here, we are not going to talk about the application level cache; we are going to talk about the second level cache.

In Hibernate, unlike with the first level cache, the second level cache is `SessionFactory` scoped; hence, it is shared by all sessions created within the same session factory. When the second level is enabled and the entity is looked up, the following applies:

1. It will first be checked in the first level cache if the instance is available, and then returned.
2. If the instance is not present in the first level, it will try to find it in the second level cache, and, if found, it is assembled and returned.
3. If the instance is not found in the second level cache, it will make the trip to the database and fetch the data. The data is then assembled and returned.

Hibernate doesn't do any caching by itself. It provides the interface `org.hibernate.cache.spi.RegionFactory`, and cache providers do the implementation of this interface. Here, we will talk about the Ehcache provider, which is mature and the most widely used cache. In order to enable second level caching, we need to add the following two lines to our persistence properties:

```
hibernate.cache.use_second_level_cache=true
hibernate.cache.region.factory_class=org.hibernate.cache.ehcache.EhCach
eRegionFactory
```

Once the level two cache is enabled, we need to define which entities we want to cache; we need to annotate those entities with `@org.hibernate.annotations.Cache`, as follows:

```
@Entity
@Cacheable
@org.hibernate.annotations.Cache(usage =
CacheConcurrencyStrategy.READ_WRITE)
public class Account implements Serializable {

}
```

Hibernate uses a separate cache region to store the states of instances of an entity. The region name is the fully qualified class name. There are different concurrency strategies provided by Hibernate, which we can use based on our requirements. The following are the different concurrency strategies:

*   `READ_ONLY`: Used only for entities that are never modified; in the case of modification, an exception is thrown. It is used for some static reference data that doesn't change.

- NONSTRICT_READ_WRITE: The cache is updated when the transaction affecting the cached data is committed. While the cache is updated, there is a chance to obtain stale data from the cache. This strategy is suitable for those requirements that can tolerate eventual consistency. This strategy is useful for data that is rarely updated.
- READ_WRITE: To avoid obtaining stale data while the cache is updated, this strategy uses soft locks. When a cached entity is updated, the entity in the cache is locked and is released after the transaction is committed. All concurrent transactions will retrieve the corresponding data directly from the database.
- TRANSACTIONAL: The transaction strategy is mainly used in distributed caches in the JTA environment.

If there is no expiration and eviction policy defined, the cache could grow indefinitely and eventually consume all of the memory. We need to set these policies, and it depends on cache providers. Here, we are using Ehcache, and the following is the method to define expiration and eviction policies in ehcache.xml:

```
<ehcache>
    <cache
    name="com.packt.springhighperformance.ch6.bankingapp.model.Account"
    maxElementsInMemory="1000" timeToIdleSeconds="0"
    timeToLiveSeconds="10"/>
</ehcache>
```

Many of us think that the cache stores entire objects. However, it doesn't store entire objects, but rather, it stores them in a disassembled state:

- The primary key is not stored, because it is the cache key
- Transient properties are not stored
- Collection associations are not stored by default
- All property values, except for associations, are stored in their original forms
- Foreign keys for @ToOne associations are stored only with IDs

Query cache

The query cache can be enabled by adding the following Hibernate property:

```
hibernate.cache.use_query_cache=true
```

Once the query cache is enabled, we can specify which query we want to cache, as follows:

```
Query query = entityManager.createQuery("SELECT a FROM Account a WHERE
a.accountId=:accountId", Account.class);
query.setParameter("accountId", 7L);
query.setHint(QueryHints.HINT_CACHEABLE, true);
Account account = (Account)query.getSingleResult();
```

If we execute the same query again which is cached by query cache, the following is the log printed with DEBUG mode:

```
2018-03-17 15:39:07 DEBUG StandardQueryCache:181 - Returning cached
query results
2018-03-17 15:39:07 DEBUG SQL:92 - select account0_.account_id as
account_1_0_0_, account0_.name as name2_0_0_ from Account account0_
where account0_.account_id=?
```

Performing updates and deletes in bulk

As we know, ORM frameworks, like Hibernate, execute two or more queries when we update or delete any entity. If we were updating or deleting a few entities, this would be fine, but think of a scenario where we want to update or delete 100 entities. Hibernate will execute 100 SELECT queries to fetch the entities, and another 100 queries to update or delete the entities.

We know that in order to achieve better performance for any application, a lower number of database statements need to be executed. If we perform the same update or delete using JPQL or native SQL, it can be done in a single statement. Hibernate provides a lot of benefits as an ORM framework and can help us keep a focus on business logic, rather than database operations. In scenarios where Hibernate could be costly such as bulk update and delete, we should use the native database queries to avoid overhead and achieve better performance.

The following is a way that we can execute the native query to UPDATE all of the user's emails in the bank inbox as read:

```
entityManager.createNativeQuery("UPDATE mails p SET read = 'Y' WHERE
user_id=?").setParameter(0, 123456).executeUpdate();
```

We can measure the performance difference using the Hibernate method and native query to update bulk data, simply by logging System.currentTimeMillis(). There should be a significant increase in performance, with the native query 10 times faster than the Hibernate approach.

The native query will definitely improve bulk operation performance, but at the same time, it comes with issues with the first level cache, and won't trigger any entity life cycle events. As we know, Hibernate stores all entities that we use within a session in the first level cache. It has benefits for write-behind optimizations and avoids duplicate select statement executions for the same entity in the same session. But, with the native query, Hibernate doesn't know which entities were updated or removed and updates the first level cache accordingly. It will keep using an outdated version of the entity in the cache if we fetch the entity before executing the native query in the same session. The following is an example of an issue with the first level cache, using the native query:

```
private void performBulkUpdateIssue(){
    Account account = this.entityManager.find(Account.class, 7L);
    entityManager.createNativeQuery("UPDATE account a SET name =
    name
    || '-updated'").executeUpdate();
    _logger.warn("Issue with Account Name: "+account.getName());

    account = this.entityManager.find(Account.class, 7L);
    _logger.warn("Issue with Account Name: "+account.getName());
}
```

A solution to this problem is to update the first level cache manually, by detaching the entity before native query execution and attaching it back after native query execution. To do so, perform the following:

```
private void performBulkUpdateResolution(){
    //make sure you are passing right account id
    Account account = this.entityManager.find(Account.class, 7L);

    //remove from persistence context
    entityManager.flush();
    entityManager.detach(account);
    entityManager.createNativeQuery("UPDATE account a SET name =
    name
    || '-changed'").executeUpdate();
    _logger.warn("Resolution Account Name: "+account.getName());
    account = this.entityManager.find(Account.class, 7L);
    _logger.warn("Resolution Account Name: "+account.getName());
}
```

Call the `flush()` and `detach()` methods before performing the native query. The `flush()` method tells Hibernate to write the changed entities from the first level cache to the database. This is to make sure that we don't lose any updates.

Hibernate programming practices

Until now, we saw problems with Hibernate when it is not used optimally, and how to use Hibernate to achieve better performance. The following are the best practices to follow (in terms of caching, and in general) to achieve better performance when using JPA and Hibernate.

Caching

The following are some programming tips in relation to the different caching levels in Hibernate:

- Make sure to use the same version of `hibernate-ehcache` as the version of Hibernate.
- Since Hibernate caches all of the objects into the session first level cache, when running bulk queries or batch updates, it's necessary to clear the cache at certain intervals to avoid memory issues.
- When caching an entity using the second level cache, collections inside of the entity are not cached by default. In order to cache the collections, annotate the collections within the entity with `@Cacheable` and `@org.hibernate.annotations.Cache(usage = CacheConcurrencyStrategy.READ_WRITE)`. Each collection is stored in a separate region in the second level cache, where the region name is the fully qualified name of the entity class, plus the name of the collection property. Define the expiration and eviction policy separately for each collection that's cached.
- When DML statements are executed using JPQL, the cache for those entities will be updated/evicted by Hibernate; however, when using the native query, the entire second level cache will be evicted, unless the following detail is added to native query execution when using Hibernate with JPA:

```
Query nativeQuery = entityManager.createNativeQuery("update Account
set name='xyz' where name='abc'");

nativeQuery.unwrap(org.hibernate.SQLQuery.class).addSynchronizedEnt
ityClass(Account.class);

nativeQuery.executeUpdate();
```

- In the case of query caching, there will be one cache entry for each combination of query and parameter values, so queries, where different combinations of parameter values are expected, are not good for caching.
- In the case of query caching, a query that fetches the entity classes for which there are frequent changes in the database is not a good candidate for caching, because the cache will be invalidated when any entity involved in the query is changed.
- All query cache results are stored in the `org.hibernate.cache.internal.StandardQueryCache` region. We can specify the expiration and eviction policies for this region. Also, if required, we can set a different region for a particular query to cache by using the query hint `org.hibernate.cacheRegion`.
- Hibernate keeps last update timestamps in a region named `org.hibernate.cache.spi.UpdateTimestampsCache` for all query cached tables. Hibernate uses this to verify that cached query results are not stale. It is best to turn off automatic eviction and expiration for this cache region, because entries in this cache must not be evicted/expired, as long as there are cached query results in cache results regions.

Miscellaneous

The following are general Hibernate best practices for achieving better performance in your application:

- Avoid enabling `generate_statistics` on the production system; rather, analyze issues by enabling `generate_statistics` on a staging or a replica of the production system.
- Hibernate always updates all database columns, even though we update one or a few columns only. All of the columns in the UPDATE statement would take more time than a few columns. In order to achieve high performance and avoid using all of the columns in an UPDATE statement, only include the columns that are actually modified and use the `@DynamicUpdate` annotation on an entity. This annotation tells Hibernate to generate a new SQL statement for each update operation, with only modified columns.
- Set the default `FetchType` as `LAZY` for all associations, and use query-specific fetching, using `JOIN FETCH`, named entity graphs, or dynamic entity graphs, to avoid the n + 1 issue and improve performance.

- Always use bind parameters to avoid SQL injections and improve performance. When used with bind parameters, Hibernate and the database optimizes queries if the same query is executed multiple times.

- Perform UPDATE or DELETE in a huge list in bulk, instead of performing them one-by-one. We already discussed this in the *Performing updates and deletes in bulk* section.

- Never use entities for read-only operations; rather, use different projections provided by JPA and Hibernate. One that we already saw was the DTO projection. For read-only requirements, changing the entity to a constructor expression in SELECT is very easy, and high performance will be achieved.

- With the introduction of the Stream API in Java 8.0, many people used its features to process huge data retrieved from a database. Stream is designed to work on huge data. But there are certain things that a database can do better than the Stream API. Don't use the Stream API for the following requirements:
  - Filter data: The database can filter data more efficiently than the Stream API, which we can do using the WHERE clause
  - Limiting data: The database provides more efficient results than the Stream API when we want to limit the number of data to be retrieved
  - Sort data: The database can sort more efficiently than the Stream API by using the ORDER BY clause

- Use order instead of sorting, especially for huge associated entities of data. Sorting is Hibernate-specific, and not a JPA specification:
  - Hibernate sorts using the Java Comparator in memory. However, the same desired order of data can be retrieved from the database by using the @OrderBy annotation on associated entities.
  - If the column name is not specified, @OrderBy will be done on the primary key.
  - Multiple columns can be specified in @OrderBy, comma-separated.
  - The database handles @OrderBy more efficiently than implementing sorting in Java. The following is a code snippet, as an example:

    ```
    @OneToMany(mappedBy = "account", fetch=FetchType.LAZY)
    @OrderBy("created DESC")
    private List<Transaction> transactions = new
    ArrayList<Transaction>();
    ```

- Hibernate regularly performs dirty checks on all entities that are associated with the current PersistenceContext, to detect required database updates. For entities that never update, such as read-only database views or tables, performing dirty checks is an overhead. Annotate these entities with @Immutable, and Hibernate will ignore them in all dirty checks, improving performance.

- Never define unidirectional one-to-many relationships; always define bidirectional relationships. If a unidirectional one-to-many relationship is defined, Hibernate will need an extra table to store the references of both of the tables, just like in many-to-many relationships. There would be many extra SQL statements executed in the case of a unidirectional approach, which would not be good for performance. For better performance, annotate @JoinColumn on the owning side of the entity, and use the mappedby attribute on the other side of the entity. This will reduce the number of SQL statements, improving performance. Adding and removing an entity from a relationship needs to be handled everywhere explicitly; hence, it is recommended to write helper methods in the parent entity, as follows:

```
@Entity
public class Account {

    @Id
    @GeneratedValue
    private Integer id;

    @OneToMany(mappedBy = "account")
    private List<Transaction> transactions = new ArrayList<>();

    public void addTransaction(Transaction transaction) {
        transactions.add(transaction);
        transaction.setPost(this);
    }

    public void removeTransaction(Transaction transaction) {
        transactions.remove(transaction);
        transaction.setPost(null);
    }
}

@Entity
public class Transaction {

    @Id
    @GeneratedValue
```

```
private Integer id;
@ManyToOne(fetch = FetchType.LAZY)
@JoinColumn(name = "account_id")
private Account account;
}
```

Summary

We started this chapter with a basic configuration of the ORM framework, Hibernate, using JPA and Spring Data. We focused on common ORM problems faced in production. In this chapter, we learned optimal solutions to the common problems faced while working on Hibernate for database operations and for achieving high performance. We learned useful tips for the best practices to follow when working on ORM-based frameworks to achieve high performance from the development stage, instead of resolving problems when facing them in the production system.

In line with optimization and high performance, the next chapter provides information on Spring messaging optimization. As you know, messaging framework enterprise applications connect multiple clients and provide reliability, asynchronous communications, and loose coupling. Frameworks are built to provide various benefits; however, we face issues if we don't use them optimally. Similarly, there are certain parameters related to queue configuration and scalability that will maximize throughput in the Spring messaging framework of our enterprise application if used effectively.

Optimizing Spring Messaging

7

In the previous chapter, we learned different advanced ways of accessing databases using **object-relational mapping** (**ORM**) frameworks such as Hibernate. We also learned how to improve database access in an optimal way when using ORM. We looked into Spring Data to remove boilerplate code for implementing the **Data Access Object** (**DAO**) interface. At the end of the chapter, we saw the Hibernate best practices.

In this chapter, we will learn about Spring's support for messaging. Messaging is a very powerful technique that helps to scale the applications and also encourages us to decouple the architecture.

Spring Framework provides an extensive support to integrate the messaging system into our application with the simplified use of the **Java Message Service** (**JMS**) API to receive messages asynchronously. Messaging solutions can be used to send messages from one point in an application to a known point, and one point from an application to many other unknown points. It is equivalent to sharing something face to face and sharing something on a loudspeaker to a group of people, respectively. If we want messages to be sent to an unknown set of clients, then we can use a queue to broadcast the messages to the people who are listening.

The following are the topics that we will cover in this chapter:

- What is messaging?
- What is AMQP?
- Why do we need AMQP?
- RabbitMQ
- Spring messaging configuration

What is messaging?

Messaging is a mode of interaction between software components or applications, where clients can send messages to, and receive messages from, any other client.

This message exchange can be done using a component called **broker**. The broker provides all the necessary support and services to exchange messages along with the capability of interacting with other interfaces. These interfaces are known as **Message Oriented Middleware** (**MOM**). The following diagram depicts a MOM-based messaging system:

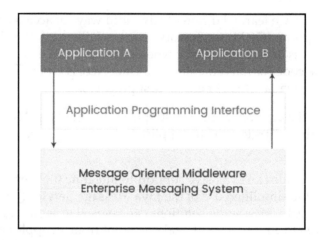

Messaging systems reduce the complexity of developing distributed applications using the AMQP, STOMP, and XMPP protocols. Let's discuss them in detail:

- **AMQP**: AMQP is an open, standard layer application protocol for asynchronous messaging systems. In AMQP, messages should be transmitted in binary format.
- **STOMP**: STOMP stands for **Simple Text Oriented Messaging Protocol**. STOMP provides a compatible medium that allows systems to communicate with almost all the available message brokers.
- **XMPP**: XMPP stands for **Extensible Messaging and Presence Protocol**. It is an XML-based, open standard communications protocol for MOM.

What is AMQP?

The **Advanced Messaging Queuing Protocol** (**AMQP**) is an open standard application layer protocol. Each byte of the transmitted message is specified, which allows it to be used in many other languages and OS architectures. Hence, this makes it a cross-platform-compatible protocol. AMQP is supported by multiple message brokers, such as RabbitMQ, ActiveMQ, Qpid, and Solace. Spring provides AMQP-based messaging implementation solutions. Spring provides a template for sending and receiving messages through the message broker.

Problems with the JMS API

JMS API is used to send and receive messages in Java platforms. Spring underpins a simple method to utilize the JMS API by providing an additional layer around the JMS layer. This layer improves the way toward sending and receiving messages and also deals with the creation and release of the connection object.

For creating Java-based messaging systems, the JMS API is widely utilized by the developers. The principal disadvantage of using the JMS API is the platform contradiction, which implies we can use the JMS API to develop messaging systems that will work with Java-based applications. The JMS API does not support other programming languages.

Why do we need AMQP?

AMQP is the solution for this JMS API problem. The fundamental advantage of using AMQP is that it underpins the exchange of messages, paying little mind to the platform's compatibility and message brokers. We can develop messaging systems using any programming language and still we can communicate with each system using AMQP-based message brokers.

Differences between AMQP and the JMS API

These are some of the important differences between AMQP and the JMS API:

- Platform compatibility
- Messaging models

- Message data type
- Message structure
- Message routing
- Workflow strategy

These are explained in more detail in the following sections.

Platform compatibility

JMS applications can work with any operating systems, but they only support the Java platform. If we want to develop a messaging system to communicate with more than one system, then all those systems should be developed using Java programming languages.

While using AMQP, we can develop a messaging system that can communicate with any system with different technologies. So it is not required for a destination system to be developed in the same technology.

Messaging models

The JMS API provides two sorts of messaging models, point-to-point, and publish-subscribe, for asynchronous messaging between different platform systems.

AMQP provides support for the following exchange types: direct, topic, fanout, and headers.

Message data type

The JMS API supports five standard messaging types:

- `StreamMessage`
- `MapMessage`
- `TextMessage`
- `ObjectMessage`
- `BytesMessage`

AMQP supports only one type of message—binary messages; messages must be transmitted in binary format only.

Message structure

The JMS API message has an essential structure that comprises three parts: headers, properties, and body. It characterizes a standard form that ought to be portable across all JMS providers.

The AMQP message comprises four parts: headers, properties, body, and footers.

Message routing

For message routing, AMQP can likewise be utilized for complex routing schemes, which is conceivable through the routing key and depends on the destination matching criteria.

The JMS API is based on more complicated routing schemes that are based on hierarchic topics and client-message selection filters.

Workflow strategy

In AMQP, producers first need to send the message to the exchange, and then it will be transferred to the queue, whereas in JMS, there is no need to exchange since messages can be sent directly to the queue or topic.

What are exchanges, queues, and bindings?

AMQP deals with Publishers and Consumers. The **Publisher** sends the message and the **Consumer** receives it. A message broker takes care of this mechanism to ensure that messages from Publishers go to the right Consumers. Two key elements used by message brokers are exchanges and queues. The following diagram illustrates how a Publisher connects to a Consumer:

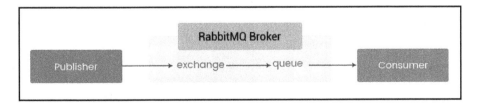

Let's understand the exchange, queue, and binding terminologies.

Exchange

An exchange is responsible for taking a message and routing it into zero or more queues. Each exchange of a broker has a unique name, as well as a few other properties within a virtual host. The message-routing algorithm used depends on the exchange type and bindings. As we mentioned earlier, there are four different types of exchanges: direct, topic, fanout, and headers.

Queue

A queue is a component from which a message consumer receives messages. A queue has a unique name so that systems can reference them. The queue name can be defined by the application or generated by the broker when requested. We cannot use a queue name beginning with `amq.`, since it is reserved by the broker for internal use.

Binding

The binding is used to connect queues to exchanges. There are certain standard headers called **routing key** headers, and they are used by the broker to match messages to queues. Each queue has a specific binding key and if that key matches the value of the routing key header, the queue receives the message.

Introducing RabbitMQ

RabbitMQ is AMQP-based and one of the most widely used lightweight, reliable, scalable, portable, and robust message brokers that is written in Erlang. The important reason behind the popularity of RabbitMQ is that it is easy to set up and fit for the cloud scale. RabbitMQ is open source and supported by most of the operating systems and platforms. The applications that use RabbitMQ can communicate with other systems via a platform neutral, wire-level protocol—the AMQP. Now, let's go through how to configure RabbitMQ.

Setting up the RabbitMQ server

Before developing a messaging system, we need to set up a message broker that will handle sending and receiving the messages. RabbitMQ is the AMQP server, which is freely available at `http://www.rabbitmq.com/download.html`.

Once you install the RabbitMQ server, depending on your installation path, you will have to set the following system variable with `RABBITMQ_HOME`:

```
RABBITMQ_HOME=D:\Apps\RabbitMQ Server\rabbitmq_server-3.6.0
```

After setting up everything, you can access the RabbitMQ console by using `http://localhost:15672/`.

You will see the default login screen, where you need to enter guest as the default **Username** `guest` and `guest` as the **Password**:

After logging in, you will see the RabbitMQ server home page, where you can manage the **Queues**, **Exchanges**, and **Bindings**:

Now we will go through an example to learn about the messaging configuration in the Spring application.

Spring messaging configuration

Before we start with the example, we need to understand the basic setup requirements to configure a messaging application. We will create a RabbitMQ messaging application and go through the different parts of the configuration. The following steps are involved in setting up messaging in Spring application:

1. Configure a Maven dependency for RabbitMQ
2. Configure RabbitMQ
3. Create a component to send and receive messages

Configuring a Maven dependency for RabbitMQ

Let's start with adding a dependency for RabbitMQ to `pom.xml`. The following code shows the dependency to be configured:

```xml
<dependency>
    <groupId>org.springframework.amqp</groupId>
    <artifactId>spring-rabbit</artifactId>
    <version>${rabbitmq.version}</version>
</dependency>
```

We have added the dependency for RabbitMQ. Now, let's create a class to configure the queue, exchange, and binding between them.

Configuring RabbitMQ

Now, we will go through the configuration parts to get a clear understanding of the configuration of `ConnectionFactory`, `RabbitTemplate`, `Queue`, `Exchange`, `Binding`, message listener container, and message converter.

Configuring ConnectionFactory

For the `ConnectionFactory` interface, there is a concrete implementation `CachingConnectionFactory` which, by default, creates a single connection proxy that can be shared by the whole application. The code used to create `CachingConnectionFactory` is as follows:

```java
@Bean
public ConnectionFactory connectionFactory() {
        CachingConnectionFactory connectionFactory = new
        CachingConnectionFactory("localhost");
        connectionFactory.setUsername("guest");
        connectionFactory.setPassword("guest");
        return connectionFactory;
}
```

We can also configure cached connections using `CachingConnectionFactory` as well as just channels. We need to set the `cacheMode` property to `CacheMode.CONNECTION` using `setCacheMode()`. We can also limit the total number of connections allowed using the `connectionLimit` property through the use of `setConnectionLimit()`. When this property is set and the limit is exceeded, the `channelCheckoutTimeLimit` is used to wait for a connection to become idle.

Configuring a queue

Now, we will configure a queue using the `Queue` class. The following code creates a queue with a specific name:

```
@Bean
public Queue queue() {
    return new Queue(RABBIT_MESSAGE_QUEUE, true);
}
```

The preceding `queue()` method creates an AMQP queue with a specific name declared using the `RABBIT_MESSAGE_QUEUE` constant. We can also set the durability using the `durable` flag. We need to pass it along with the second constructor argument as a Boolean type.

Configuring an exchange

Now, we need to create an AMQP exchange, to which a message producer will send a message. The `Exchange` interface represents an AMQP exchange. There are four implementations of the `Exchange` interface type: `DirectExchange`, `TopicExchange`, `FanoutExchange`, and `HeadersExchange`. We can use any exchange type based on our requirements. We will use `DirectExchange` using the following code:

```
@Bean
public DirectExchange exchange() {
    return new DirectExchange(RABBIT_MESSAGE_EXCHANGE);
}
```

The `exchange()` method creates `DirectExchange` with a specific name defined under `RABBIT_MESSAGE_EXCHANGE`. We can also set the durability using the durable flag. We need to pass it along with the second constructor argument as a Boolean type.

Configuring a binding

Now, we need to create a binding using the `BindingBuilder` class to connect `queue` to `Exchange`. The following code is used to create a binding:

```
@Bean
Binding exchangeBinding(DirectExchange directExchange, Queue queue) {
    return BindingBuilder.bind(queue).
        to(directExchange)
        .with(ROUTING_KEY);
}
```

The `exchangeBinding()` method creates a binding of `queue` and `Exchange` with the `ROUTING_KEY` routing key value.

Configuring RabbitAdmin

`RabbitAdmin` is used to declare the exchanges, queues, and binding that needs to be ready on startup. `RabbitAdmin` does the automatic declaration of the queues, exchanges, and binding. The main benefit of this auto-declaration is that if the connection is disconnected for some reason, they will be applied automatically when the connection is re-established. The following code configures `RabbitAdmin`:

```
@Bean
public RabbitAdmin rabbitAdmin() {
    RabbitAdmin admin = new RabbitAdmin(connectionFactory());
    admin.declareQueue(queue());
    admin.declareExchange(exchange());
    admin.declareBinding(exchangeBinding(exchange(), queue()));
    return admin;
}
```

`rabbitAdmin()` will declare the `Queue`, `Exchange`, and `Binding`. The `RabbitAdmin` constructor creates an instance using the `connectionFactory()` bean and it must not be null.

> `RabbitAdmin` performs automatic declaration only when the `CachingConnectionFactory` cache mode is `CHANNEL` (it is by default). The reason for this limitation is because it may be the case that exclusive and autodelete queues may be bound to the connection.

Configuring a message converter

At the precise time a message is received by the listener, two change steps happen. In the initial step, the incoming AMQP message is changed over to a Spring messaging `Message` using `MessageConverter`. In the second step, when the target method is executed, the payload of the message is changed over to the parameter type if necessary. By default, in the initial step, `MessageConverter` is utilized as Spring AMQP `SimpleMessageConverter` that handles the transformation to String and `java.io.Serializable`.

In the second step, by default, `GenericMessageConverter` is used for conversion. We have used `Jackson2JsonMessageConverter` in the following code:

```
@Bean
public MessageConverter messageConverter() {
    return new Jackson2JsonMessageConverter();
}
```

We will use this message converter as a property to change the default message converter while configuring a `RabbitTemplate` in the next section.

Creating a RabbitTemplate

Spring AMQP's `RabbitTemplate` provides everything for the basic AMQP operations. The following code creates an instance of `RabbitTemplate` using `connectionFactory`:

```
@Bean
public RabbitTemplate rabbitTemplate() {
    RabbitTemplate template = new RabbitTemplate(connectionFactory());
    template.setRoutingKey(ROUTING_KEY);
    template.setExchange(RABBIT_MESSAGE_EXCHANGE);
    template.setMessageConverter(messageConverter());
    return template;
}
```

`RabbitTemplate` acts as a helper class for the producer to send, and the consumer to receive, the messages.

Configuring a listener container

To receive the message asynchronously, the easiest way is to use an annotated listener endpoint. We will use the @RabbitListener annotation as a message listener endpoint. To create this listener endpoint, we have to configure a message listener container using the SimpleRabbitListenerContainerFactory class, which is an implementation of the RabbitListenerContainerFactory interface. The following code is used to configure SimpleRabbitListenerContainerFactory:

```
@Bean
public SimpleRabbitListenerContainerFactory listenerContainer() {
    SimpleRabbitListenerContainerFactory factory = new
    SimpleRabbitListenerContainerFactory();
    factory.setConnectionFactory(connectionFactory());
    factory.setMaxConcurrentConsumers(5);
    return factory;
}
```

The listenerContainer() method will instantiate SimpleRabbitListenerContainerFactory. You can set the maximum number of consumers with the maxConcurrentConsumers property using the setMaxConcurrentConsumers() method.

The following is the class that contains all the previously discussed configuration methods:

```
@Configuration
@ComponentScan("com.packt.springhighperformance.ch7.bankingapp")
@EnableRabbit
public class RabbitMqConfiguration {

    public static final String RABBIT_MESSAGE_QUEUE =
    "rabbit.queue.name";
    private static final String RABBIT_MESSAGE_EXCHANGE =
    "rabbit.exchange.name";
    private static final String ROUTING_KEY = "messages.key";

    @Bean
    public ConnectionFactory connectionFactory() {
      CachingConnectionFactory connectionFactory = new
      CachingConnectionFactory("127.0.0.1");
      connectionFactory.setUsername("guest");
      connectionFactory.setPassword("guest");
      return connectionFactory;
    }

    @Bean
```

```java
    public Queue queue() {
      return new Queue(RABBIT_MESSAGE_QUEUE, true);
    }

    @Bean
    public DirectExchange exchange() {
      return new DirectExchange(RABBIT_MESSAGE_EXCHANGE);
    }

    @Bean
    Binding exchangeBinding(DirectExchange directExchange, Queue queue) {
      return
      BindingBuilder.bind(queue).to(directExchange).with(ROUTING_KEY);
    }

    @Bean
    public RabbitAdmin rabbitAdmin() {
      RabbitAdmin admin = new RabbitAdmin(connectionFactory());
      admin.declareQueue(queue());
      admin.declareExchange(exchange());
      admin.declareBinding(exchangeBinding(exchange(), queue()));
      return admin;
    }

    @Bean
    public MessageConverter messageConverter() {
      return new Jackson2JsonMessageConverter();
    }

    @Bean
    public RabbitTemplate rabbitTemplate() {
      RabbitTemplate template = new RabbitTemplate(connectionFactory());
      template.setRoutingKey(ROUTING_KEY);
      template.setExchange(RABBIT_MESSAGE_EXCHANGE);
      template.setMessageConverter(messageConverter());
      return template;
    }

    @Bean
    public SimpleRabbitListenerContainerFactory listenerContainer() {
      SimpleRabbitListenerContainerFactory factory = new
      SimpleRabbitListenerContainerFactory();
      factory.setConnectionFactory(connectionFactory());
      factory.setMaxConcurrentConsumers(5);
      return factory;
    }

}
```

Creating a message receiver

Now, we will create a `Consumer` listener class with the `@RabbitListener` annotated method, which will receive the message from RabbitMQ:

```
@Service
public class Consumer {

    private static final Logger LOGGER =
    Logger.getLogger(Consumer.class);

    @RabbitListener(containerFactory = "listenerContainer",
    queues = RabbitMqConfiguration.RABBIT_MESSAGE_QUEUE)
    public void onMessage(Message message) {
        LOGGER.info("Received Message: " +
        new String(message.getBody()));
    }
}
```

This is the message `listenerContainer` class. Whenever, producer sends a message to the `queue`, this class will receive it and only the method with the `@RabbitListener(containerFactory = "listenerContainer", queues = RabbitMqConfiguration.RABBIT_MESSAGE_QUEUE)` annotation will receive the message. In this annotation, we mentioned the `containerFactory` attribute, which points to the message listener factory defined in the `listenerContainer` bean.

Creating a message producer

To run this application, we will use the `RabbitTemplate.convertAndSend()` method to send the message. This method also converts custom Java objects to AMQP messages and is sent to direct exchange. The following `BankAccount` class is created as a custom class to populate the message properties:

```java
public class BankAccount {

    private int accountId;
    private String accountType;

    public BankAccount(int accountId, String accountType) {
        this.accountId = accountId;
        this.accountType = accountType;
    }

    public int getAccountId() {
        return accountId;
    }

    public String getAccountType() {
        return accountType;
    }

    @Override
    public String toString() {
        return "BankAccount{" +
                "Account Id=" + accountId +
                ", Account Type='" + accountType + '\'' +
                '}';
    }
}
```

In the following class, we will initialize the preceding class with some proper values and send it to the exchange using `RabbitTemplate.convertAndSend()`:

```
public class Producer {

  private static final Logger LOGGER =
  Logger.getLogger(Producer.class);
  @SuppressWarnings("resource")
  public static void main(String[] args) {
      ApplicationContext ctx = new
      AnnotationConfigApplication
      Context(RabbitMqConfiguration.class);
      RabbitTemplate rabbitTemplate =
      ctx.getBean(RabbitTemplate.class);
      LOGGER.info("Sending bank account information....");
      rabbitTemplate.convertAndSend(new BankAccount(100, "Savings
      Account"));
      rabbitTemplate.convertAndSend(new BankAccount(101, "Current
      Account"));
    }

}
```

When we run the preceding code, the producer will send two objects of `BankAccount` using the `convertAndSend()` method and the following output will be displayed:

```
2018-05-13 19:46:58 INFO Producer:17 - Sending bank account
information....
2018-05-13 19:46:58 INFO Consumer:17 - Received Message:
{"accountId":100,"accountType":"Savings Account"}
2018-05-13 19:46:58 INFO Consumer:17 - Received Message:
{"accountId":101,"accountType":"Current Account"}
```

Maximizing throughput with RabbitMQ

The following are the configuration options for optimal performance in relation to maximum message passing throughput:

- Keep your queues short
- Avoid the use of lazy queues
- Avoid persistent messages
- Create multiple queues and consumers
- Divide queues into different cores
- Disable acknowledgment
- Disable unnecessary plugins

Performance and scalability with RabbitMQ

There are many important points that we should consider for achieving optimal performance with RabbitMQ:

- Payload message size
- Exchange management
- Configure prefetch properly
- RabbitMQ HiPE
- Clustering of nodes
- Disable RabbitMQ statistics
- Update the RabbitMQ libraries

Summary

In this chapter, we learned about the concept of messaging. We also went through the advantages of using messaging systems. We learned about AMQP. We went through the needs of AMQP by understanding the JMS API problem. We also saw the differences between AMQP and the JMS API. We learned about the exchanges, queues, and binding related to AMQP. We also went through the setup aspect of RabbitMQ and different configurations related to the Spring application.

In the next chapter, we will learn about the cover core concept of Java threads and then we will move to the advanced thread support provided by the `java.util.concurrent` package. We will also go through the various classes and interfaces of `java.util.concurrent`. We will learn how we can use Java thread pool to improve performance. We will walk through useful functionality provided by the Spring framework, such as task executing, scheduling, and running as asynchronous. Finally, we will look into Spring transaction management with threads and various best programming practices for threads.

Multithreading and Concurrent Programming

8

In the previous chapter, we learned how we can optimize Spring messaging. We also learned various configuration tips and tricks that help us to improve the performance of our application. We also looked at the monitoring and configuration of JMS and RabbitMQ for optimal performance.

In this chapter, we will cover the core concept of Java threads and then will move to advanced thread support provided by the `java.util.concurrent` package. For this package, we will see various classes and interfaces that help us write multithreaded and concurrent programming. We will also learn how we can use Java `ThreadPool` to improve performance. We will walk through useful functionalities provided by the Spring Framework, such as task executing, scheduling, and running as asynchronous. Finally, we will look into Spring transaction management with threads and various best programming practices for threads.

The following topics will be covered in this chapter:

- Java classical threads
- The `java.util.concurrent` package
- Using the thread pools for asynchronous processing
- Spring task execution and scheduling
- Spring Async
- Spring and threads—transactions
- Java threads best programming practices

Java classical threads

Java applications execute via threads, which are an independent path of execution within a program. Any Java program has at least one thread, known as the main thread, which is created by **Java Virtual Machine (JVM)**. Java is a multithreaded application that allows multiple thread execution at any particular time and these threads can run concurrently, either asynchronously or synchronously. When multiple threads are executing, each thread's path can differ from the other thread's paths.

The JVM provides each thread with its own stack to prevent threads from interfering with each other. Separate stacks help threads keep track of their next instructions to execute, which can differ from thread to thread. The stack also gives a thread its own copy of method parameters, local variables, and the return value.

Threads live within a process and share their resources, such as memory and open files, with the other threads of the process. The ability to share resources between different threads makes them more susceptible to errors where performance is a significant requirement. Every thread in Java is created and controlled by the `java.lang.Thread` class and the `java.lang.Runnable` interface.

Creating threads

Threads are objects in the Java language. They can be created using the following mechanisms:

- Create a class that implements the `Runnable` interface
- Create a class that extends the `Thread` class

There are two ways to create a `Runnable` object. The first way is to create a class that implements the `Runnable` interface as follows:

```
public class ThreadExample {
  public static void main(String[] args) {
    Thread t = new Thread(new MyThread());
    t.start();
  }
}
class MyThread implements Runnable {
  private static final Logger LOGGER =
  Logger.getLogger(MyThread.class);
  public void run() {
    //perform some task
```

```
      LOGGER.info("Hello from thread...");
    }
  }
```

Before Java 8, we only had this way to create a `Runnable` object. But since Java 8, we can create a `Runnable` object using a Lambda expression.

After creating the `Runnable` object, we need to pass it to a `Thread` constructor that receives a `Runnable` object as an argument:

```
Runnable runnable = () -> LOGGER.info("Hello from thread...");
Thread t = new Thread(runnable);
```

Some constructors don't take the `Runnable` object as an argument, such as `Thread()`. In that case, we need to take another approach in order to create a thread:

```
public class ThreadExample1 {
  public static void main(String[] args) {
    MyThread t = new MyThread1();
    t.start();
  }

}
class MyThread1 extends Thread {
  private static final Logger LOGGER =
  Logger.getLogger(MyThread1.class);
  public void run() {
    LOGGER.info("Hello from thread...");
  }
}
```

Thread life cycle and states

Understanding the thread life cycle and states is very important when working with threads and multithreaded environments. In the previous examples, we saw how we can create the Java thread object using the `Thread` class and the `Runnable` interface. But to start the thread, we have to first create the thread object and call its `start()` method to execute the `run()` method as a thread.

The following are different states of the thread life cycle in Java:

- **New**: The thread is in the new state when it is created with a `new` operator. At this stage, the thread is not alive.

- **Runnable**: The thread is in the runnable state when we call the `start()` method of the thread object. At this stage, the thread scheduler still does not pick it for running.
- **Running**: The thread state is changed from runnable to running when the thread scheduler has selected it.
- **Blocked/waiting**: The thread state is blocked/waiting when it is currently not eligible to run.
- **Terminated/dead**: The thread state is terminated/dead when it executes its run method. At this stage, it's considered to be not alive.

More advanced thread tasks

We have seen the thread life cycle and its states, but threads also support some advanced tasks, such as sleeping, joining, and interrupting. Let's discuss them:

- **Sleeping**: The `sleep()` thread method can be used to pause the execution of the current thread for the specified amount of time.
- **Joining**: The `join()` thread method can be used to pause the execution of the current thread until the thread it joins completes its task.
- **Interrupting**: The `interrupt()` thread method can be used to break out the sleeping or waiting state of the thread. It throws `InterruptedException` if the thread is in the sleeping or waiting state, otherwise, it doesn't interrupt the thread but sets the interrupted flag to true.

Synchronizing threads

In multithreaded applications, there might be situations where multiple threads try to access a shared resource and produce erroneous and unexpected results. We need to ensure that the resource will be used by only one thread at a time, and that can be achieved by synchronization. The `synchronized` keyword is used to achieve synchronization; when we define any synchronized block in Java, only one thread can access that block and other threads are blocked until the thread inside the block exits that block.

The `synchronized` keyword can be used with the following different types of blocks:

- Instance methods
- Static methods

- Code blocks inside instance methods
- Code blocks inside static methods

In Java, a synchronized block degrades performance. We must use the `synchronized` keyword when required, otherwise, we should use the synchronized block of the critical section only where it is required.

Issues with multithreading

Multithreading is a very powerful mechanism that helps us to better utilize the system's resources, but we need to take special care while reading and writing data shared by multiple threads. There are two basic problems with multithreading programming—visibility and access problems. A visibility problem occurs when the effects of one thread can be seen by another. An access problem can occur when the same shared resources are accessed by multiple threads at the same time.

Due to visibility and access problems, a program does not react any more and it leads to deadlocks or generates incorrect data.

The java.util.concurrent package

In the previous section, we focused on Java's low-level support for threads. In this section, we will move on to look at Java's high-level thread support provided by the `java.util.concurrent` package. This package has various classes and interfaces that provide very useful functionalities to help us implement multithreaded and concurrent programming. In this section, we will mainly focus on some of the most useful utilities of this package.

The following diagram shows the high-level overview of the `java.util.concurrent` API:

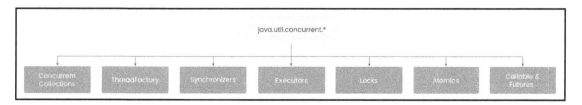

Let's discuss the interfaces in detail.

Executors

`Executor` provides an abstraction layer over all the internal thread management tasks and manages the entire concurrent execution flow of the threads. An `Executor` is an object that executes tasks provided.

The Java concurrency API provides the following three basic interfaces for executors:

- `Executor`: This is a simple interface that is used to launch a new task. It does not strictly require the execution to be asynchronous.
- `ExecutorService`: This is a subinterface of the `Executor` interface. It allows us to pass a task to be executed by a thread asynchronously. It provides methods to manage the termination of previously sublimed tasks through `shutdown()`, `shutdownNow()`, and `awaitTermination(long timeout, TimeUnit unit)`. It also provides methods that return the `Future` object for tracking the progress of one or more asynchronous tasks.
- `ScheduledExecutorService`: This is a subinterface of `ExecutorService`. It provides various key methods, such as `schedule()`, `scheduleAtFixedRate()` and `scheduleWithFixedDelay()`. All schedule methods can accept relative delays and periods as arguments, and this helps us to schedule tasks to execute after a given delay or period.

The following is a simple example showing how to create `Executor` in order to execute a `Runnable` task:

```
public class ExecutorExample {
    private static final Logger LOGGER =
    Logger.getLogger(ExecutorExample.class);

    public static void main(String[] args) {
        ExecutorService pool = Executors.newSingleThreadExecutor();

            Runnable task = new Runnable() {
            public void run() {
                LOGGER.info(Thread.currentThread().getName());
            }
        };

        pool.execute(task);
        pool.shutdown();
    }
}
```

In the previous example, a `Runnable` object is created by an anonymous class and executes a task by means of a single-threaded `Executor` interface. When we compile and run the preceding class, we will get the following output:

```
pool-1-thread-1
```

ThreadFactory

The `ThreadFactory` interface is used to create a new thread on demand and also helps us to eliminate lots of boilerplate code for creating threads.

The following example shows how we can use the `ThreadFactory` interface to create new threads:

```
public class ThreadFactoryExample implements ThreadFactory {
  private static final Logger LOGGER =
  Logger.getLogger(ThreadFactoryExample.class);

  public static void main(String[] args) {
    ThreadFactoryExample factory = new ThreadFactoryExample();

    Runnable task = new Runnable() {
      public void run() {
        LOGGER.info(Thread.currentThread().getName());
      }
    };
    for (int i = 0; i < 5; i++) {
      Thread t = factory.newThread(task);
      t.start();
    }
  }

  @Override
  public Thread newThread(Runnable r) {
    Thread t = new Thread(r);
    return t;
  }
}
```

When we compile and run the preceding class, we will get the following output:

```
Thread-0
Thread-1
```

Synchronizers

Java provides a `synchronized` keyword to write synchronized code, but it is difficult to correctly write synchronized code through the `synchronized` keyword alone. The `java.util.concurrent` package provides various utility classes, such as `CountDownLatch`, `CyclicBarrier`, `Exchanger`, `Semaphore`, and `Phaser`, which are known as synchronizers. Synchronizers are concurrency utilities that provide thread synchronization without using the `wait()` and `notify()` methods. Let's have a look at the following classes:

- `CountDownLatch`: This allows one thread to wait for one or more threads to complete before it can start processing.
- `CyclicBarrier`: This is very similar to `CountdownLatch`, but it allows multiple threads to wait for each other before they can start processing.
- `Semaphore`: This maintains a set of permits for restricting the number of threads that can access a shared resource. Threads require a permit from `Semaphore` before accessing a shared resource. It provides two main methods, `acquire()` and `release()`, for getting and releasing permits, respectively.
- `Exchanger`: This provides a synchronization point where threads can exchange objects.
- `Phaser`: This provides a thread synchronization mechanism similar to `CyclicBarrier` and `CountDownLatch`, but it supports more flexible usage. It allows a group of threads to wait on a barrier and then proceed after the last thread arrives, and it also supports multiple phases of execution.

Concurrent collection classes

The concurrent collection classes provide more scalability and performance than other collection classes, such as `HashMap` or `Hashtable`. The following are useful concurrent classes provided in the `java.util.concurrent` package:

- `ConcurrentHashMap`: This is similar to `HashMap` and `Hashtable`, but it has been designed to work in concurrent programming without the need for explicit synchronization. `Hashtable` and `ConcurrentHashMap` are both thread-safe collections, but `ConcurrentHashMap` is more advanced than `Hashtable`. It does not lock the entire collection for synchronization, so it is very useful when there are a lot of updates and fewer concurrent reads.

- `BlockingQueue`: The producer-consumer pattern is the most common design pattern in asynchronous programming, and the `BlockingQueue` data structure can be very useful in these asynchronous scenarios.
- `DelayQueue`: This is an infinite size blocking queue of elements where an element can only be taken when its delay has expired. If multiple elements delay expiry, then the element with the longest delay expiration will be taken first.

Lock

The `Lock` interface provides more advanced locking mechanisms than the synchronized block. The main difference between the synchronized block and `Lock` is that the synchronized block is fully contained in a method while the `Lock` interface has separate methods, `lock()` and `unlock()`, that can be called in a different method.

Callable and Future

The `Callable` interface is similar to the `Runnable` object, but it can return any type of object, which helps us to get a result or status from a `Callable` task.

The `Callable` task returns the `Future` object, which is used for getting the result of an asynchronous operation. Its uses include providing a couple of methods to check whether the asynchronous execution is completed or not and retrieving the result of the computation.

Atomic variables

Atomic variables are non-blocking algorithms introduced in the `java.util.concurrent.atomic` package. The main benefits of using atomic variables is that we don't need to worry about synchronization. Atomic variables are a necessity in multithreaded environments to avoid data inconsistency. It supports lock-free, thread-safe operations on single variables.

Using thread pools for asynchronous processing

Thread pool is a core concept in multithreaded programming that serves a collection of idle threads that can be used to execute a task. A thread pool can reuse previously created threads to execute the current task so that the thread is already available when the request arrives, which can reduce the time of thread creation and improve the performance of the application. Normally, thread pool can be used in a web server to handle client requests and also to maintain open connections to the database.

We can configure the maximum number of concurrent threads in the pool, which is useful for preventing overload. If all threads are busy executing a task, then a new task is placed in a queue and waits for a thread to become available.

The Java concurrency API supports the following types of thread pools:

- **Fixed-thread pool**: A thread pool with a fixed number of threads. A task will only execute if a thread is available, otherwise, it is waiting in a queue. The `Executors.newFixedThreadPool()` method is used to create a fixed-thread pool.
- **Cached-thread pool**: A thread pool where we can create new threads as required, but also reuse previously created threads. A thread will be terminated and removed from the pool if it is ideal for 60 seconds. The `Executors.newCachedThreadPool()` method is used to create a cached-thread pool.
- **Single-thread pool**: A thread pool with one thread. It executes tasks one by one. The `Executors.newSingleThreadExecutor()` method is used to create a single-thread pool.
- **Fork/join pool**: A thread pool that is used to perform heavy tasks faster, by splitting the task into smaller pieces recursively. To create a fork/join pool, we need to create an instance of the `ForkJoinPool` class.

The following is a simple example of the fixed-thread pool:

```
public class ThreadPoolExample {
  private static final Logger LOGGER =
  Logger.getLogger(ThreadPoolExample.class);
  public static void main(String[] args) {
    ExecutorService executor = Executors.newFixedThreadPool(3);

    for (int i = 1; i <= 6; i++) {
```

```
        Runnable task = new Task(" " + i);
        executor.execute(task);
      }
      executor.shutdown();
      while (!executor.isTerminated()) {
      }
      LOGGER.info("All threads finished");
    }
}
```

The following demonstrates how the task is implemented:

```
public class Task implements Runnable {
  private static final Logger LOGGER = Logger.getLogger(Task.class);
  private String taskNumber;

  public Task(String taskNumber) {
    this.taskNumber = taskNumber;
  }

  @Override
  public void run() {
    LOGGER.info(Thread.currentThread().getName() + ", Execute Task = "
    + taskNumber);
    taskProcess();
    LOGGER.info(Thread.currentThread().getName() + ", End");
  }

  private void taskProcess() {
    try {
      Thread.sleep(2000);
    } catch (InterruptedException e) {
      e.printStackTrace();
    }
  }
}
```

In the previous example, we created a pool with a maximum of three concurrent threads and submitted 6 tasks to the `executor` object. When we compile and run the preceding class, we know that only three threads execute the tasks.

Here is the output:

```
pool-1-thread-1, Execute Task = 1
pool-1-thread-2, Execute Task = 2
pool-1-thread-3, Execute Task = 3
pool-1-thread-1, End
```

```
pool-1-thread-1, Execute Task = 4
pool-1-thread-3, End
pool-1-thread-2, End
pool-1-thread-2, Execute Task = 5
pool-1-thread-3, Execute Task = 6
pool-1-thread-1, End
pool-1-thread-2, End
pool-1-thread-3, End
All threads finished
```

Spring task execution and scheduling

Using threads in any web application is not easy when we are dealing with a long-running task. Sometimes, we need to run a task asynchronously or after a specific delay, and that can be accomplished by Spring's task execution and scheduling. The Spring Framework introduced abstractions for asynchronous execution and scheduling of tasks with the `TaskExecutor` and `TaskScheduler` interfaces.

TaskExecutor

Spring provides the `TaskExecutor` interface as an abstraction for dealing with `Executor`. The implementation classes of `TaskExecutor` are as follows:

- `SimpleAsyncTaskExecutor`: This starts a new thread and executes it asynchronously. It does not reuse the thread.
- `SyncTaskExecutor`: This executes each task synchronously in the calling thread. It does not reuse the thread.
- `ConcurrentTaskExecutor`: This exposes bean properties for configuring `java.util.concurrent.Executor`.
- `SimpleThreadPoolTaskExecutor`: This is a subclass of `SimpleThreadPool` of `Quartz`, which listens to Spring's life cycle callbacks.
- `ThreadPoolTaskExecutor`: This exposes bean properties for configuring `java.util.concurrent.ThreadPoolExecutor` and wraps it in `TaskExecutor`.
- `TimerTaskExecutor`: This implements a single `TimerTask` class as its backing implementation. It executes methods as synchronous in a separate thread.

- `WorkManagerTaskExecutor`: This uses the `CommonJ WorkManager` interface as its backing implementation.

Let's see a simple example of executing a task with `SimpleAsyncTaskExecutor` in the Spring application. It creates a new thread for each task submission and runs as asynchronous.

Here is the configuration file:

```
@Configuration
public class AppConfig {
  @Bean
  AsyncTask myBean() {
    return new AsyncTask();
  }
  @Bean
  AsyncTaskExecutor taskExecutor() {
    SimpleAsyncTaskExecutor t = new SimpleAsyncTaskExecutor();
    return t;
  }
}
```

Here is the bean class where we have assigned 5 tasks to `TaskExecutor`:

```
public class AsyncTask {
  @Autowired
  private AsyncTaskExecutor executor;
  public void runTasks() throws Exception {
    for (int i = 1; i <= 5; i++) {
      Runnable task = new Task(" " + i);
      executor.execute(task);
    }
  }
}
```

The following is the code for executing the task from the `main` method:

```
public class TaskExecutorExample {
  public static void main(String[] args) throws Exception {
    ApplicationContext context = new
    AnnotationConfigApplicationContext(AppConfig.class);
    AsyncTask bean = context.getBean(AsyncTask.class);
    bean.runTasks();
  }
}
```

When we compile and run the preceding class, we will get the following output. Here, we can see five threads are created and they execute the task asynchronously:

```
SimpleAsyncTaskExecutor-1, Execute Task = 1
SimpleAsyncTaskExecutor-4, Execute Task = 4
SimpleAsyncTaskExecutor-3, Execute Task = 3
SimpleAsyncTaskExecutor-2, Execute Task = 2
SimpleAsyncTaskExecutor-5, Execute Task = 5
SimpleAsyncTaskExecutor-2, End
SimpleAsyncTaskExecutor-1, End
SimpleAsyncTaskExecutor-4, End
SimpleAsyncTaskExecutor-3, End
SimpleAsyncTaskExecutor-5, End
```

TaskScheduler

Sometimes, we need to perform a task at fixed intervals, and this can be achieved with the Spring scheduler framework. In this section, we will see how we can schedule a task in Spring with the use of a few annotations.

Let's see a simple example of scheduling a task in the Spring application:

```
@Configuration
@EnableScheduling
public class SpringSchedulingExample {
    private static final Logger LOGGER =
    Logger.getLogger(SpringSchedulingExample.class);
    @Scheduled(fixedDelay = 2000)
    public void scheduledTask() {
        LOGGER.info("Execute task " + new Date());
    }

    public static void main(String[] args) {
        AnnotationConfigApplicationContext context = new
        AnnotationConfigApplicationContext(
        SpringSchedulingExample.class);
        String scheduledAnnotationProcessor =
        "org.springframework.context.annotation.
        internalScheduledAnnotationProcessor";
        LOGGER.info("ContainsBean : " + scheduledAnnotationProcessor +
        ": " + context.containsBean(scheduledAnnotationProcessor));
        try {
            Thread.sleep(12000);
        } catch (InterruptedException e) {
            e.printStackTrace();
```

```
        } finally {
            context.close();
        }
    }
}
```

In Spring, we can enable task scheduling with the help of the @EnableScheduling annotation. Once task scheduling is enabled, Spring will automatically register an internal bean post processor, which will find the @Scheduled annotated methods on a Spring-managed bean.

In the previous example, we annotated the scheduledTask() method with the @Scheduled annotation with the fixedDelay attribute to be invoked every 2 seconds. We can also use other attributes, such as fixedRate and cron:

```
@Scheduled(fixedRate = 2000)
@Scheduled(cron = "*/2 * * * * SAT,SUN,MON")
```

When we compile and run the previous class, we will get the following output:

```
Execute task Thu May 10 20:18:04 IST 2018
ContainsBean :
org.springframework.context.annotation.internalScheduledAnnotationProce
ssor: true
Execute task Thu May 10 20:18:06 IST 2018
Execute task Thu May 10 20:18:08 IST 2018
Execute task Thu May 10 20:18:10 IST 2018
Execute task Thu May 10 20:18:12 IST 2018
Execute task Thu May 10 20:18:14 IST 2018
```

Spring Async

In this section, we will see the asynchronous execution support in Spring. In certain cases, we need to execute some tasks asynchronously, because the result of that task does not require the user, so we can process that task in a separate thread. The main benefit of asynchronous programming is that we can increase the performance and responsiveness of our application.

Spring provides annotation support for asynchronous method execution via @EnableAsync and @Async. Let's discuss them in detail.

The @EnableAsync annotation

We can enable asynchronous processing by simply adding `@EnableAsync` to a configuration class, as follows:

```
@Configuration
@EnableAsync
public class AppConfig {
  @Bean
  public AsyncTask asyncTask() {
    return new AsyncTask();
  }
}
```

In the previous code, we have not provided `TaskExecutor` as a bean, so Spring will use a default `SimpleAsyncTaskExecutor` implicitly.

The @Async annotation

Once asynchronous processing is enabled, then the methods that are annotated with the `@Async` annotation will execute asynchronously.

The following is a simple example of the `@Async` annotation:

```
public class AsyncTask {
  private static final Logger LOGGER =
  Logger.getLogger(AsyncTask.class);
  @Async
  public void doAsyncTask() {
    try {
      LOGGER.info("Running Async task thread : " +
      Thread.currentThread().getName());
    } catch (Exception e) {
    }
  }
}
```

We can also annotate the @Async annotation to a method with the return type, as follows:

```
@Async
  public Future<String> doAsyncTaskWithReturnType() {
    try
    {
      return new AsyncResult<String>("Running Async task thread : " +
      Thread.currentThread().getName());
    }
    catch (Exception e) {
    }
    return null;
  }
```

In the previous code, we used the AsyncResult class, which implements Future. This can be used to get the results of the execution of the asynchronous method.

The following is the code to call the asynchronous method from the main method:

```
public class asyncExample {
  private static final Logger LOGGER =
  Logger.getLogger(asyncExample.class);
  public static void main(String[] args) throws InterruptedException {
    AnnotationConfigApplicationContext ctx = new
    AnnotationConfigApplicationContext();
    ctx.register(AppConfig.class);
    ctx.refresh();
    AsyncTask task = ctx.getBean(AsyncTask.class);
    LOGGER.info("calling async method from thread : " +
    Thread.currentThread().getName());
    task.doAsyncTask();
    LOGGER.info("Continue doing something else. ");
    Thread.sleep(1000);
  }
}
```

When we compile and run the preceding class, we will get the following output:

```
calling async method from thread : main
Continue doing something else.
Running Async Task thread : SimpleAsyncTaskExecutor-1
```

@Async with CompletableFuture

In the previous section, we saw how we can use `java.util.Future` to get the result of asynchronous method execution. It provides an `isDone()` method to check whether the computation is done or not, and a `get()` method to retrieve the result of the computation when it is done. But there are certain limitations to using the `Future` API:

- Suppose we have written code to fetch the latest product price from an e-commerce system through a remote API. This task is time-consuming, so we need to run it asynchronously and use `Future` to get the result of that task. Now, the problem will occur when the remote API service is down. At that time, we need to complete `Future` manually by the last cached price of the product and that is not possible with `Future`.
- `Future` only provides a `get()` method that notifies us when a result is available. We cannot attach a callback function to `Future` and have it get called automatically when the `Future` result is available.
- Sometimes we have requirements, such as the result of the long-running task is needed to send another long-running task. We can't create such asynchronous workflow with `Future`.
- We cannot run multiple `Future` in parallel.
- The `Future` API does not have any exception handling.

Because of these limitations, Java 8 introduced a better abstraction than `java.util.Future`, called `CompletableFuture`. We can create `CompletableFuture` simply using the following no-arg constructor:

```
CompletableFuture<String> completableFuture = new
CompletableFuture<String>();
```

Here is the list of methods provided by `CompletableFuture`, which help us to resolve the limitations of `Future`:

- The `complete()` method is used to complete the task manually.
- The `runAsync()` method is used to run background tasks asynchronously that do not return anything. It takes a `Runnable` object and returns `CompletableFuture<Void>`.
- The `supplyAsync()` method is used to run background tasks asynchronously and return a value. It takes `Supplier<T>` and returns `CompletableFuture<T>`, where `T` is the type of the value given by the supplier.

- The `thenApply()`, `thenAccept()`, and `thenRun()` methods are used to attach a callback to `CompletableFuture`.
- The `thenCompose()` method is used to combine two dependent `CompletableFuture` together.
- The `thenCombine()` method is used to combine two independent `CompletableFuture` together.
- The `allOf()` and `anyOf()` methods are used to combine multiple `CompletableFuture` together.
- The `exceptionally()` method is used to get the generated error from `Future`. We can log the error and set a default value.
- The `handle()` method is used to handle the exception.

Spring and threads – transactions

The Spring Framework offers an extensive API for database transaction management. Spring takes care of all basic transaction management control and provides a consistent programming model for different transaction APIs, such as JDBC, Hibernate, **Java Transaction API (JTA)**, **Java Persistence API (JPA)**, and **Java Data Objects (JDO)**. There are two types of transactions provided by Spring: one is declarative and the other is programmatic transaction management. Declarative is very high-level, while programmatic is more advanced but flexible.

Spring transaction management works very well with a single thread. But it cannot manage a transaction across multiple threads. If we try to use the transaction with multiple threads, our program gives a runtime error or an unexpected result.

To understand why a Spring transaction fails with multiple threads, first, we need to understand how transactions work with Spring. Spring stores all transaction information in the `ThreadLocal` variables inside the `org.springframework.transaction.support.TransactionSynchronizationManag er` class:

```
public abstract class TransactionSynchronizationManager {
  private static final Log logger =
  LogFactory.getLog(TransactionSynchronizationManager.class);
  private static final ThreadLocal<Map<Object, Object>> resources = new
  NamedThreadLocal("Transactional resources");
  private static final ThreadLocal<Set<TransactionSynchronization>>
  synchronizations = new NamedThreadLocal("Transaction
  synchronizations");
```

```
    private static final ThreadLocal<String> currentTransactionName = new
    NamedThreadLocal("Current transaction name");
    private static final ThreadLocal<Boolean> currentTransactionReadOnly
    = new NamedThreadLocal("Current transaction read-only status");
    private static final ThreadLocal<Integer>
    currentTransactionIsolationLevel = new NamedThreadLocal("Current
    transaction isolation level");
    private static final ThreadLocal<Boolean> actualTransactionActive =
    new NamedThreadLocal("Actual transaction active");
}
```

The thread's local variable holds the information of a specific transaction for a single thread only and that cannot be accessed by another thread. So, an ongoing transaction's information is not passed to the newly created thread. The result will be an error indicating that the transaction is missing.

Now we are able to understand the problem of a Spring transaction with multiple threads. Spring cannot maintain the transaction state to old threads from newly created threads. To solve the transaction problem with multiple threads, we need to manually pass the thread's local variable values to the newly created thread.

Java threads best programming practices

The purpose of using multithreading and concurrent programming is to improve performance, but we need to always remember that speed comes after correctness. The Java programming language provides lots of synchronization and concurrency support from the language to API level, but it depends on an individual's expertise in writing bug-free Java concurrency code. The following are Java concurrency and multithreading best practices, which help us write better concurrency code in Java:

- **Use immutable classes**: We should always prefer the immutable class in multithreading programming because immutable classes make sure that values are not changed in the middle of an operation without using synchronized blocks. For example, in an immutable class, such as `java.lang.String`, any modification on `String`, such as adding something or converting into uppercase, always creates another string object, keeping the original object unbroken.

- **Use local variables**: Always try to use local variables instead of an instance or class-level variables because local variables are never shared between threads.

- **Use thread pool**: Thread pool can reuse previously created threads and eliminate the time of thread creation, which improves the performance of the application.

- **Use the synchronization utility**: Here, we can use the synchronization utility instead of the `wait` and `notify` methods. The `java.util.concurrent` package provides better synchronization utilities, such as `CycicBariier`, `CountDownLatch`, `Sempahore`, and `BlockingQueue`. It is very easy to wait for five threads using `CountDownLatch` to complete its task instead of implementing the same utility using the `wait` and `notify` methods. It is also easier to implement the producer-consumer design with the help of `BlockingQueue` rather than the `wait` and `notify` methods.

- **Use concurrent collections instead of synchronized collection**: Concurrent collections are implemented with the new locking mechanism provided by the `Lock` interface and designed in such a way that we can take advantage of the native concurrency construct provided by the underlying hardware and JVM. Concurrent collections give more scalability and performance than their synchronized counterparts. `ConcurrentHashMap` provides better performance than synchronized `HashMap` or `Hashtable` classes if there are many updates and fewer reads concurrently.

- **Minimize locking scope**: We should always try to reduce the locking scope as much as possible because locking block will not be executed concurrently and it impacts the application's performance. We should always first try to use atomic and volatile variables to achieve our synchronization requirement if our requirement is not satisfied with them, and then we need to use the functionality provided by the `Lock` interface. We can also reduce the locking scope to use a synchronized block instead of the synchronized method.

- **Use Java Executor framework**: It provides an abstraction layer on the Java threading framework and provides better control in terms of creating and executing threads in a multithreaded environment.

Summary

In this chapter, we explored Java thread and learned how we can implement multithreading and concurrent programming with the help of the `java.util.concurrent` package. We also learned how we can improve performance using a thread pools in our application. We saw the task executing and scheduling functionalities provided by Spring and also learned about `@Async` support by Spring, which can increase the performance and responsiveness of our application. We reviewed how Spring transaction management creates an issue while working with multiple threads, and also looked at the best programming practices for multithreading and concurrent programming.

In the next chapter, we will learn about profiling an application to figure out the performance of an application. It is very useful for identifying performance issues. We will also learn about logging, which is an important tool for identifying issues in the application.

Profiling and Logging

9

In the previous chapter, we dove into the details of multithreading and concurrent programming. We looked at the `java.util.concurrent` package API. The chapter covered thread pooling for asynchronous programming, Spring task execution, scheduling, and Spring Async API. In the latter part of the chapter, we compared Spring Async with `CompletableFuture`.

Along similar lines, this chapter will focus on profiling and logging. This chapter starts by defining profiling and logging, and how they are useful for assessing application performance. In the latter part of the chapter, the focus will be on learning about software tools that can be used to study application performance.

The following topics will be covered in this chapter:

- Performance profiling
- Application logging and monitoring
- Profiling tools

Performance profiling

This section will focus on performance and application profiling for performance measurement. Profiling is an important step in any application development and deployment life cycle. It helps us to perform the following two things:

1. Defining a benchmark for expected performance outcomes
2. Measuring and comparing the current performance outcome against benchmarks

The second step defines further actions to be taken, in order to take performance to the benchmark level.

Application performance

Performance means different things to different people when used in terms of software applications. It must have some context for better understanding. Application performance is measured against two sets of performance metrics. The actual performance observed or experienced by the application users remains one of the most important metrics for measuring application performance. It includes the average response time during peak and normal loads. Measurements related to average response time include the time taken by the application to respond to a user's action, such as a page refresh, navigation, or a button click. They also include the time taken to perform certain operations, such as sorting, searching for, or loading data.

This section is meant to provide technical teams a perspective on some of the aspects of configurations and internals that can be set or altered to optimize effects, in order to improve the performance of the application. In usual cases, technical teams never keep an eye on the memory that the application uses or the CPU utilization unless they are stuck with a performance issue. Application transactions include requests received by the application per second, database transactions per second, and pages served per second. The load on the system is usually measured in terms of volume of transactions that the application processes.

There is another set of measurements that involves measuring the computational resources utilized by the application while performing operations. It is a very good way of identifying whether the application has enough resources to sustain the given load. It also helps in identifying whether the application utilizes more resources than it is expected to. If so, it can be concluded that the application is not optimized on the performance side. Cloud-hosted applications are popular these days. In this era, it is important for users to have the same experiences on applications deployed over the cloud or a non-cloud infrastructure, and on the local environment.

Application performance monitoring and improvements may not be necessary for an application, as long as it performs per expectations. However, as part of the application development life cycle, new requirements come up, new features are added, and the application becomes more complex by the day. This starts impacting the application's performance, as the main focus is kept on new feature development. A time will come when the performance is not up to marks, because no one actually works on application performance enhancement.

Application logging and monitoring

This section focuses on logging important information while the application is running. It helps to debug the application from various aspects, which we will look at in detail. Another important aspect covered in this section is application monitoring. In some cases, application monitoring is considered no different from application profiling; these are certainly different aspects in application performance measurement.

Application logging

Before we dive into the details of Java application logging, it is mandatory to understand what logs and logging are. A **log** is a statement that displays information to help us understand the state of the application. Log statements are written in the log files, in an application-specific format. The log statements may include information such as the date and time of execution of a particular statement, the values of various variables, and the states of the objects. The process of writing log statements to log files is known as **logging**.

Every application produces logs for various purposes. Applications produce logs to keep track of application events, including access-related events, login and logout events, events when errors occur in an application, and system configuration modifications. Operating systems also produce log files. Log files can be processed to bifurcate required information. Logging is one of the most fundamental parts of software applications. A well-written log and well-designed logging mechanism become a huge utility for developers and administrators. It is most useful to teams working on application support activities. Well, designed logging saves a lot of time for development and support teams. As the frontend programs are executed, the system builds log files in an invisible manner.

The following are common log files, usually generated in applications:

- **Error/Exception logs**: Any unexpected situation in an application flow is termed as an **error**. Errors may occur for different reasons. Errors are categorized based on severity and impact on the application. If the user cannot proceed further in the application, such an error is categorized as a **blocker**. If the web page does not have an appropriate label, it is categorized as a low severity issue. An error log is a recording of critical errors that have occurred while the application is executing. An application without errors virtually doesn't exist. In Java, it is not required to log all exceptions. Java supports managed exceptions, which can be taken care of and thrown as a warning or error message to the user. This could be a validation error or a user input error, which can be thrown using managed exceptions.

- **Access logs**: At an abstract level, any request that comes to a web application can be considered a request to access a resource on the web application server. The resource could be a web page, a PDF file on the server, an image file, or a report from the data in the database. From a security point of view, every resource must be protected by access rights. Access rights define who can access the resource from the web application. Access logs are written information on who tried to access which resource. They may also include information about the location from which the resource was accessed. Access logs write access information for every request coming into the web application. Access logs can also be used to find information about the number of visitors, the number of visitors accessing the application for the first time, the number of visitors from a specific location, the number of requests for a particular page, and the application usage patterns.

- **Transaction logs**: Transactions are related to databases. A sequence of database commands or statements executed in order to maintain atomicity and database integrity is known as a **transaction**. Transactions are maintained to guarantee protection over crashes or failures. A **transaction log** is a file where all such transactions are recorded or written. At a particular time, if the database is found to be inconsistent, then transaction logs become helpful in debugging the issue. Transaction logs can also be used to record any rollback operations performed. Usually, transaction logs also record the time of database statements to execute, along with passed in parameters. This information is very helpful in profiling database performance issues.

- **Audit logs**: **Auditing** is the process of inspecting how the application is used. It inspects the application resources being used, the users who access or use application resources, and the authentication and authorization information for the users. The **audit log** records every event that the application passes through, along with the previously mentioned details.

Logging best practices

Having described what should be logged and common logging information, this section details the best practices for logging:

- It is very important to assign appropriate log levels to each of the log statements.
- Logging should also be considered in a cluster environment. We can use the same type of log files, with the cluster node name as a suffix to the filename. This will prevent the log entries from being overwritten or wrongly considered when analyzing logs.

- Building log files impacts the application's performance. If an application starts logging every minor piece of information, the application's performance will be slow. We must ensure that the size of the log files and frequency of writing log entries are low.

- All exceptions, except for validations and input errors, must be logged. The exception messages must be logged in a way that highlights the problems clearly. The best practice is to let the framework log all of the exceptions.

- Logs must be user-friendly and easily parsed. Logs can be used in two ways. One way is that the users read the logs to build understanding. Another way is that the utility programs parse the application logs, based on the log formats, to filter out unimportant information.

- Every log entry must be different from other log entries, though they represent the same information. Every log entry can have a unique identifier, most often based on the timestamp, which can be used to differentiate it from other logs.

- Sensitive information must not be logged in log files. Passwords, credentials, and authentication keys are a few examples.

In most cases, best practices work as general guidelines and can be followed in a customized manner, based on the project.

Logging tools

In the preceding sections of this chapter, we learned about the importance of logging. We also learned logging best practices. Now is the time to add logging tools to our skill sets. This section focuses on logging tools. Logging tools are helpful because of the features they provide. In the past, log files consisted of log statements, written in a plain text format. Plain text log files are still useful in specific situations, like analyzing infrastructure data, but they are no longer sufficient in logging information for an application. Java has built-in support for standard logging in the `java.util.logging` API. Log4j is another well-known and widely used logging tool in the Java community.

Before we jump into the details of logging tools, it is important to understand the key elements of the logging mechanism. The following are key logging components:

- **Log Level**: The Java logging levels are used to control the logging output. They provide flexibility in enabling or disabling the various logging levels. This makes it possible to choose which logs will be displayed in the log files. With this, it is possible that the application running on the production has a different logging level than the same application running on the staging environment. Enabling one level of logging will make all higher-level logs enabled for printing in the log files. The following are the log levels and effective logging levels for the Java logging API:

Request level	Effective logging level						
	SEVERE	WARNING	INFO	CONFIG	FINE	FINER	FINEST
SEVERE	Yes	Yes	Yes	Yes	Yes	Yes	Yes
WARNING	No	Yes	Yes	Yes	Yes	Yes	Yes
INFO	No	No	Yes	Yes	Yes	Yes	Yes
CONFIG	No	No	No	Yes	Yes	Yes	Yes
FINE	No	No	No	No	Yes	Yes	Yes
FINER	No	No	No	No	No	Yes	Yes
FINEST	No	No	No	No	No	No	Yes

- **Logger**: The job of the `Logger` object is to log application messages. The application can create anonymous loggers, which are stored differently than in the `Logger` namespace. The application must be sure to keep a reference to the `Logger` object, as the `Logger` may get garbage collected at any point in time. The `Logger` object is associated with a parent `Logger` object, which is the nearest ancestor in `Logger` namespace. During the logging process, log messages are sent to `Handler` objects. The `Handler` objects forward the log messages to files, logs, or consoles. Every `Logger` object has a log level associated with it. It indicates the minimum level `Logger` will print logs for.

- **Handler**: The responsibility of a `Handler` object is to get log messages from `Logger` objects, and send those log messages for printing to the appropriate destination. Examples include writing the log messages on the console, writing the log messages into a file, or writing the log messages to a network logging service. It is possible to enable or disable a `Handler`, which, in essence, stops printing those logs on the output medium.

- **Formatter:** The log `Formatter` formats the log messages before writing them to the output medium. Java supports two types of `Formatter` objects: `SimpleFormatter` and `XMLFormatter`. The `XMLFormatter` object is required to include a head and tail around formatted records. It is also possible to create custom `Formatter` objects.

- **LogManager:** `LogManager` is a singleton object, used to maintain a shared state of loggers and log services. Apart from this, the `LogManager` object manages logging properties and the `Logger` namespace. The `LogManager` object is instantiated while class initialization takes place. The object cannot be subsequently changed. `LogManager` reads the initial configuration from the `lib/logging.properties` file by default, which can be modified.

The following diagram shows the logging process with one `Handler`:

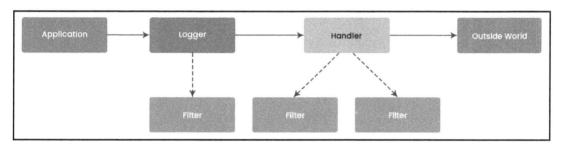

The following diagram shows the logging process with multiple handlers:

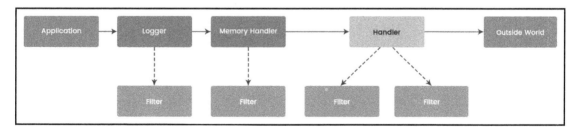

Java standard logging

This section explains Java's built-in logging mechanism. The Java logging API is comprised of the `java.util.logging` package. The core package includes support for writing plain text or XML log entries to output streams, files, memory, the console, or sockets. The logging API is also capable of interacting with already existing logging services on the operating system.

The following code example is used for printing log messages using the standard logging API:

```java
package com.packt.springhighperformance.ch9.logging;

import java.io.FileInputStream;
import java.io.IOException;
import java.sql.Timestamp;
import java.util.logging.Level;
import java.util.logging.LogManager;
import java.util.logging.Logger;

public class SampleLoggingOne {
  private static Logger logger =
  Logger.getLogger("com.packt.springhighperformance.ch4.logging");

  public static void main(String argv[]) throws SecurityException,
  IOException {
    FileInputStream fis = new FileInputStream("D:\\projects\\spring-
    high-performance\\SampleProject\\src\\main\\resources
    \\logging.properties");
    LogManager.getLogManager().readConfiguration(fis);
    Timestamp tOne = new Timestamp(System.currentTimeMillis());
    for(int i=0; i < 100000; i++) {
        logger.fine("doing stuff");
    }
    Timestamp tTwo = new Timestamp(System.currentTimeMillis());
    System.out.println("Time: " + (tTwo.getTime() - tOne.getTime()));
    try {
      Bird.fly();
    } catch (Exception ex) {
      logger.log(Level.WARNING, "trouble flying", ex);
    }
    logger.fine("done");
  }
}
```

The following is an example of the `logging.properties` file referenced in the preceding code example:

```
# Logging
handlers = java.util.logging.ConsoleHandler
.level = ALL

# Console Logging
java.util.logging.ConsoleHandler.level = ALL
```

The following is the output after executing the preceding example:

```
Feb 19, 2018 12:35:58 AM
com.packt.springhighperformance.ch9.logging.SampleLoggingOne main
FINE: doing stuff
Feb 19, 2018 12:35:58 AM
com.packt.springhighperformance.ch9.logging.SampleLoggingOne main
FINE: done
```

The benefit of using Java standard logging is that you don't need separate JAR dependencies to be installed in the project. Though logging is related to troubleshooting issues that we come across on servers, we also have to make sure that logging does not impact the application performance in a negative way. The following points must be taken care of to make sure that logging does not impact application performance:

- `Logger.log` methods are used to print log records on the output medium via a `Handler`. We can use `Logger.isLoggable` to ensure that `Logger` is enabled for the log level. If we pass a custom object as an argument to the `Logger.log` method, the `toString` method of the custom object is called from deep inside of the library classes. So, if we want to perform heavy operations in order to prepare an object for logging, we should do that from either within the block which checks `Logger.isLoggable`, or from within the object's `toString` method.
- We must not call the `toString` method on any object to get the log message contents. We must not pass the `toString` method call as an argument to `Logger.log`, either. The `Logger` object and logging framework take care of calling the `toString` method on a custom object.

- The mixing of format string concatenation and log arguments must be avoided. It is possible for an application user with wrong intentions to break the log and access data that is not permitted to the user using a malicious concatenated string.

One of the major drawbacks of Java standard logging is comparative performance. Standard logging takes more time as compared to other Java-based logging frameworks, like Apache Log4j 2, commons logging, or **Simple Logging Facade for Java** (SLF4J).

Apache Log4j 2

Apache Log4j is one of the most widely used logging frameworks in the Java community. It is written in Java and distributed under the Apache software license. Apache Log4j 2 is the revision of an earlier version. The most notable features include thread safety, performance optimization, a named logger hierarchy, and internationalization support.

In order to set up Log4j 2, the following Maven dependencies must be added in the Maven `pom.xml` file:

```
<dependency>
  <groupId>org.apache.logging.log4j</groupId>
  <artifactId>log4j-core</artifactId>
  <version>2.7</version>
</dependency>

<dependency>
  <groupId>org.apache.logging.log4j</groupId>
  <artifactId>log4j-core</artifactId>
  <version>2.7</version>
  <type>test-jar</type>
  <scope>test</scope>
</dependency>
```

In order to gain access to the context rule that is required for testing of the named configuration files, we must include the `test` JAR, along with the main `log4j-core` package.

Log4j 2 has three major logging components:

- `Loggers`: The `Loggers` are responsible for capturing logging information.
- `Appenders`: These are similar to that of the `Handler` objects in Java standard logging. `Appenders` are responsible for broadcasting logging information or messages to configured output mediums.
- `Layouts`: The `Layouts` are responsible for formatting the log messages into configured styles.

The following is an example of the `log4j2.xml` file:

```xml
<?xml version="1.0" encoding="UTF-8"?>
<Configuration status="WARN">
  <Appenders>
    <Console name="ConsoleAppender" target="SYSTEM_OUT">
      <PatternLayout pattern="%d [%t] %-5level %logger{36} -
      %msg%n%throwable" />
    </Console>
  </Appenders>
  <Loggers>
    <Root level="ERROR">
      <AppenderRef ref="ConsoleAppender" />
    </Root>
  </Loggers>
</Configuration>
```

The following is an example of Log4j 2 Java code:

```java
package com.packt.springhighperformance.ch9.logging;

import org.apache.log4j.Logger;

public class SampleLog4j2Example {
  private static Logger logger =
  Logger.getLogger(SampleLog4j2Example.class);

  public static void main(String argv[]) {
    logger.info("example info log");
    try {
      Bird.fly();
    } catch (Exception ex) {
      logger.error("example error log", ex);
    }
    logger.warn("example warning log");
  }
}
```

When we execute the preceding example, the following output is produced:

```
2018-02-22 01:18:09 INFO SampleLog4j2Example:9 - example info log
2018-02-22 01:18:09 WARN SampleLog4j2Example:15 - example warning log
```

Apache Log4j 2 has additional log levels, beyond common log levels. These are `ALL` and `OFF` levels. The `ALL` log level is used when we want to enable logs at `ALL` log levels. If the `ALL` log level is configured, while the levels are not considered. The `OFF` log level is the opposite of the `ALL` log level. It disables all logging.

Application monitoring

As discussed earlier, application performance is considered one of the most important milestones in any software application life cycle. It is also required that the application performs well consistently. This is one of the ways that we can ensure that application users will have the best experience with the application. It also means that the application is up and running well. An application performance monitoring tool tracks every request and response coming in and out of the application, processes information from the requests, and responds and displays in a graphical user interface. It means monitoring tools provide the administrators with the data necessary for quickly discovering, isolating, and solving problems impacting the performance.

The monitoring tools usually collect data about CPU utilization, memory requirements, bandwidth, and throughput. It is possible to have multiple monitoring systems for disparate monitoring. One of the important aspects of any application performance monitoring is to combine data from such monitoring systems into a statistical analysis engine and display it on a dashboard. The dashboard makes it easy to read the data logs for analysis. Application monitoring tools help administrators monitor application servers in order to comply with **service level agreements (SLA)**. Business rules are set to send administrators an alert in the event of a problem. This ensures that business-critical features and applications are considered with higher priority. With the fast changing environments, it has become very important to have rapid deployments in production systems. Rapid deployments mean more chances to introduce errors impacting system architecture or to slow the system down.

Many implementations and tools are available based on these basic concepts. There is a huge and crowded market for application monitoring tools, including industry-leading and well-known tools like AppDynamics, New Relic, and Dynatrace. Apart from these known tools, there also exist open source application monitoring tools. The open source tools include Stagemonitor, Pinpoint, MoSKito, Glowroot, Kamon, and many more. We will look at each of these tools in detail in the following sections.

Stagemonitor

Stagemonitor has a monitoring agent built with support for clustered application stacks. The purpose of the tool is to monitor applications running on a number of servers, which is a usual production scenario. Stagemonitor is optimized for integration with time series databases. It is optimized for time series data management, which includes arrays of numbers, indexed by time. Such databases include elasticsearch, graphite, and InfluxDB. Stagemonitor can also be set up in private networks. It uses the open tracking API to correlate requests in distributed systems. It features defining thresholds for the metrics. Stagemonitor also supports creating new plugins and integrating third-party plugins.

Stagemonitor contains a Java-based agent. The agent sits in the Java application. The agent connects to the central database and sends metrics and request traces and statistics. Stagemonitor requires one instance for monitoring all applications, instances, and hosts.

In the browser, on the monitoring side, we can see historical or current data from the cluster. We can also create custom alerts. It is also possible to define a threshold for each metric. Stagemonitor has a dashboard. The dashboard is utilized for visualizing and analyzing different metrics and requests of interest. Stagemonitor supports creating custom dashboards, writing custom plugins, and using third-party plugins. It has in-browser widget support, as well. The widget does not require a backend and is injected automatically into the monitored web page.

Following is the screenshot of Stagemonitor dashboard for reference:

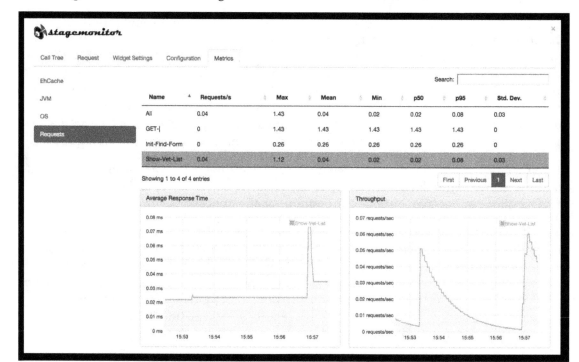

The Stagemonitor dashboard view (source: http://www.stagemonitor.org/)

Pinpoint

Pinpoint is different from Stagemonitor, in that it was developed with large-scale applications in mind. It was developed after Dapper (a distributed systems tracing infrastructure developed by Google) in order to provide developers with more information about how complex distributed systems behave.

Pinpoint helps in analyzing the overall system structure and how different components of the system are interconnected. Pinpoint does this by tracing transactions across distributed applications. It is aimed at explaining how each transaction is executed, tracing the flow between components and potential bottlenecks and problematic areas.

Pinpoint, similar to Stagemonitor, has a dashboard for visualization. The dashboard helps in visualizing the interconnection between components. The dashboard also lets users monitor active threads in the applications at particular points in time. Pinpoint features a tracing request count and response patterns. This helps in identifying potential problems. It provides support for viewing critical information, including CPU utilization, memory utilization, garbage collection, and JVM arguments.

Pinpoint consists of four components, named Collector, Web, Sample TestApp, and HBase. We can run an instance by executing a script for each of the components separately.

Following is the Pinpoint dashboard for reference:

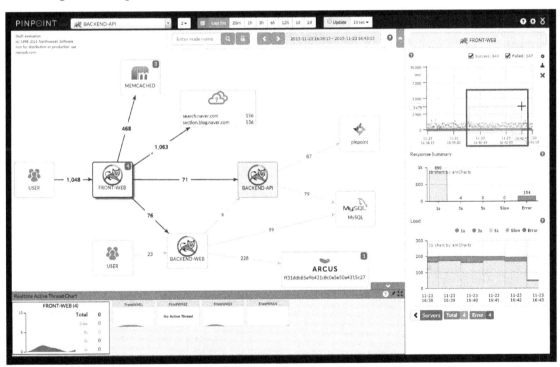

The Pinpoint dashboard reference view (source: http://www.testingtoolsguide.net/tools/pinpoint-apm/)

MoSKito

MoSKito is a group of three tools:

- **MoSKito-Essential**: This standalone project is the core of MoSKito. It makes it possible to monitor the application.
- **MoSKito-Central**: This works as a centralized storage server. It stores all of the performance-related information.
- **MoSKito-Control**: This tool works for multi-node web applications. It provides support for monitoring multi-node web applications.

In order to set up MoSKito, we need to install a JAR file in the application's `WEB-INF/lib` directory, which is a common folder for keeping API libraries. It can also be set up by adding a new section in the `web.xml` file.

The tool is capable of collecting all of the application performance metrics, including memory, threads, storage, caches, registrations, payments, conversions, SQL, services, load distribution, and many more. It does not require users to make any code changes in the application. It supports all major application servers, including Tomcat, Jetty, JBoss, and Weblogic. It stores the data locally.

MoSKito also has a notification feature to broadcast an alert when a threshold is met. It also records a user's actions, which might be of interest for monitoring purposes. MoSKito offers a mobile application for monitoring the application on the go. It also has web-based dashboards.

One of the distinguishing points for MoSKito is that it is very stable and well-known in the Java community. It is supported by the community and team, which includes paid support, as well.

Following is the MoSKito dashboard for reference:

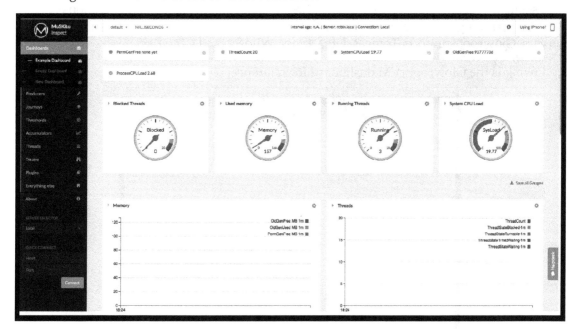

The MoSKito dashboard view (source: https://confluence.opensource.anotheria.net/display/MSK/Javaagent+light+and+multiple+java+processes)

Glowroot

One of the fast, clean, and simple application performance monitoring tools is Glowroot. It has a feature which allows tracing for slow requests and errors. With Glowroot, it is also possible to log the time taken for each user action. Glowroot supports SQL capture and aggregation. Historical rollup of the data with retention configuration is one of the additional features that Glowroot provides.

Glowroot provides support for visualizing response time breakdown and response time percentiles in charts. It has a responsive user interface, which allows one to monitor the application using mobile devices, as well as from desktop systems, without any additional installations.

Glowroot comes in a ZIP file bundle. In order to get started with Glowroot, we have to download and unzip the ZIP file bundle. Glowroot requires changes in the JVM parameters of the application. We have to add `-javaagent:<path to glowroot.jar>` in the JVM arguments for the application.

Glowroot provides continuous profiling with filtering once it is set up and running. We can also set up alerts for response time percentiles and MBean attributes. Asynchronous requests spanning multiple threads are also supported by Glowroot. In terms of application servers, Glowroot supports Tomcat, Jetty, JBoss, Wildfly, and Glassfish.

Following is the Glowroot JVM dashboard for reference:

The Glowroot JVM dashboard view (source: https://demo.glowroot.org)

New Relic

New Relic is another widely used application performance monitoring tool in the Java community. New Relic provides grouped views for application and network performance statistics. This helps in the quick diagnosis of domain level problems. It also provides features for drilling down into specific requests for viewing performance metrics by response time, data transfer size, and throughput.

New Relic supports applications developed in Java, Scala, Ruby, Python, PHP, .NET, and Node.js. New Relic offers four different approaches for backend monitoring:

- **Application performance management**: In application performance management, New Relic features high-level metrics with the ability to drill down to the code level to see how the application is performing. On the dashboard, New Relic displays a response time graph. New Relic uses the Apdex index score method to distill metrics into performance indicators. New Relic requires the user to manually set the threshold values.
- **Server monitoring**: New Relic focuses on the hardware the application servers are running on. The measurements include CPU usage, memory utilization, disk I/O, and network I/O. New Relic provides brief details on the heap memory and garbage collection attributes.
- **Database monitoring**: In New Relic, the dashboard for the database is a part of the application performance management dashboard. It is possible to view database monitoring metrics through plugins.
- **Insights and analytics**: New Relic has a built-in, opt-in database, which stores statistics and enables querying the database.

Following is the New Relic dashboard for reference:

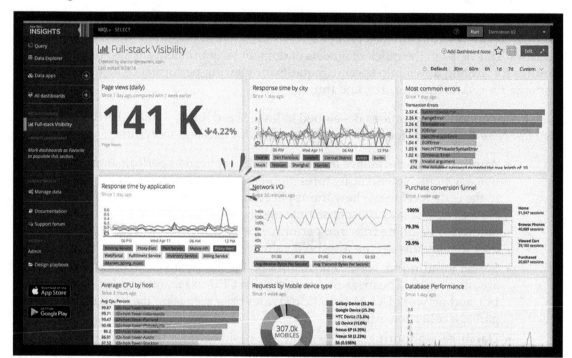

The New Relic dashboard view (source: https://newrelic.com/)

Profiling tools

Profiling tools, or profilers, are software tools used by application developers to investigate and identify characteristics of and issues in the code. Profiling tools are also useful in identifying performance problems. Profiling tools answer questions like what JVM parameters are set, what the status of the heap memory is, what the generation-based classification of memory utilization is, which threads are active, and so on. Some profilers also track methods in the code to understand how frequently SQL statements are called, or how frequently web services are called.

Similar to application performance monitoring tools, many profiling tools are available on the market. VisualVM, JConsole, and HeapAnalyzer are a few of them. We will discuss each of the profiling tools in detail in the following sections.

VisualVM

VisualVM is a Java profiling and performance analysis tool. It has a visual interface to analyze detailed information for Java applications running in local and remote environments on JVMs. It integrates and utilizes JDK provided command-line tools like `jstack`, `jconsole`, `jmap`, `jstat`, and `jinfo`. These tools are part of the standard JDK distribution. VisualVM is instrumental in solving runtime problems, with features such as heap dump and thread analysis. It helps in identifying application performance and where it stands against the benchmark. It also helps in ensuring optimal memory usage. It further helps in monitoring the garbage collector, profiling CPU usage, analyzing heap data, and tracking memory leaks. The following are the purposes of each of the command-line tools used by VisualVM:

- `jstack`: This tool is used to capture the thread dumps of a Java application
- `jmap`: This tool prints shared object memory maps and heap memory details for a given process
- `jstat`: This tool displays performance statistics for JVMs running the application
- `jinfo`: This tool prints Java configuration information

VisualVM is part of the standard JDK bundle. It was first bundled with the JDK platform in JDK version 6, update 7. It can also be installed separately. Let's look at each section in detail:

The Applications window view of VisualVM

As can be seen in the preceding screenshot, on the left-side of the window, there is an **Applications** window. The **Applications** window has nodes and subnodes. The nodes and subnodes can be expanded in order to view configured applications and saved files. We can view additional information or perform actions by right-clicking the nodes and choosing items from the pop-up menus that appear. The pop-up menu options vary, depending on the selected node.

Inside of the **Applications** window, we can see a menu for **Local** nodes. A local node displays information about the name of the process and process identifier for the Java processes running on the same machine as VisualVM. After launching VisualVM, the local nodes are automatically populated when the **Local** root node is expanded. VisualVM is always loaded as one of the local nodes. The nodes automatically disappear when the service is terminated. If we take thread dumps and heap dumps of an application, those are displayed like subnodes.

It is possible to connect to JVM running on a remote machine using VisualVM. All such running processes or applications are displayed under the **Remote** node. After a connection is established with the remote node, we can expand the **Remote** node to see all Java applications running on the remote machine.

The **VM Coredumps** node is only visible if the application is running on Linux or Solaris operating systems. When a core dump file is opened in VisualVM, the **VM Coredumps** node shows the open core dump file. It is a binary file containing information about the runtime status of the machine.

The last section in the **Applications** window is labeled **Snapshots**. The **Snapshots** section displays all of the saved snapshots taken while the application is running.

The data for local or remote applications is presented in tabs in VisualVM. The **Overview** tab is opened by default when viewing application data. The **Overview** tab displays information including the process ID, the location of the system, the main class for the application, the path to the Java installation, JVM arguments passed, JVM flags, and system properties.

The next tab in the list is the **Monitor** tab. The **Monitor** tab can be used to view real-time information about heap memory, permanent generation heap memory, and the number of classes and threads. The classes here indicate classes loaded into the virtual machine. The application monitoring process puts on low overhead.

The heap graph on the **Monitor** tab displays the total heap size and currently used heap size. The changes in the permanent generation area over a period of time are displayed in the PermGen graph. The classes graph displays the total number of loaded and shared classes. The number of live and daemon threads information is displayed in the **Threads** section. VisualVM can be used to take a thread dump, which shows exact information on threads at a specific time.

From within the **Monitor** tab, we can forcefully perform garbage collection. The action will immediately run garbage collection. It is also possible to capture a heap dump from the **Monitor** tab:

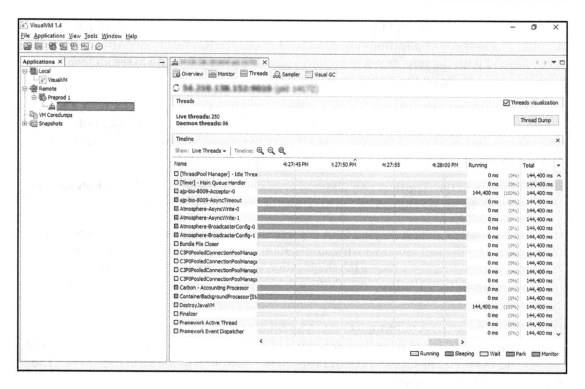

VisualVM displays real-time thread activity in the **Threads** tab. As a default, the **Threads** tab shows the timeline of current thread activity. By clicking on a particular thread, we can view details about that particular thread in the **Details** tab.

The **Timeline** section shows a timeline with real-time thread states. We can filter the types of threads displayed by choosing the appropriate values in the drop-down menu. In the preceding screenshot, it shows the **Live threads** timeline. We can also view all of the threads, or finished threads, by selecting this from the drop-down menu.

We can choose to take a thread dump of the application while the application is running. The thread dump, when printed, shows a thread stack that includes thread states for Java applications.

The **Profiler** tab makes it possible to start and stop the profiling sessions of an application. The results are displayed in the **Profiler** tab itself. Profiling can be done for CPU profiling or memory profiling. Upon starting the profiling session, VisualVM connects to the application to start collecting the profiling data. Once the results are available, they are displayed in the **Profiler** tab automatically.

JConsole

JConsole is another Java profiling tool. It compiles to **Java Management Extension (JMX)** specifications. JConsole extensively uses instrumentation in JVM to collect and display information about the performance and resource consumption of applications running on the Java platform. JConsole is updated to a GNOME and Windows look and feel in Java SE 6.

Similar to VisualVM, JConsole comes bundled with the Java development kit. The executable file for JConsole can be found in the JDK_HOME/bin directory. JConsole can be started from the Command Prompt or console window with the following command:

```
jconsole
```

Upon executing the preceding command, JConsole presents the user with a choice of all of the Java applications running on the system. We can choose to connect to any running application.

It is also possible to supply the process ID, if we know the process ID of the Java application that we want JConsole to connect to. The following is the command to boot JConsole up, with a connection to a specific Java application identified by its process ID:

```
jconsole <process-id>
```

The following command can be used to connect to a Java application running on a remote machine:

```
jconsole hostname:portnumber
```

JConsole presents information in the following tabs:

- **Overview**: This tab displays information about the JVM and values to be monitored. It presents the information in a graphical monitoring format. The information contains overview details on CPU usage, memory usage, thread counts, and the number of classes loaded in JVM.

- **Memory**: This tab displays information about memory consumption and usage. The memory tab contains a **Perform GC** button, which can be clicked to activate immediate garbage collection. For the HotSpot Java VM, the memory pools are Eden Space, Survivor Space, Tenured Generation, Permanent Generation, and Code Cache. It is possible to display various charts for depicting the consumption of memory pools.

- **Threads**: This tab displays information about thread usage. The threads include active threads, Live threads, and all threads. The chart's representation shows the peak number of threads and the number of live threads on two different lines. MXBean provides other information not covered by the **Threads** tab. With MXBean, it is possible to detect deadlocked threads.

- **Classes**: This tab displays information about classes loaded in the Java virtual machine. The class information includes the total number of classes loaded so far, including those which are unloaded later on and the current number of classes loaded.

- **VM**: This tab displays statistical information about the Java virtual machine. The summary includes uptime, indicating the amount of time since the JVM started; the process CPU time, indicating the amount of CPU time that JVM has consumed since it started; and the total compile time, indicating the time spent on the compilation process.

- **MBeans**: This tab displays information about MBeans. The **MBeans** include those currently running. We can get `MBeanInfo` descriptor information by selecting the **MBean**.

Following screenshot shows how the JConsole dashboard looks like:

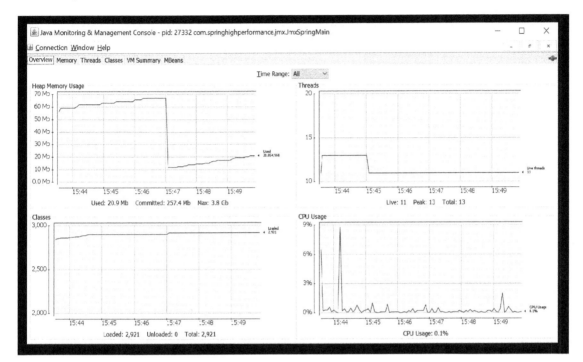

Summary

This chapter was full of information on application performance measurement techniques. The chapter is useful for development teams working on application performance enhancement tasks. At the same time, it can be referred to by technical teams setting up their application logging mechanisms.

The chapter started with introductory details on performance profiling and logging. Moving ahead, we learned about specific application performance monitoring and application logging. We learned what the key elements of logging are. We also looked into logging tools, like standard Java logging and Log4j. In the latter part of the chapter, we learned about VisualVM as a performance profiling tool. VisualVM is one of the most widely used Java-based performance profiling tools, available as a standard Java distribution package. That was it for this chapter.

The next chapter will focus on optimizing application performance. One can leverage the knowledge and information provided in this chapter in the next chapter while working on performance optimization. This chapter provides a base for the next chapter. The next chapter covers details for identifying the symptoms of performance issues, the performance tuning life cycle, and JMX support in Spring. Pretty exciting stuff, isn't it?

10
Application Performance Optimization

In the previous chapter, we focused on how to profile an application to figure out the performance issue of an application. We also covered logging, which is a useful tool in identifying issues in the application. It was an essential part and will be part of our daily routine when we work on Spring applications.

Now let's look at what we've got in this chapter. This is a crucial chapter in this book; it provides you with ways to improve application performance. In this chapter, we will discuss the fundamental approach for application performance optimization, which is key for any application, including Spring-based applications. We'll discuss Spring's support for **Java Management Extension (JMX)**, improvements in database interactions, and the performance tuning of Spring applications. By the end of this chapter, you will be able to identify performance bottlenecks in a Spring-based application and resolve them.

Let's look at important aspects of application performance optimization with a structured approach. We'll cover the following topics:

- Performance issue symptoms
- Performance tuning life cycle
- Performance tuning patterns and anti-patterns
- The iterative performance-tuning process
- Spring support of JMX

Performance issue symptoms

Let's start with performance issue symptoms. This is an obvious place to start, as it's like consulting a doctor where symptoms are discussed and then a diagnosis is made. Application performance is the behavior experienced by the end users in terms of speed, accuracy in delivering the content, and average response times under the highest load. The load is referred to by the number of transactions processed by the application per unit time. The response times are the times required for an application to respond to a user's actions at such a load.

Whenever performance needs an improvement, the first thing that comes to mind is the problems that are affecting the performance of our application. To find the issues with performance, we need to look for certain symptoms that can lead us to the issue.

Some common symptoms that can be observed in a Spring application are as follows:

- Timeouts
- Running out of worker threads
- Threads waiting on class loaders
- A major amount of time spent on loading classes even under normal load
- Class loader attempts to load non-existing classes

In the following sections, we will understand these symptoms with an example context. The details will help us identify the symptom when it occurs.

Timeouts

Timeouts occur in two different ways. One is the request timeout, which is represented by `HTTP response status code 408`. Another flavor of timeout is the gateway timeout, which is represented by `HTTP response status code 504`.

The request timeout indicates that the server did not receive the complete request from the client within the specified time. In such a case, the server chose to close the connection with the client. The request timeout is an error message directly from the server.

The gateway timeout indicates that the gateway or the proxy server timed out while processing the request. In most cases, this is because the proxy or gateway do not receive a timely response from the actual server in the upstream.

Running out of worker threads

Consider the example of a bank; the bank has a web application with a monitoring system on top of it. The monitoring system keeps an eye on the strength of the JVMs. The parameters for measurement are memory, CPU, I/O, heap memory, and various other attributes. The monitoring system provides distinctive dashboards that show and highlight the measurements for the aforementioned attributes. There exists an accompanying dashboard that demonstrates the group of activities performed in the banking application. This dashboard also identifies the group of activities on which the JVM starts running low while accessing specialized application resources, such as threads. The application is running in multiple JVM environments. The following is a screenshot of a sample dashboard for reference:

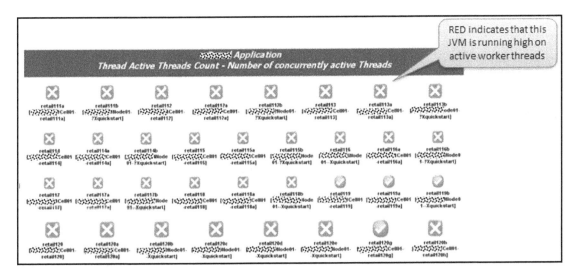

The monitoring system is configured with threshold values. For example, the maximum threads utilized by a JVM at a time should be no more than 250. When the JVM is utilizing less than 150 threads at a time, the corresponding JVM indicator in the dashboard is green. At the time when the JVM starts utilizing more than 150 threads, the monitoring system indicates that JVM in red. It is a symptom indicating that a failure might occur or that performance is impacted beyond normal.

The following is a timeline-based screenshot showing JVMs maxed out of worker threads:

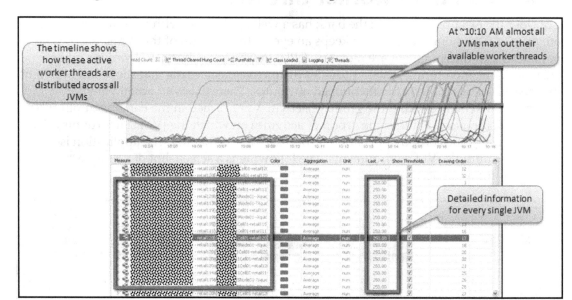

Threads waiting on class loaders

Continuing with the same example as described in the previous section, the first question that arises is, what is wrong with these threads? Taking a deeper look into the threads and breaking down the state, it was discerned that these threads (approximately 242 out of 250) were looking out for the server's `CompoundClassLoader`. These threads were stacking extra objects and that's what they were looking out for the class loader. Because of the high number of threads endeavoring to get to that common asset—the class loader—most threads got stuck in pause.

The following screenshot from the monitoring shows the number of threads waiting for `CompoundClassLoader`:

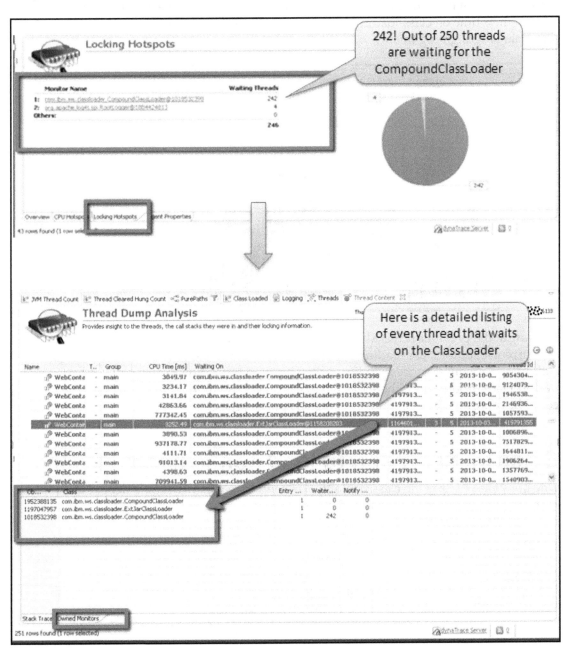

Time spent on class-loading activities

Another thing that came out of the analysis in the monitoring system is that threads spend most of their time on class-loading activities. The following is the monitoring system screenshot highlighting this:

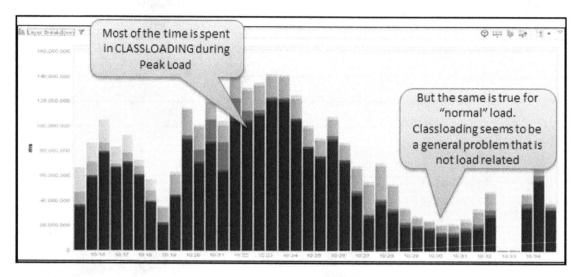

Looking at the previous screenshot of the monitoring system, it is clear that regardless of the current load, the class-loading activities take considerable time compared to other activities in a request-processing life cycle. This is an indication or symptom of a performance problem as it increases the overall response time. In the case of a bank, it could be confirmed by evaluating average response times.

Class loader trying to load non-existent classes

One question arises: Is the class stacking extremely important? Digging deeper and looking at the requests processed, it demonstrated that each request tried to stack a class that did not exist. The application server was prompting a huge amount of the ClassNotFoundException class. The main driver of the issue is that the class could never be effectively stacked, but the application server continued attempting to stack it for each request. This should not be a problem for quick and moderate requests and features. This level of detail for each incoming request or feature may clutch the rare asset—the class loader—and, accordingly, affect the response time for requests.

The ability, adaptability, and capacity of the monitoring system is to catch each and every request and response with the data on stacking classes to help recognize the symptoms. The following screenshot displays one such scenario in the application framework:

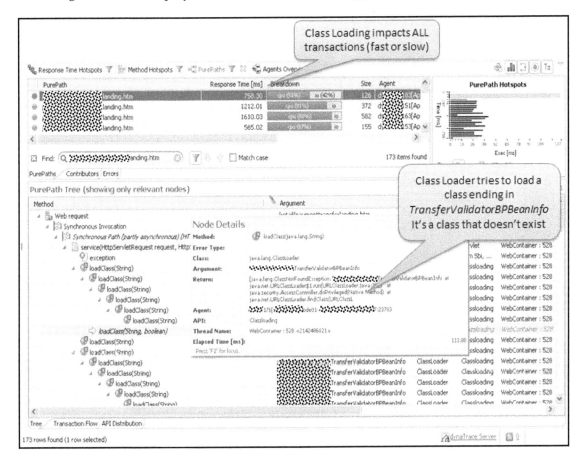

The symptoms of a potential performance issue must be clear by now. It is specifically applicable to any JVM-based web application, not only a Spring-based web application. The following screenshot shows us the pointers that would basically help us identify the impact of performance issues:

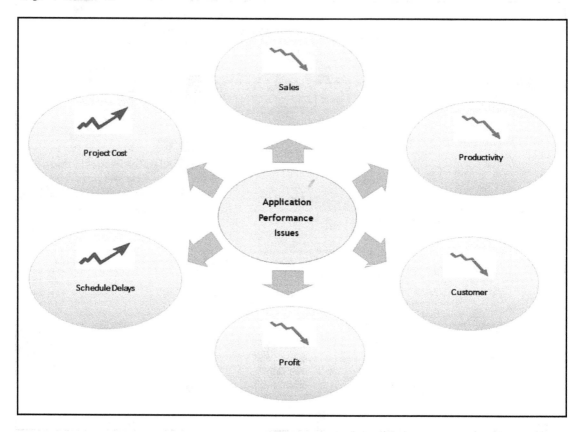

Poorly performing applications matter a lot to businesses, as they have seen dips in sales because of application performance. An application can also notice productivity or business loss because of performance issues.

Let's understand the business impact of performance issues with a basic illustration:

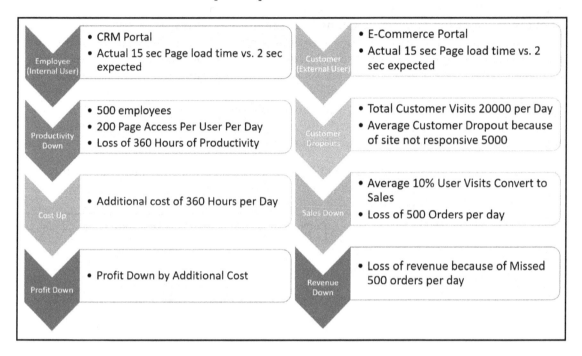

As we can understand from the previous diagram, bad application behavior can impact business, which can be described in either high project costs, a decrease in conversion ratios, fewer repeat visits and poor customer retention, a decline in sales, a decline in productivity, losing customers, increases in project cost, and delays or declines in profit and returns on investments. Performance matters a lot to businesses.

What do we need to do to avoid or address performance issues? Don't wait for performance issues to occur. Get architecture, design, and code reviewed, and plan out for load testing, tuning, and benchmarking in advance. Today, in the world of competitive marketing, an organization's key point is to have their system up and running with the best performance. Any failure or downtime directly impacts the business and revenue; performance of an application is a factor that cannot be overlooked. Day by day, the mountain of data is growing because of the extensive use of technology in numerous ways. Due to this, the load average is going through the roof. For some cases, it cannot be assured that data will not exceed the limit or the number of users will not go out of bounds.

At any point, we can meet unexpected demands to scale. For any organization, it is very important for its application to provide scalability, performance, availability, and security. Application scalability in terms of scaling horizontally and vertically by spreading database to cater to different application queries across multiple servers, is quite feasible. It is easy to add horsepower to the cluster to handle the load. Cluster servers instantly handle failures and manage the failover part to keep your system available almost all the time. If one server goes down, it will redirect the user's request to another node and perform the requested operation. Today, in the world of competitive marketing, an organization's key point is to have their system up and running. Any failure or downtime directly impacts business and revenue; high availability is a factor that cannot be overlooked.

The following diagram shows us some of the common performance issues that we might come across:

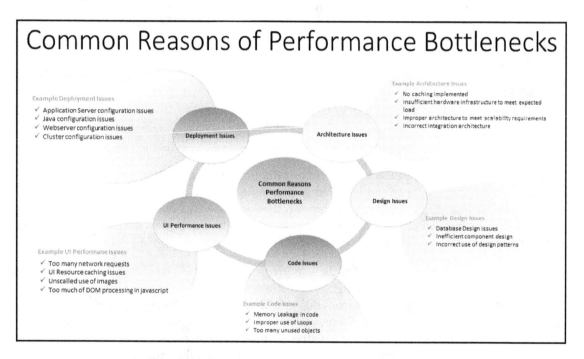

Now, let's move towards the phases of the performance tuning life cycle.

Performance tuning life cycle

Speed is at the heart of every business. In this hyper-connected modern world, the thing that fascinates the majority of people is speed; be it the fastest car, fastest computer processor, or even the fastest website. Website performance has become the highest priority of each and every business. User's expectations are higher than ever. If your website doesn't respond instantly, there are high chances that your users will switch to your competitors.

A study by Walmart (`https://www.slideshare.net/devonauerswald/walmart-pagespeedslide`) found that for every 1 second of page performance improvement, there's a 2% increase in conversions.

A study by Akamai (`https://www.akamai.com/us/en/about/news/`) found that:

- 47% of people expect a web page to load in two seconds or fewer
- 40% will abandon a web page if it takes more than three seconds to load
- 52% of online shoppers say quick page loads are important for their loyalty to a site

In 2007, Amazon reported that for every 100-millisecond increase in the load time of Amazon (`https://www.amazon.com/`), their sales decreased by 1%.

With help of the following figure, we can easily understand the different phases of the life cycle of performance tuning:

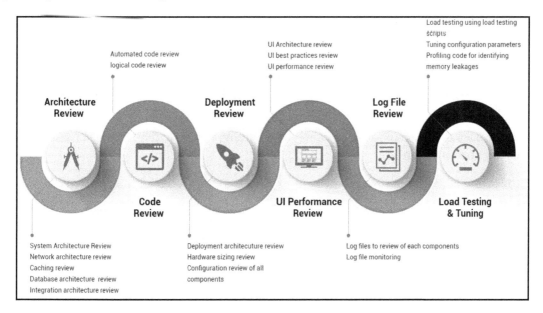

In most of these cases, performance issues can be avoided by reviewing the following artifacts at the right time:

- Architecture
- Design
- Code
- Engage expert consultants to perform application reviews at the right time
- Engage any time before the development phase is completed
- It is strongly recommended to identify performance optimization issues beforehand, which can start before the completion of the architecture phase
- It's always better to prevent performance issues before making applications available to users
- Conduct various reviews and tests to avoid performance issues in production
- The performance tuning life cycle can also be done after going to production or when facing performance issues in the production environment

In order to tune the performance of a Spring application, the strategies described in the following sections can be pretty handy.

Connection pooling

Connection pooling is a strategy to help an application's execution where N connections with the database are opened and overseen in a pool. The application just requests a connection, utilizes it, and afterward drops it back to the pool. At the point when the application requests a connection, the prepared connections are kept accessible to be utilized as part of the pool. The pool deals with the connection life cycle to such an extent that the developer really doesn't have to sit tight for the connection and shift through the stale ones.

Hibernate uses its magic to identify which connection pool provider to use—based on the properties you configure.

The following is the properties configuration for the c3p0 connection pooling:

```
<property name="hibernate.c3p0.min_size">5</property>
<property name="hibernate.c3p0.max_size">20</property>
<property name="hibernate.c3p0.timeout">300</property>
<property name="hibernate.c3p0.max_statements">50</property>
<property name="hibernate.c3p0.idle_test_period">3000</property>
```

The following is the example connection pooling properties configuration for the Apache Commons DBCP:

```
<property name="hibernate.dbcp.initialSize">8</property>
<property name="hibernate.dbcp.maxActive">20</property>
<property name="hibernate.dbcp.maxIdle">20</property>
<property name="hibernate.dbcp.minIdle">0</property>
```

When using either of the connection pooling mechanisms, we have to place the JAR dependencies in the server classpath manually or by using a dependency management tool such as Maven.

It is also possible to specify the connection provider explicitly with the `hibernate.connection.provider_class` property, though it is not mandatory.

If we do not configure a connection pool with Hibernate, the default is used. It is visible in the log or console output when we start the application:

```
org.hibernate.engine.jdbc.connections.internal.DriverManagerConnectionP
roviderImpl configure
```

The default connection pool of Hibernate is a good option for the development environment, but when it comes to production, it is recommended to configure the pool based on the requirements and the use cases.

If you are using an application server, you may wish to use the built-in pool (typically, a connection is obtained using the **Java Naming and Directory Interface (JNDI)**).

To use the server's built-in pool with Hibernate session using JNDI configuration, we need to set the following property in the Hibernate configuration file:

```
hibernate.connection.datasource=java:/comp/env/jdbc/AB_DB
```

It is assumed that `AB_DB` is the JNDI name of the Tomcat JDBC Connection Pool `DataSource`.

If you cannot or do not wish to use your application server's built-in connection pool, Hibernate supports several other connection pools, such as:

- c3p0
- Proxool

After Apache DBCP, the second most preferred connection pool implementation is c3p0, which easily integrates with Hibernate, and is said to deliver good performance.

Hibernate

The connection pooling mechanism ensures that the application does not run out of database connections when it needs one badly. Hibernate is one of the finest ORM frameworks for Java-based applications. When used, it must be tuned for performance optimization.

Transaction

Hibernate does the grimy checking just when it needs to, to keep in mind the execution cost. The cost increments when a specific substance has a relating table with an expansive number of segments. To try and limit the filthy checking cost, it's better we help Spring by determining an exchange to be perused, which enhances the execution stunningly better, wiping out the requirement for any grimy checks.

The following is an example use of the @Transactional annotation, which indicates that the method runs within the Hibernate transaction:

```
@Transactional(readOnly=true)
public void someBusinessMethod() {
    ....
}
```

Periodical clearing of Hibernate sessions

While including/adjusting information in the database, Hibernate maintains sessions. In the session, it stores a form of the instances which are to be held on. If these instances or records are altered or modified before the session is closed, it is known as **filthy checking.** Nonetheless, we can keep Hibernate from holding the elements in its session longer than really required. So once the requirements are done, we will not have to keep the instances in the session any longer. For this situation, we can securely flush and clear the EntityManager to adjust the condition of elements in the database and expel the instances from the session. This will keep the application far from memory requirements and beyond any doubt to affect the execution on a higher side.

The following is a piece of code that can be used to flush() and clear() the Hibernate session:

```
entityManager.flush();
entityManager.clear();
```

Lazy initialization

In case you are using Hibernate, you should take care that the IN statements are used adequately. It lazily loads the records only when it's required. When such custom records are loaded into memory inefficiently, every record will be stacked independently with separate utilization. Consequently, if there are excessively numerous instances loaded in memory, the same number of queries will execute consecutively, which may result into a major execution hit.

Constructor-based HQLs

In typical situations, when an application is utilizing Hibernate, we don't try to recover the entire substance with every one of its properties despite the fact that we need not bother with every one of them for a specific use case. A solitary substance may have 30 properties, while we may only need a couple to be set in our feature or shown to the client. In such a case, a huge number of records are retrieved with the query to the database. It adds up to a significant load considering the unused fields sticking with the application, which will eventually be a gigantic execution or performance hit.

To manage this, HQL/JPA gives us a select new constructor call, which is frequently utilized for detailing inquiries, which also enables the designer to choose collected esteems.

Entity and query caching

In the event that a similar inquiry is conjured each time for a specific element and the table information isn't subject to change for a specific availability, we can store the question and the elements with Hibernate.

In the event that an inquiry store is connected, at that point, no resulting SQL articulation is sent to the database for execution. If the inquiry store or first-level cache cannot find the elements based on the identifier, the stored element identifiers are utilized to get to Hibernate's second-level store where comparing real elements are reserved. This highly affects the reaction time. When we do this, we are likewise worried about when the reserve invigorates itself. We can do that effortlessly with some basic setups.

Native queries

In spite of the fact that the local inquiries have a mishap, they are the fastest where execution is concerned. At the point when HQL changes don't resist enhancing the execution of your application, local questions can essentially enhance the execution by around 40%.

Primary key generation

While indicating Hibernate comments into substance classes or composing .hbm documents, we should abstain from utilizing the auto key age methodology, which prompts a gigantic measure of succession calls.

The following is an example code for defining the key generation strategy:

```
@Id
@GeneratedValue(strategy = GenerationType.SEQUENCE, generator =
"your_key_generator")
private Long id;
```

With this simple change, an improvement in the range of 10-20% can be noticed in insert-intensive applications, with basically no code changes.

Database

Once the Hibernate performance optimization life cycle is performed, the next step would be to perform an optimization life cycle at a database level. The following sections define performance improvement techniques for database components.

Indexing

Lists become an imperative factor if the tables included in the query have a large number of columns. Also, it impacts when complex database queries get terminated by the application. The most ideal approach to get recommendations on required indexes is to check the query execution plan. While analyzing the SQL queries for indexing, we must anticipate every one of the genuine queries separately.

While working with indexes, it must be noted that:

- Indexes might slow down inserts and updates, so apply them carefully on columns that are frequently updated

- Indexes are meant to speed up search operations that use WHERE and ORDER BY clauses in the query

Views

Database views are another procedure that we explore or think of when we are highly encompassed with longer execution time issues. Until SQL Server 2000, views were implied only for accommodation, and not speed. Later forms of SQL server included an uncommon component called recorded views that is said to monstrously expand the execution, however, ordered views must be made utilizing an arrangement of rules.

Spring Security

Spring Security is one of the most important aspects for any application, especially those running over the internet. While Spring Security provides an application with a secure facade and prevents the application from unwanted access, it adds up to a lot of overhead if not managed properly. We will focus on Spring Security best practices in the sections to follow.

Authentication cache

Spring Security execution is one of the worries that occasionally comes into the picture, when the demand-handling time is seen to be on the high, and therefore inadmissible, side. There may be circumstances where you see that the real demand handling takes around 120 milliseconds, while Spring Security validation/verification includes another 500-600 milliseconds.

LDAP custom authorities

This won't be the approach that you would need to consider, yet it does provide you with another option to enhance the execution of your Spring Security implementation.

In this approach, we set the user authorities with our own custom usage, as opposed to confirming it from LDAP. There are a few good reasons to do this, and the application's execution is one of them.

Native LDAP

Spring Security provides us with the most standard and solid usage to LDAP verification. With Center Spring LDAP, the approach turns somewhat terrible, yet shows signs of streamlined improvements. The last approach (with Center Spring LDAP) has been seen to radically enhance the execution of your application when contrasted with that of Spring Security. This is not a preferred approach, still we can consider it to be one of the options for development.

Multithreading

Every application nowadays is multithreaded, meaning it is capable of performing multiple operations at the same time.

With every conceivable streamline, the single hits to your application may look fulfilling. Be that as it may, the heap tests with a few simultaneous hits to your application begin to obstruct your application's execution. In such highly simultaneous situations, you may need to tune up the thread defaults on the Tomcat server. On the off-chance that there is high simultaneousness, the HTTP asks to put it on hold until the point that a thread winds up to process it. In more outrageous cases, the hold-up lines hoist and the solicitations time out.

The default server thread usage can be additionally supplemented with the use of agent structure inside your business rationale, to additionally make simultaneous non-concurrent calls from inside a strategy in a solitary string execution stream.

Performance tuning patterns and anti-patterns

Performance tuning is the change of the framework execution. Regularly in PC frameworks, the inspiration for such an action is known as a performance issue, which can be either genuine or assumed. Most frameworks will react to expanded load with some level of diminishing execution. A framework's capacity to acknowledge a higher load is called versatility, and altering a framework to deal with a higher load is synonymous with execution tuning.

The performance tuning involves the following mentioned steps:

1. The issue should be surveyed and checked against expected numeric counts for satisfaction.
2. Measure the execution of the framework before alteration.
3. Distinguish the piece of the framework that is basic for enhancing the execution. This is known as the **bottleneck**.
4. Alter that piece of the framework to evacuate the bottleneck.
5. Measure the execution of the framework after alteration.
6. In the event that the adjustment improves the execution, receive it. In the event that the change aggravates the execution, set it back the way it was.

Anti-patterns

As there are patterns, there are also anti-patterns in software development. Patterns help to ensure the betterment of the application in terms of performance, scalability, and optimized processing. On the other hand, the existence of anti-patterns in the code indicates that challenges exist in application execution. Anti-patterns impact the application with a similar degree to patterns but in a negative way. Performance anti-patterns mostly degrade the application's performance. We are discussing anti-patterns because, along with following patterns and best practices, we have to ensure that we do not follow or use anti-patterns.

Architectural anti-patterns

There are many types of performance anti-patterns in architecture. The multi-layering anti-pattern describes an architecture that attempts to achieve high abstraction through as many independent, logical application layers as possible. As a developer, such an architecture quickly becomes recognizable by the fact that much of the time spent mapping and converting data is lost, and that a simple pass from the interface to the database is complex.

Such architectures usually arise because the application should be kept as flexible as possible so that, for example, GUIs can be exchanged easily and quickly, and the dependencies on other systems and components can be kept low. The decoupling of the layers leads to performance losses during the mapping and exchange of the data—especially if the layers are also physically separated and the data exchange takes place via remoting technologies, such as **Simple Object Access Protocol (SOAP)** or **Remote Method Invocation (RMI)**, **Internet Inter-ORB Protocol (IIOP)**.

The many mapping and conversion operations can also result in higher garbage collection activity, known as the cycling object problem. As a solution to this anti-pattern, the architecture drivers should be scrutinized to clarify what flexibility and decoupling is needed. New framework approaches, such as JBoss Seam, have addressed the problem and try to avoid mapping data as much as possible.

Another architectural anti-pattern is the so-called **session cache**. In doing so, the web session of an application is misused as a large data cache, which severely limits the scalability of the application. Session sizes have often been measured to be well larger than 1 MB in tuning jobs—in most cases, no team member knows the exact content of the session. Large sessions cause the Java heap to be very busy and only a small number of parallel users are possible. Especially when clustering applications with session replication, depending on the technology used, the performance loss due to serialization and data transfer is very high. Some projects help to acquire new hardware and more memory, but in the long run, this is a very expensive and risky solution.

Session caches arise because the architecture of the application has not clearly defined which data is session-dependent and which is persistent, that is, recoverable at any time. During development, all data is quickly stored in the session, because this is a very convenient solution—often this data is no longer removed from the session. To solve this problem, you should first memory-analyze the session using a production heap dump and clean up the session for data that is not session-dependent. Caching can positively impact performance if the process of getting data is performance critical, for example, with database accesses. Optimally, the caching is then transparent to the developer within the framework. For example, Hibernate provides a first and second-level cache to optimize access to data, but be careful; the configuration and tuning of such frameworks should be done by experts, otherwise, you'll quickly get a new performance anti-pattern.

Implementing anti-patterns

There are many Java performance anti-patterns and tuning tips available, but the problem with these technological anti-patterns is that they are heavily dependent on the Java version and manufacturer, and especially on the use case. A very common anti-pattern is the underrated frontend. For web applications, the frontend is often the performance Achilles heel. HTML and JavaScript development are often a nuisance to real application developers and are therefore often under-optimized for performance. Even with the increasing use of DSL, the connection is often still a bottleneck, especially if it is a mobile connection via **Universal Mobile Telecommunications System** (**UMTS**) or **General Packet Radio Service** (**GPRS**). Web applications are becoming increasingly complex, driven by the Web 2.0 hype, and are increasingly approaching desktop applications.

This comfort leads to extended waiting times and higher server and network load through many server round trips and large pages. There is a whole range of solutions to optimize web-based interfaces. Compressing HTML pages with GZip significantly reduces the amount of data transferred and has been supported by all browsers since HTTP 1.1. Web servers, such as Apache, have modules (`mod_ gzip`) to perform the compression without changing the application. However, page sizes can also be reduced quickly in HTML by consistently using CSS and swapping CSS and JavaScript sources into your own files so that they can be better cached by the browser. Also, AJAX can, when correctly used, improve the performance significantly, because the complete reloading of web pages can be saved; for example, only the contents of lists are retransmitted.

But even in the analysis, the performance of the surfaces can be significantly improved by adapting the contents of the pages to the requirements of the user. For example, if only those fields that are needed 80% of the time appear on a page, the average transfer rate can be significantly reduced; the dropped fields are offloaded to separate pages. As an example, in many web applications, there are forms with more than 30 input fields. In 90% of the instances when users fill in those forms, they fill in values for only two fields but we display all these 30 fields in the listing pages or reports, including all lists for the selection boxes. Another common anti-pattern is **phantom logging**, which can be found in almost all projects. Phantom logging generates log messages that do not actually have to be created in the active log level. The following code is an example of the problem:

```
logger.debug ("one log message" + param_1 + "text" + param_2);
```

Although the message would not be logged in the `INFO` level, the string is assembled. Depending on the number and complexity of the debug and trace messages, this can lead to enormous performance losses, especially if objects have an over-written and costly `toString()` method. The solution is simple:

```
if (logger.isDebugEnabled ()) {
   logger.debug ("One log message" + param_1 + "Text" + param_2);
}
```

In this case, the log level is first queried and the log message is only generated if the DEBUG log level is active. In order to avoid performance bottlenecks during development, the used frameworks in particular should be understood correctly. Most commercial and open source solutions have sufficient performance documentation, and experts should be consulted at regular intervals to implement the solution. Even if profiling finds the bottleneck within a framework, it does not mean that the problem lies within the framework. In most cases, the problem is misuse or configuration.

The iterative performance-tuning process

The iterative performance-tuning process is a set of guidelines that will help improve application performance drastically. These guidelines can be applied in iterations until the desired output is achieved. These guidelines can also be applied to a variety of web applications, regardless of the technology used to build the application.

The first and most important part of any application is the rendering of static content. The delivery of static content is one of the most common performance bottlenecks. The static content includes images, logos, browser executable scripts, cascaded style sheets, and themes. As this content remains the same all the time, it is unnecessary to serve this content dynamically. Instead, the web server, such as Apache, should be configured to have a long browser cache time while serving static resources to the response. This improvement in static content delivery can significantly improve the application's overall performance. The web server must also be configured to compress static resources. Web accelerators can be used for caching a web resource. For content-driven public portals, it is highly recommended to cache whole pages through the web accelerator. Varnish is an open source web accelerator tool.

Server resource monitoring must be included as part of iterative performance analysis. The reason is that as the application grows, it starts occupying more resources at a particular instance in time. The higher demand for server resources, such as CPU, memory, and disk I/O, can cause it to exceed the operating system limits and become prone to failure. The monitoring systems must be set up in order to observe resource utilization. Resource monitoring usually includes:

- Web servers
- Application servers
- Processes—Maximum versus actual
- Threads—Maximum versus actual

- Memory usage
- CPU utilization
- Heap memory as a separate measurement
- Disk I/O operations
- Database connections—Maximum versus busy
- JVM garbage collection
- Database slow queries
- Cache
- Cache hits—Number of times the result is found from the cache
- Cache misses—Number of times the result is not found from the cache

In order to monitor the resources, the following tools can be used:

- `jconsole` and `jvisualvm` come bundled with the standard **Java Development Kit** (**JDK**). Using these tools, we can monitor JVM, garbage collection execution, cache statistics, threads, CPU usage, memory usage, and database-connection pooling statistics.
- `mpstat` and `vmstat` are available on Linux-based operating systems. Both of these are command-line tools and are used for collecting and reporting processor-related statistics.
- `ifstat` and `iostat` are useful for monitoring system input/output operations.

There might be a question on why we should do this iterative performance tuning process while we follow best practices. The goals of the iterative performance tuning process are as follows:

- Identify bottlenecks in the system's performance at various levels
- Improve the performance of the portal as per the expectations
- Find the solution and approach
- Put the solution workflow in place
- Understand the performance pain areas of the system
- Define the performance strategy for the application
- Identify the performance measurement tool based on the technologies
- Understand application key user scenarios
- Document key scenarios

- Prepare sufficient data to generate considerable distributed load on all flavors in a single execution
- Customize and combine load testing scripts to prepare a performance test suite that can be used for execution on any single flavor or on all flavors at a time
- Execute performance scripts with different scenarios and load combinations to identify bottlenecks using response times

The iterative performance tuning process is followed at all stages of the application development life cycle. The following table demonstrates the items being reviewed with input and output expectations:

Review item	Input	Output
Architecture • High availability • Scalability • Caching • Integration • Network • Search Engine • Database	System architecture diagram	Recommendations on best practices
User interface	• Frontend code • Existing technology selection criteria	• Review of the code • Recommendations for the change
Hardware configuration	• Web server details • App server details • Database details • Server type (Virtual or Physical) • Number of CPU • Hard disk space • Memory configuration	Changes recommended in hardware configuration
Software configuration	• Framework configuration • Dependent modules/integrations configuration, if any	Recommendations on configuration change
Application server configuration	• App server configuration files	Recommendations on configuration change
Web server configuration	• Web server configuration files • Cache control settings • Static resource-handling settings	Recommendations on configuration change
Deployment architecture	• Deployment diagram • Software installation details • Configuration details	Recommendation on deployment architecture changes

Code and database	• Code review • DB design review • Code duplication • Modularization of code • Any third-party libraries/APIs • Coding standard implemented • Loops and conditions • Data normalization • Indexing • Long-running queries • Relations between tables	• Code review results • Recommendations for improvement

Spring support of JMX

JMX is the standard component in the Java platform. It was first released in J2SE 5.0. Basically, JMX is a set of specifications defined for application and network management. It empowers developers to assign management attributes to the Java objects used in the applications. By assigning management attributes, it makes the Java objects capable of working with network management software in use. It provides a standard way for developers to manage applications, devices, and services.

JMX has a three-layer architecture. The three layers are defined here:

- **The probe or instrumentation layer**: This layer contains managed beans. The application resources to be managed are enabled for JMX.
- **The agent or MBeanServer layer**: This layer forms the core of the JMX. It works as an intermediary between managed beans and the application.
- **The remote management layer**: This layer enables the remote applications to connect to and access MBeanServer using connectors or adapters. The connector provides full access to mBeanServer whereas an adapter adapts the API.

The following diagram shows the architecture of JMX:

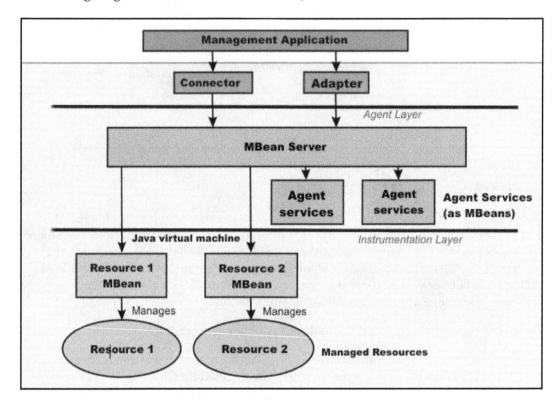

Source: https://www.ibm.com/support/knowledgecenter/en/SSAW57_8.5.5/com.ibm.websphere.nd.multiplatform.doc/ae/cxml_javamanagementx.html

Managed beans

The managed bean is a type of Java bean. It is used specifically in JMX technology and it is created using the **dependency injection** (**DI**) technique. In JMX, a resource is represented as a **managed bean** (**MBean**). These managed beans are registered with a core managed beans server. So, a managed bean can be visualized as a wrapper around Java services, components, or devices. As all the managed components are registered with the MBeans server, it is used for managing all of the managed beans. The managed beans server allows server components to wire in and find managed beans. A typical JMX agent consists of a managed beans server and services required to interact with managed beans.

The JMX specification describes standard connectors. These connectors are also known as **JMX connectors**. JMX connectors allow us to access JMX agents from remote management applications. The connectors can use different protocols to work with the same management interface.

The following are the reasons why JMX should be used:

- It provides a way to manage applications on different devices
- It provides a standard way to manage Java applications and networks
- It can be used to manage JVM
- It provides a scalable and dynamic management interface

With the basic understanding of JMX, let's move on to check how it is supported in Spring. The JMX support for Spring enables us to transform the spring application into JMX architecture quite easily.

The following are the features provided by Spring's JMX support:

- Automatic registration of a Spring bean as a managed bean
- A flexible structure for controlling the management interface for Spring beans
- A declarative approach for managed beans over remote connectors
- Proxying of local and remote managed bean resources

These features work without coupling with either of Spring or JMX's classes or interfaces. Spring JMX support has a class called `MBeanExporter`. This class is responsible for collecting Spring beans and registering them with the managed beans server.

The following is an example of a Spring bean:

```
package com.springhighperformance.jmx;

public class Calculator {
  private String name;
  private int lastCalculation;

  public String getName() {
    return name;
  }

  public void setName(String name) {
    this.name = name;
  }

  public int getLastCalculation() {
```

```
        return lastCalculation;
    }

    public void calculate(int x, int y) {
        lastCalculation = x + y;
    }
}
```

In order to expose this bean and its properties as managed attributes and operations, the following configurations should be done in the configuration file:

```
<beans>
  <bean id="exporter"
    class="org.springframework.jmx.export.MBeanExporter
    " lazy-init="false">
    <property name="beans">
      <map>
        <entry key="bean:name=calculatorBean1" value-
        ref="calculatorBean"/>
      </map>
    </property>
  </bean>

  <bean id="calculatorBean"
    class="com.springhighperformance.jmx.Calculator">
    <property name="name" value="Test"/>
    <property name="lastCalculation" value="10"/>
  </bean>
</beans>
```

An important bean definition, from the preceding configuration, to look for is the exporter bean. The beans map property of the exporter bean indicates the Spring beans to be exposed as JMX beans to the JMX-managed beans server.

With the preceding configuration, it is assumed that the managed beans server must be running in the environment accessible to the Spring application. If the managed beans server or MBeanServer is running, Spring will attempt to find it and register all the beans. This default behavior is useful when the application is running inside Tomcat or IBM WebSphere that has a bundled MBeanServer.

In other cases, we have to create an MBeanServer instance, as follows:

```
<beans>
  <bean id="mbeanServer" class="org.springframework.jmx.support.
    MBeanServerFactoryBean"/>
```

```
<bean id="exporter"
 class="org.springframework.jmx.export.MBeanExporter">
  <property name="beans">
    <map>
      <entry key="bean:name=calculatorBean1" value-
        ref="calculatorBean"/>
    </map>
  </property>
  <property name="server" ref="mbeanServer"/>
</bean>

<bean id="calculatorBean"
 class="com.springhighperformance.jmx.Calculator">
  <property name="name" value="Test"/>
  <property name="lastCalculation" value="10"/>
</bean>
</beans>
```

We have to specify the server property on the MBeanExporter bean to associate it with the MBeanServer that has been created.

With the inception of annotations in JDK 5.0, Spring enabled the provision for setting annotations to register Spring beans as JMX beans.

The following is an example Calculator bean defined using the @ManagedResource annotation:

```
package com.springhighperformance.jmx;

import org.springframework.jmx.export.annotation.ManagedAttribute;
import org.springframework.jmx.export.annotation.ManagedOperation;
import
org.springframework.jmx.export.annotation.ManagedOperationParameter;
import
org.springframework.jmx.export.annotation.ManagedOperationParameters;
import org.springframework.jmx.export.annotation.ManagedResource;

  @ManagedResource(objectName = "Examples:type=JMX,name=Calculator",
    description = "A calculator to demonstrate JMX in the
    SpringFramework")
  public class Calculator {
  private String name;
  private int lastCalculation;

  @ManagedAttribute(description = "Calculator name")
  public String getName() {
    return name;
```

```
  }

  @ManagedAttribute(description = "Calculator name")
  public void setName(String name) {
    this.name = name;
  }

  @ManagedAttribute(description = "The last calculation")
  public int getLastCalculation() {
    return lastCalculation;
  }

  @ManagedOperation(description = "Calculate two numbers")
  @ManagedOperationParameters({
      @ManagedOperationParameter(name = "x",
          description = "The first number"),
      @ManagedOperationParameter(name = "y",
          description = "The second number") })
  public void calculate(int x, int y) {
    lastCalculation = x + y;
  }
}
```

The `@ManagedAttribute` and `@ManagedOperation` annotations are used to expose the bean properties and methods to manage the beans server.

The following is the client code that instantiates the managed beans, which can be monitored by tools such as JConsole or VisualVM:

```
package com.springhighperformance.jmx;
import java.util.Random;

import org.springframework.context.ApplicationContext;
import
org.springframework.context.annotation.AnnotationConfigApplicationConte
xt;
import org.springframework.context.annotation.Bean;
import org.springframework.context.annotation.Configuration;
import org.springframework.context.annotation.EnableMBeanExport;

@Configuration
@EnableMBeanExport
public class JmxSpringMain {
  private static final Random rand = new Random();
    @Bean
    public Resource jmxResource() {
        return new Resource();
```

```
    }

    @Bean
    public Calculator calculator() {
        return new Calculator();
    }

    public static void main(String[] args) throws InterruptedException
{
        ApplicationContext context = new
        AnnotationConfigApplicationContext(JmxSpringMain.class);
        do {
          Calculator cal = context.getBean(Calculator.class);
          cal.calculate(rand.nextInt(), rand.nextInt());
          Thread.sleep(Long.MAX_VALUE);
        } while(true);
    }
}
```

Once exposed as managed beans, these resources can be monitored for various parameters, such as the number of objects, memory occupied by the objects, and heap memory space occupied by the objects, using tools such as JConsole or VisualVM.

The following is a screenshot from Java VisualVM highlighting the exposure of the Calculator as a managed bean:

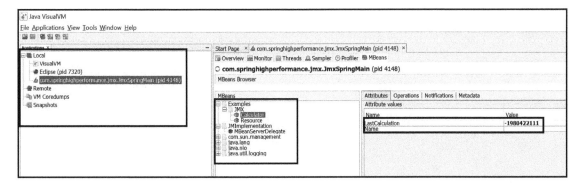

Summary

This is one of the most important chapters in this book. It solely focuses on performance measurement and enhancement strategies. This chapter resembles a real-life health checkup scenario. If a person is unwell, the first step is to identify the symptoms in order to identify and cure the disease. Similarly, this chapter started by identifying the symptoms of performance degradation, moving on to the performance tuning life cycle. Performance tuning patterns and anti-patterns were described, which resemble the best practices to be followed. This was followed by the iterative performance tuning process and JMX support in the Spring framework. We saw an example of Spring beans turned into JMX-managed beans.

The next chapter focuses on fine-tuning the JVM. This will not be tuning that is specific to a Spring application, but is applicable to any application running on JVM. This chapter will do a deep dive into the inside details of JVM, which are not very well-known to developers. Let's get ready to dive into JVM.

11
Inside JVM

The previous chapter gave us knowledge on how to tune an application's performance by understanding the symptoms of the performance issues. We walked through the performance tuning life cycle, learning at what stages of the application performance can be tuned and how. We also learned how to connect JMX to the Spring application, observed the application's bottleneck, and tuned it.

In this chapter, we will walk through the insides of **Java Virtual Machine** (**JVM**) and tuning JVM to achieve high performance. JVM performs two primary jobs—executing code and managing memory. JVM allocates memory from OS, manages to do heap compaction, and performs **garbage collection** (**GC**) of unreferenced objects. GC is important because proper GC improves the memory management of the application and the performance.

The following are the topics we will go through in this chapter:

- Understanding JVM internals
- Understanding memory leak
- Common pitfalls
- GC
- GC methods and policies
- Tools to analyze GC logs

Understanding JVM internals

Being a Java developer, we know that Java bytecode runs in a **Java Runtime Environment (JRE)** and the most important part of the JRE is JVM, which analyzes and executes the Java bytecode. When we create a Java program and compile it, the result is a file with the `.class` extension. It contains Java bytecode. JVM converts Java bytecode into machine instructions that are executed on the hardware platform where we run our application. When a JVM runs a program, it needs memory to store bytecodes and other information it extracts from loaded class files, instantiated objects, method parameters, return values, local variables, and intermediate results of computations. The JVM organizes the memory it needs into several runtime data areas.

JVM consist of three parts:

- Class loader subsystem
- Memory areas
- Execution engine

The following diagram illustrates the high-level JVM architecture:

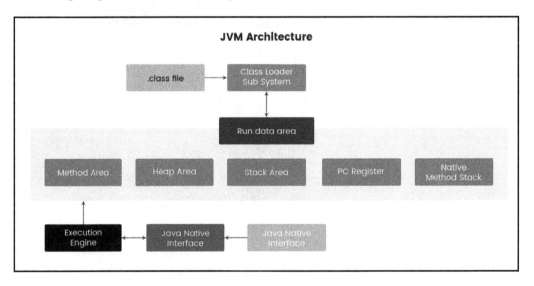

JVM architecture

Let's briefly understand the three different parts of JVM we saw in the diagram.

Class loader subsystem

The class loader subsystem's responsibilities are not limited to just locating and importing the binary data for classes. It also verifies that the imported classes are correct, allocates and initializes memory for class variables, and assists in resolving symbolic references. These activities are performed in a strict order:

1. **Loading**: The class loader reads the `.class` file and finds and imports binary data for a type.
2. **Linking**: It performs verification, preparation, and (optionally) resolution:

    - **Verification**: Ensures the correctness of the imported type
    - **Preparation**: Allocates memory to class variables and initializes the memory to default values
    - **Resolution**: Transforms symbolic references from the type into direct references

3. **Initialization**: Assigns values to all static variables defined in the code and executes static block (if any). Execution occurs from top to bottom in a class, and from parent to child in a class hierarchy.

In general, there are three class loaders:

- **Bootstrap class loader**: This loads core-trusted Java API classes located in the `JAVA_HOME/jre/lib` directory. These Java APIs are implemented in native languages, such as C or C++.
- **Extension class loader**: This inherits the Bootstrap class loader. It loads the classes from extension directories located at `JAVA_HOME/jre/lib/ext`, or any other directory specified by the `java.ext.dirs` system property. It is implemented in Java by the `sun.misc.Launcher$ExtClassLoader` class.
- **System class loader**: This inherits the extension class loader. It loads classes from our application classpath. It uses the `java.class.path` environment variable.

To load classes, JVM follows the delegation hierarchy principle. The system class loader delegates a request to the extension class loader, and the extension class loader delegates the request to the Bootstrap class loader. If a class is found in the Bootstrap path, the class is loaded, otherwise, the request will be transferred to the extension class loader and then to the system class loader. At the end, if the system class loader fails to load the class, then a `java.lang.ClassNotFoundException` exception is generated.

The following diagram illustrates the delegation hierarchy principle:

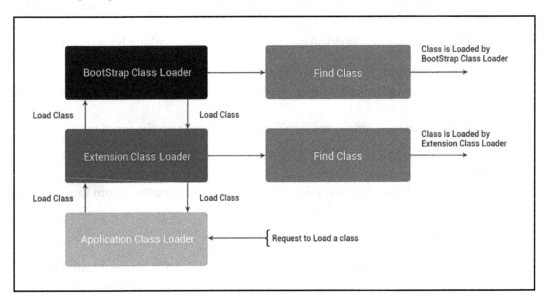

Delegation hierarchy principle

Memory areas

Java runtime memory is divided into five different areas, as shown in the following diagram:

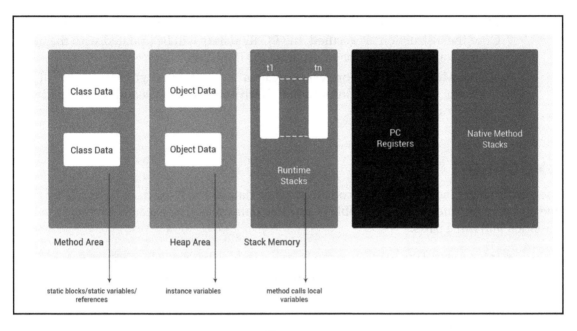

Memory areas

Let's look into a brief description of each component:

- **Method Area**: This contains all the class-level information, such as class name, parent class, methods, instance, and static variables. There is only one method area per JVM, and it is a shared resource.
- **Heap Area**: This contains the information of all the objects. There is one **Heap Area** per JVM. It is also a shared resource. As **Method Area** and **Heap Area** are shared memory between multiple threads, the data stored is not thread-safe.
- **Stack Memory**: JVM creates one runtime stack for every thread in execution and stores it in the stack area. Every block of this stack is called an **activation record** that stores methods call. All local variables of that method are stored in their corresponding frame. The stack area is thread-safe since it is not a shared resource. The runtime stack will be destroyed by the JVM up on termination of the thread. So, in the case of infinite loops of method calls, we might see `StackOverFlowError`, which is due to no memory in the stack for storing method calls.

- **PC Registers**: These hold the addresses of current instructions under execution. Once the instruction is executed, the **PC Registers** will be updated with the next instruction. Each thread has a separate **PC Registers**.
- **Native Method Stacks**: For every thread, a separate native stack is created. It stores the native method information. Native information is nothing but native method calls.

Execution engine

The execution engine executes bytecode in runtime data areas. It executes bytecode by each line and uses the information available in runtime data areas. The execution engine can be classified into three parts:

- **Interpreter**: This reads, interprets, and executes bytecode by each line. It interprets and executes bytecode quickly; however, it can be very slow in executing interpreted results.
- **Just-In-Time (JIT)**: In order to overcome the interpreter's slowness in executing interpreted results, the JIT compiler converts the bytecode to native code once the interpreter interprets the code the first time. Execution happens fast with native code; it executes instructions one by one.
- **Garbage collector**: This destroys anything that is not referenced. This is very important, so anything not required will be destroyed to create room for new execution.

Understanding memory leak

Java's best benefit is the JVM, which offers memory management out of the box. We can create objects and Java's garbage collector takes care of freeing up memory for us. Still, memory leaks occur in Java applications. In the following section, we will see some common causes of memory leaks and walk through a few solutions to detect/avoid them.

Memory leak in Java

A memory leak occurs when the garbage collector could not collect the objects any longer being used/referenced by an application. If the objects are not garbage collected, the application uses more memory and, once the entire heap is full, the object cannot be allocated, which leads to OutOfMemoryError.

Heap memory has two types of objects—referenced objects and unreferenced objects. The garbage collector will remove all unreferenced objects. However, the garbage collector would not be able to remove referenced objects even though they aren't used by the application.

Common reasons for memory leaks

The following are the most common reasons for memory leaks:

- **Open streams**: While working on streams and readers, we often forget to close the streams, which eventually results in the memory leak. There are two types of leaks that result from unclosed streams—low-level resource leak and memory leak. Low-level resource leak includes OS-level resources, such as file descriptor and open connection. As JVM consumes memory to track these resources, it leads to memory leak. To avoid leaks, use the `finally` block to close the stream or use the autoclose feature of Java 8.
- **Open connections**: We often forget to close opened HTTP, database, or FTP connections, which results in the memory leak. Similar to closing streams, close the connections.
- **Static variables referencing instance objects**: Any static variable referencing a heavy object could lead to memory leak because even if the variable is not in use, it won't be garbage collected. To prevent this, try not to have heavy static variables; use local variables instead.
- **Missing methods for objects in collection**: Adding objects having no implementation of the `equals` and `hashcode` methods to `HashSet` will add the number of duplicate objects in `HashSet` and we would not be able to remove these objects once added. To prevent this, implement the `equals` and `hashcode` methods in the object added to `HashSet`.

Diagnosing memory leaks is a lengthy process that requires a lot of practical experience, debugging skills, and detailed knowledge of the application. The following are the ways to diagnose memory leaks:

- Enable GC logs and fine-tune GC parameters
- Profiling
- Code review

In the following sections, we will see GC's common pitfalls, GC methods, and tools to analyze GC logs.

Common pitfalls

Performance tuning is critical, and things can start getting hairy with one small JVM flag. JVM is subject to GC pauses, which vary in frequency and duration. During a pause, everything stops and all kinds of unexpected behaviors start. During pauses and unstable behavior where JVM gets stuck, performance is impacted. We can see the symptoms of slow response times, high CPU, and memory utilization, or the system acts normally most of the time but behaves weirdly, such as performing extremely slow transactions and disconnections.

The majority of the time, we measure the average transaction time and ignore the outliers that cause unstable behavior. Most of the time a system behaves normally, however at certain points, system responsiveness degrades. The majority of the time, the reason for this low performance is due to low awareness of GC overhead and focusing on only average response times.

When defining performance requirements, an important question we need to answer is: What are the acceptable criteria for our application related to GC pause frequency and duration? Requirements vary from application to application, so based on our application and user experience, we need to first define these criteria.

A few common misunderstandings we usually have are as follows.

Number of garbage collectors

Most of the time, people are not aware that there isn't only one, but four, garbage collectors. The four garbage collectors are—**Serial**, **Parallel**, **Concurrent**, and **Garbage First** (**G1**). We will see them in the following section. There are some third-party garbage collectors, such as **Shenandoah**. JVM HotSpot's default garbage collector is Parallel up to Java 8, while from Java 9, the default collector is **Garbage First Garbage Collector** (**G1 GC**). A Parallel garbage collector isn't best most of the time; however, it depends on our application requirements. For example, the **Concurrent Mark Sweep** (**CMS**) and G1 collectors cause less frequent GC pauses. But when they do cause a pause, the pause duration will most likely be longer than a pause caused by the Parallel collector. On the other hand, the Parallel collector usually achieves higher throughput for the same heap size.

Wrong garbage collector

A common reason for the GC issue is the wrong choice of garbage collector for the type of application. Each collector has their own significance and benefits. We need to find our application's behavior and priorities and based on which we need to choose right garbage collector. The default garbage collector of HotSpot's is Parallel/Throughput and, most of time, it hasn't proven to be a good choice. The CMS and G1 collector are concurrent and cause less frequent pauses, but when a pause does come, its duration is longer than the Parallel collector. So the choice of the collector is a common mistake we often make.

Parallel / Concurrent keywords

A GC can either cause a **stop-the-world** (**STW**) situation, or objects can be collected concurrently without stopping the application. The GC algorithm can be executed in a single thread or in multithread. So, Concurrent GC does not mean it executes in parallel, whereas Serial GC doesn't mean it causes more pauses due to serial execution. Concurrent and Parallel are different, where Concurrent means the GC cycle, and Parallel means the GC algorithm.

G1 is a problem solver

With the introduction of the new garbage collector in Java 7, many people think that it is the problem solver to all previous garbage collectors. An important problem solved by G1 GC is the fragmentation problem, which is common to the CMS collector. However, in many cases other collectors can outperform G1 GC. So it all depends on our application's behavior and requirements.

Average transaction time

Mostly, while testing performance, we tend to measure average transaction time and, by only doing that, we miss the outliers. At some point, when GC causes pauses for a long duration, the application's response time increases drastically, which affects users accessing the application. This can go unnoticed, as we are only looking at the average transaction time. When the GC pause frequency increases, response time becomes a serious problem that we might have ignored by just measuring the average response time.

Reducing new object allocation rates improves GC behavior

Instead of focusing or reducing the new object allocation rate, we should focus on the life of objects. There are three different types of objects lives: long-lived objects, we cannot do much about them; mid-lived objects, these cause the biggest issues; and short-lived objects, which usually get freed and allocated quickly so they are collected by the next GC cycle. So instead of concentrating on long-lived and short-lived objects, focusing on the mid-lived objects allocation rate could bring positive results. It's not the object allocation rate alone; it's the type of objects in play that causes all the trouble.

GC logs cause overhead

It is not true that GC logs cause overhead, especially in the default log settings. The data is extremely valuable and Java 7 introduced hooks to control the size of their log files. If we don't collect GC logs with timestamps, then we are missing out on a critical source of data to analyze and solve pausing issues. GC logs are the richest source of data for the state of GC in a system. We can get data about all GC events in our application; say, it is completed concurrently or caused an STW pause: how long did it take, how much CPU it consumed, and how much memory was freed. From this data, we would be able to understand the frequency and duration of pauses, their overhead, and move on to take action to reduce them.

Enable GC by adding following arguments:

```
-XX:+PrintGCDetails -XX:+PrintGCDateStamps -Xloggc:`date +%F_%H-%M-%S`-
gc.log -XX:+UseGCLogFileRotation -XX:NumberOfGCLogFiles=10 -
XX:GCLogFileSize=10M
```

GC

One of Java's best achievements is GC. The GC process automatically manages memory and heap allocation that tracks down dead objects, removes them, and reallocates memory to a new object. Theoretically, as garbage collector automatically manages memory, it makes developers create new objects without thinking about the allocation and deallocation of memory to eliminate memory leaks and other problems related to memory.

How GC works

We usually think that GC collects and removes the unreferenced objects. Instead, GC in Java tracks live objects and marks all unreferenced objects as garbage.

The heap area of the memory is where objects are allocated dynamically. We should allocate heap memory to JVM before running the application. Allocating heap to JVM in advance has a couple of consequences:

- Improves object creation rate because JVM doesn't need to communicate with the OS to get memory for each new object. Once the JVM allocates memory to an object, JVM moves the pointer toward the next available memory.
- Garbage collectors collect the object when there is no object reference and reuse its memory for new object allocation. As the garbage collector doesn't delete the object, no memory is returned to the OS.

Until the objects are being referenced, JVM considers them live objects. When an object is no longer referenced and is not reachable by the application code, the garbage collector removes it and reclaims its memory. We get a question in our mind, who is the first reference in the tree of objects, right? Let's see the object tree and its roots.

GC roots

Each tree of an object has one or more objects at the root. If the garbage collector can reach the root, the tree is reachable. Any object that is not reached by, or referenced by, GC roots is considered dead and the garbage collector removes it.

Here are the different kinds of GC roots in Java:

- **Local variables:** Variables or parameters of a Java method.
- **Active threads:** A running thread is a live object.
- **Static variables:** Classes referencing static variables. When the garbage collector collects classes, it removes references to static variables.
- **JNI references:** Object reference created during the JNI call. They are kept alive because JVM is unaware that the native code has references of it.

Please have a look at the following diagram:

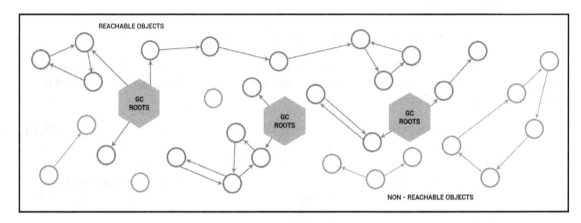

GC roots

GC methods and policies

As we learned in the preceding section, there isn't one but four different garbage collectors. Each one has its own advantages and disadvantages. The one thing these collectors have in common is that they split the managed heap into different segments with the assumption that objects are short-lived and should be removed shortly. Let's see four different algorithms of GC.

Serial collector

The Serial collector is the simplest GC implementation, mainly designed for single-threaded environments and small heaps. This GC implementation freezes all application threads whenever it's working. Hence, it's not a good idea to use it in multithreaded applications, such as server environments.

To enable the Serial garbage collector, set $-XX:+UseSerialGC$ to VM arguments

Parallel/Throughput collector

The Parallel collector is the JVM's default collector and is also known as the Throughput collector. As the name suggests, this collector, unlike the Serial collector, uses multithread to manage the heap memory. The Parallel garbage collector still freezes all the application threads when performing either minor or full GC. If we want to use the Parallel garbage collector, we should specify the tuning parameters, such as threads, pause time, throughput, and footprints.

The following are the arguments to specify the tuning parameters:

- Threads: $-XX:ParallelGCThreads=<N>$
- Pause time: $-XX:MaxGCPauseMillis=<N>$
- Throughput: $-XX:GCTimeRatio=<N>$
- Footprint (maximum heap size): $-Xmx<N>$

To enable the Parallel garbage collector in our application, set the $-XX:+UseParallelGC$ option.

CMS garbage collector

The CMS implementation uses multiple garbage collector threads to scan (mark) the unused objects that can be removed (sweep). This garbage collector is preferable for applications that require short GC pauses, and who can share processor resources with the garbage collector while the application is running.

The CMS algorithm enters into STW mode in only two cases: when objects in Old Generations are still referenced from the thread entry point or static variables, and when the application changed the state of the heap while CMS is running which makes the algorithm go back and reiterate the object tree to validate that it had marked the correct objects.

With this collector, promotion failure is the greatest cause for concern. Promotion failure occurs when a race condition occurs between a collection of objects from the Young and Old Generations. If the collector needs to promote objects from the Young Generation to the Old Generation and there is not enough space, it has to first STW to create the space. In order to make sure this doesn't happen in the case of the CMS collector, increase the size of the Old Generation or allocate more background thread to the collector to compete with the allocation rate.

In order to provide high throughput, CMS uses more CPU to scan and collect objects. It is good for long-running server applications, which are adverse to application freezes. So, if we can allocate more CPU to avoid application pauses, we can choose the CMS collector for GC in our application. To enable the CMS collector, set the -`XX:+UseConcMarkSweepGC` option.

G1 collector

This is the new collector, introduced in JDK 7 update 4. The G1 collector is designed for an application willing to allocate heap memory of more than 4 GB. G1 divides the heap into multiple regions, spanning from 1 MB to 32 MB, depending on the heap we configure and uses multiple background threads to scan through the heap regions. The benefit of dividing the heap into multiple regions is that G1 will scan through regions where there is plenty of garbage first in order to meet a given pause time.

G1 reduces the change of low-heap availability before the background threads have finished scanning for unused objects. This reduced the chances to STW. G1 compacts the heap on-the-go, unlike CMS, which does this during STW.

In order to enable the G1 garbage collector in our application, we need to set the –`XX:+UseG1GC` option in the JVM parameters.

Java 8 update 20 introduced a new JVM argument, –`XX:+UseStringDeduplication`, for the G1 collector. With this argument, G1 identifies duplicate strings and creates the pointer to the same integral `char[]` array to avoid multiple copies of the same string.

From Java 8 `PermGen`, part of the heap is removed. This was the part that was allocated for class metadata, static variables, and interned strings. This parameter-tuning caused many `OutOfMemory` exceptions, which would be fine from Java 8 onward, where JVM would take care of it.

Heap memory

Heap memory is divided into primarily two generations: Young Generation and Old Generation. There is a **PERM GENERATION** that is a part of heap memory until Java 7, while from Java 8, the **PERM GENERATION** is replaced by **METASPACE**. **METASPACE** is not part of the heap memory but is part of the **Native Memory**. Set size of **METASPACE** using the `-XX:MaxMetaspaceSize` option. It is critical to consider this setting when going to production since if **METASPACE** takes up excessive memory, it affects the application's performance:

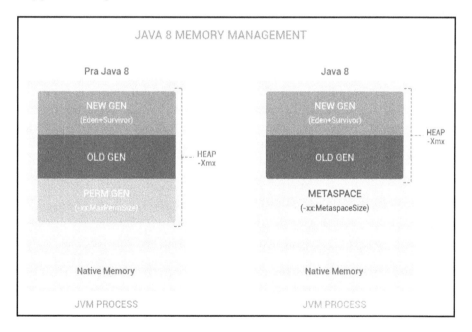

Java 8 memory management

The **Young Generation** is where objects are created and allocated; it's for young objects. The **Young Generation** is further divided into **Survivor Space**. The following is the **Hotspot Heap Structure**:

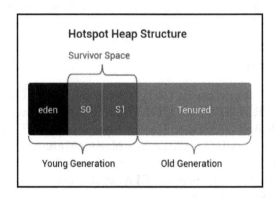

The **eden** area is, by default, bigger than **Survivor Space**. All the objects are created first in the **eden** area. When **eden** is full, minor GC is triggered, which will quickly scan the object's references, and unreferenced objects are marked dead and collected. The **Survivor Space** area in either of them would always be empty. Objects that survived in **eden** during minor GC will be moved to the empty **Survivor Space**. We might wonder why there are two **Survivor Space** areas and not one. The reason is to avoid memory fragmentation. When the **Young Generation** runs through and removes dead objects from the **Survivor Space**, it leaves holes in the memory and needs compaction. To avoid compaction, JVM moves surviving objects from one **Survivor Space** to another. This ping-pong of live objects from **eden** and one **Survivor Space** to another happens until the following conditions occur:

- Objects reach maximum tenuring threshold. This means objects are no longer young.
- **Survivor Space** is full and cannot accommodate any new objects.

When the preceding conditions happen, objects are moved to the **Old Generation**.

JVM flags

The following are the JVM parameters/flags commonly used in applications to tune the JVM for better performance. Tuning values depend on our application's behavior and the rate at which it is generated. So there is no defined guideline to use specific values for JVM flags in order to achieve better performance.

-Xms and -Xmx

The $-Xms$ and $-Xmx$ are known as the minimum and maximum heap size. Setting $-Xms$ equal to $-Xmx$ prevents GC pauses during heap expansion and improves performance.

-XX:NewSize and -XX:MaxNewSize

We can set the size of the Young Generation using $-XX:MaxNewSize$. The Young Generation resides under the total heap memory and the Old Generation size will be smaller if we set the size of the Young Generation as large. The Young Generation size should never be larger than the Old Generation for stability reasons. Thus, $-Xmx/2$ is the maximum size we can set for $-XX:MaxNewSize$.

To achieve better performance, set the initial size of the Young Generation by setting the $-XX:NewSize$ flag. This saves some costs in terms of the Young Generation growing to that size over time.

-XX:NewRatio

We can set the size of the Young Generation as a ratio of the Old Generation using the $-XX:NewRatio$ option. The benefit we can get with this option could be that the Young Generation can grow and shrink when JVM adjusts the total heap size during execution. $-XX:NewRatio$ means the ratio of Old Generation is larger than the Young Generation. $-XX:NewRatio=2$ means the size of the Old Generation is twice that of the Young Generation, which further means that the Young Generation is 1/3 of the total heap.

If we specify ratio and a fixed size for the Young Generation, then the fixed size will take precedence. There is no generation rule regarding which method of specifying the size of the Young Generation is preferable. The rule of thumb here is that if you know the size of the objects generated by our application, then specify the fixed size, otherwise, specify the ratio.

-XX:SurvivorRatio

The `-XX:SurvivorRatio` value is the ratio of eden relative to Survivor Spaces. There will be two Survivor Spaces and each one would be equal to the other. If `-XX:SurvivorRatio=8`, then eden occupies 3/4 and each Survivor Spaces occupies 1/4 of the total Old Generation size.

If we set a ratio such that Survivor Spaces are small, then eden will make more space for new objects. During minor GC, unreferenced objects will be collected and eden will be empty for new objects, however, if the object still has references, then the garbage collector moves them to the Survivor Space. If the Survivor Space is small and cannot accommodate the new object, then the objects will be moved to the Old Generation. Objects in the Old Generation can only be collected during full GC, which creates long pauses in the application. And if the Survivor Space is large enough, then more objects can live in the Survivor Space but die young. If the Survivor Spaces are large, eden would be small, and a small eden would cause frequent young GC.

-XX:InitialTenuringThreshold, -XX:MaxTenuringThreshold, and -XX:TargetSurvivorRatio

The tenuring threshold decides when an object can be promoted/moved from the Young Generation to the Old Generation. We can set the initial and maximum value of the tenuring threshold using the `-XX:InitialTenuringThreshold` and `-XX:MaxTenuringThreshold` JVM flags. We can also use `-XX:TargetSurvivorRatio` to specify the target utilization (as a percentage) of the Survivor Space at the end of a Young Generation GC.

-XX:CMSInitiatingOccupancyFraction

Use the `-XX:CMSInitiatingOccupancyFraction=85` option when using the CMS collector (`-XX:+UseConcMarkSweepGC`). If the flag is set and the Old Generation is 85% full, the CMS collector starts collecting unreferenced objects. It is not necessary that CMS will start collection only after the Old Generation 85% occupied. If we want CMS to start only at 85%, then we need to set `-XX:+UseCMSInitiatingOccupancyOnly`. The default value of the `-XX:CMSInitiatingOccupancyFraction` flag is 65%.

-XX:+PrintGCDetails, -XX:+PrintGCDateStamps, and -XX:+PrintTenuringDistribution

Flags are set to generate GC logs. In order to fine-tune JVM parameters to achieve better performance, it is important to understand GC logs and the behavior of the application. `-XX:+PrintTenuringDistribution` reports the statistics of an object (how old they are) and the desired threshold of objects when they are promoted. This is very important to understand how our application is holding the objects.

Tools to analyze GC logs

The Java GC logs are one of the places where we can start debugging an application in the event of a performance issue. The GC logs provide important information, such as:

- The last time the GC ran
- The number of GC cycles run
- The interval at which the GC ran
- The amount of memory freed up after the GC ran
- The time the GC took to run
- The amount of time for which the JVM paused when the garbage collector ran
- The amount of memory allocated to each generation

The following is the sample GC logs:

```
2018-05-09T14:02:17.676+0530: 0.315: Total time for which application
threads were stopped: 0.0001783 seconds, Stopping threads took:
0.0000239 seconds
2018-05-09T14:02:17.964+0530: 0.603: Application time: 0.2881052
seconds
.....
2018-05-09T14:02:18.940+0530: 1.579: Total time for which application
threads were stopped: 0.0003113 seconds, Stopping threads took:
0.0000517 seconds
2018-05-09T14:02:19.028+0530: 1.667: Application time: 0.0877361
seconds
2018-05-09T14:02:19.028+0530: 1.667: [GC (Allocation Failure)
[PSYoungGen: 65536K->10723K(76288K)] 65536K->13509K(251392K), 0.0176650
secs] [Times: user=0.05 sys=0.00, real=0.02 secs]
2018-05-09T14:02:19.045+0530: 1.685: Total time for which application
threads were stopped: 0.0179326 seconds, Stopping threads took:
0.0000525 seconds
2018-05-09T14:02:20.045+0530: 2.684: Application time: 0.9992739
seconds
.....
2018-05-09T14:03:54.109+0530: 96.748: Total time for which application
threads were stopped: 0.0000498 seconds, Stopping threads took:
0.0000171 seconds
Heap
 PSYoungGen total 76288K, used 39291K [0x000000076b200000,
0x0000000774700000, 0x00000007c0000000)
  eden space 65536K, 43% used
[0x000000076b200000,0x000000076cde5e30,0x000000076f200000)
  from space 10752K, 99% used
[0x000000076f200000,0x000000076fc78e28,0x000000076fc80000)
  to space 10752K, 0% used
[0x0000000773c80000,0x0000000773c80000,0x0000000774700000)
 ParOldGen total 175104K, used 2785K [0x00000006c1600000,
0x00000006cc100000, 0x000000076b200000)
  object space 175104K, 1% used
[0x00000006c1600000,0x00000006c18b86c8,0x00000006cc100000)
 Metaspace used 18365K, capacity 19154K, committed 19456K, reserved
1067008K
  class space used 2516K, capacity 2690K, committed 2816K, reserved
1048576K
2018-05-09T14:03:54.123+0530: 96.761: Application time: 0.0131957
seconds
```

These logs are very difficult to interpret quickly. If we have a tool that can render these logs in a visual interface, it would be easy and quick to understand what is going on with the GC. We will take a look at one such tool to interpret the GC logs in the next section.

GCeasy

GCeasy is one of the most popular garbage collection log analysis tools. GCeasy is developed to identify problems from the GC logs automatically. It is intelligent enough to provide alternative ways to solve problems.

The following are the important basic features provided by GCeasy:

- Uses machine learning algorithms to analyze the logs
- Quickly detects memory leaks, premature object promotions, long JVM pauses, and many other performance issues
- Powerful and informative visual analyzer
- Provides the REST API for proactive log analysis
- Free cloud-based tool for log analysis
- Provides suggestions on the JVM heap size
- Equipped to analyze all formats of GC logs

GCeasy.io (`http://www.gceasy.io/`) is the online garbage collection log analysis tool. It requires the log files to be uploaded on the GCeasy public cloud.

The following are the steps to gather detailed log analysis using the online tool:

1. Enable GC logs in the application by adding `XX:+PrintGCDetails -XX:+PrintGCDateStamps -Xloggc:<GC-log-file-path>` in the JVM parameters on the server.
2. Once the GC log file is generated at a specified location, upload the file to the GCeasy cloud by navigating to `http://gceasy.io/`. It is also possible to upload a compressed ZIP file in case there are multiple log files to be analyzed.
3. Once the log files are processed, the detailed analysis report will be generated.

The report is properly organized and detailed enough to highlight every possible problem causing the performance hit. The following section explains the important sections in the report generated by GCeasy.

Tips on JVM tuning

The top section in the report provides suggestions based on the garbage-collection-log analysis. The suggestions are generated dynamically by machine learning algorithms after a thorough analysis of the log files. The details in the suggestion also include the probable cause of the issue. The following is an example suggestion provided by GCeasy after GC log analysis:

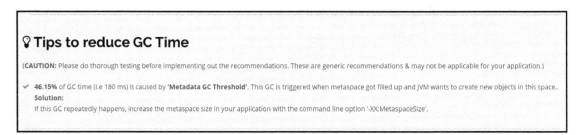

💡 Tips to reduce GC Time

(**CAUTION:** Please do thorough testing before implementing out the recommendations. These are generic recommendations & may not be applicable for your application.)

✔ **46.15%** of GC time (i.e 180 ms) is caused by '**Metadata GC Threshold**'. This GC is triggered when metaspace got filled up and JVM wants to create new objects in this space..
Solution:
If this GC repeatedly happens, increase the metaspace size in your application with the command line option '-XX:MetaspaceSize'.

JVM Heap Size

This section in the report provides information on the heap allocation and peak memory usage for each memory generation. It is possible that the allocated heap size may not match the one defined in the JVM parameters. This is because the GCeasy tool obtains the allocated memory information from the logs. It is possible that we have allocated 2 GB of heap memory, but at runtime, JVM could allocate only 1 GB of heap memory. In such a case, the report will show the allocated memory as 1 GB. The report shows the heap allocation in tabular and graphical formats. The following is an example heap size section from the report:

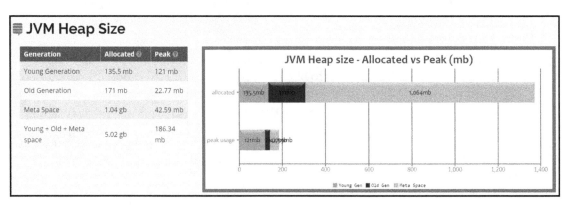

🖥 JVM Heap Size

Generation	Allocated	Peak
Young Generation	135.5 mb	121 mb
Old Generation	171 mb	22.77 mb
Meta Space	1.04 gb	42.59 mb
Young + Old + Meta space	5.02 gb	186.34 mb

JVM Heap size - Allocated vs Peak (mb)

Key Performance Indicators

Key Performance Indicators (**KPIs**) help make profound decisions for improving the application's performance. Throughput, latency, and footprint are a few of the important KPIs. The KPIs in the report include **Throughput** and **Latency**. The footprint basically describes the amount of time CPU was occupied. It can be obtained from a performance-monitoring tool, such as JVisualVM.

The **Throughput** option indicates the amount of productive work done by the application during a specified time period. The **Latency** option indicates the average time taken by the GC to run.

The following is an example of KPIs from the report:

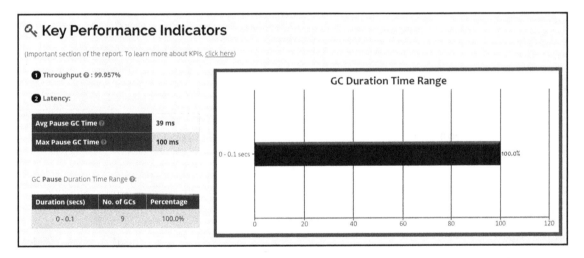

GC Statistics

The GC statistics section provides information on the behavior of the garbage collector over a period of time. The period is the time duration for which the logs are analyzed. The GC statistics are provided based on real-time analysis. The statistics include the bytes reclaimed after the garbage collector ran, the cumulative GC time in seconds, and the average GC time in seconds. This section also provides information on total GC statistics, minor and full GC statistics, and GC pause statistics in a tabular format.

GC Causes

The **GC Causes** section provides information on what caused the garbage collector to run. The information is provided in tabular as well as graphical format. Along with the reasons, it also provides information on the time it took for the garbage collector to execute. The following is an example from the report:

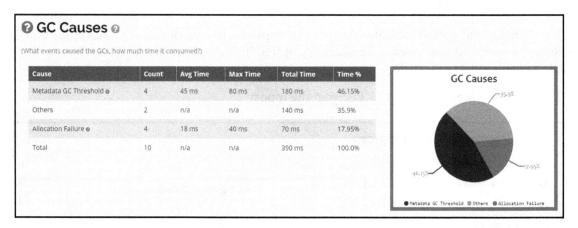

Based on the preceding details, GCeasy is an important tool in helping developers to interpret GC logs in a visual manner.

Summary

In this chapter, we learned about JVM and its parameters. We learned about memory leaks and common misunderstandings related to GC. We learned about different GC methods and their importance. We learned about import JVM flags, which are tuned to achieve better performance.

In the next chapter, we will learn about Spring Boot microservices and its performance tuning. Microservice is an architecture of an application with loosely coupled services that implements business capabilities. Spring Boot enables us to build production-ready applications.

12
Spring Boot Microservice Performance Tuning

In the previous chapter, we learned about **Java Virtual Machine** (**JVM**). Starting with the internals of JVM and Java's class-loading mechanism, we learned how memory management is performed in Java. The last section of the chapter focused on garbage collection and JVM tuning. The chapter was full of pretty important details for application performance optimization.

In this chapter, we will move toward solving performance problems. The approach is to develop microservices. Microservices are having a boom in the software development industry right now. There is a lot of buzz around microservices and related keywords. This approach basically works at an application-architecture level to tune the application's performance. It describes how we can improve application performance by setting up the architecture in a different manner. We will cover the following topics in this chapter:

- Spring Boot configuration
- Metrics with the Spring Boot Actuator
- Health checks
- Microservices using Spring Boot
- Microservices with Spring Cloud
- Spring microservice configuration example
- Monitoring microservices with Spring Boot admin
- Spring Boot performance tuning

Spring Boot configuration

In this section, we will focus on making Spring Boot work for us. Before jumping on to Spring Boot configuration, we will understand what Spring Boot is, why we should use it, and what Spring Boot brings to the table. We will move quickly to the how to do it part of it.

What is Spring Boot?

It is necessary for software development processes to be faster, more accurate, and more robust. Software teams are asked to develop quick prototypes for showcasing the application's features to prospective clients. The same applies to production-grade applications. The following are a few areas where software architects focus on to improve the effectiveness of development teams:

- Use the right set of tools, which includes frameworks, IDEs, and build tools
- Reduce code clutter
- Reduce the amount of time spent writing repetitive code
- Spend the majority of the time implementing business features

Let's think for a moment. Why are we discussing this? The reason is that this is the foundation for Spring Boot. These thoughts are the founding stones for the creation of any framework or tool that helps teams to improve their productivity. Spring Boot is found with exactly the same reason—to improve productivity!

With Spring Boot, it becomes easy to create production-grade applications that are powered by the Spring Framework. It also makes it easy to create production-ready services with minimal challenges. Spring Boot helps new and existing users get to their productive tasks quickly by taking an opinionated view of the Spring Framework. Spring Boot is a tool that facilitates creating a standalone Java application, which can be run using the `java -jar` command, or a web application, which can be deployed to web servers. The Spring Boot setup is bundled with command-line tools to run Spring programs.

The major goals of Spring Boot are:

- To gain an extremely fast experience to get started with Spring-powered projects
- Broad accessibility
- Major support from out-of-the-box configuration
- Flexibility to deviate from Spring default as the need may arise

- That it does not generate any code
- That it does not require XML configuration

Along with previously listed primary features, Spring Boot also provides support for non-functional features, listed as follows:

- Support for versioning and configuration for widely known and used frameworks
- Support for application security
- Support for monitoring application health check parameters
- Support for monitoring of performance metrics
- Support for externalized configurations

Though Spring Boot provides defaults for the primary and non-functional features, it is flexible enough to allow developers to use the frameworks, servers, and tools of their choice.

Spring Initializr

Spring Boot applications can be kickstarted in multiple ways. One of the ways is to use the Eclipse-based Spring Tools Suite IDE (`https://spring.io/tools/sts`). Another way is to use `https://start.spring.io`, also known as Spring Initializr. First things first, Spring Initializr is not Spring Boot or an equivalent. Spring Initializr is a tool that has simple web UI support to configure the Spring Boot application. It can be considered a tool for a quick-start generation of Spring projects. It provides APIs that can be extended for customization in order to generate the projects.

The Spring Initializr tool provides a configuration structure to define a list of dependencies, supported Java and Spring Boot versions, and supported dependency versioning.

Basically, Spring Initializr creates an initial Spring project based on the configuration provided and allows the developer to download the project in a ZIP file. Here are the steps to be followed:

1. Navigate to `https://start.spring.io/`.
2. Choose the dependency management tool from Maven or Gradle.
3. Choose the JVM-based programming language from Java, Kotlin, and Groovy.
4. Choose the **Spring Boot** version to be used.
5. Provide the **Group** artifact by inputting the group name as `com.packt.springhighperformance`.

6. Input **Artifact**, which is the artifact ID for the Maven project. This will become the name of the project WAR or JAR file to be deployed or executed.

7. Choose a packaging type from **Jar** and **War**.

8. Click on the **Switch to the full version** link. This will open up a list of starter projects to choose from. The starter project will be explained in detail in the following section.

9. Once we have chosen the starters or dependencies, click on the **Generate Project** button. This will download the ZIP file containing the initial project configuration.

The following is the Spring Initializr screen with a few configurations:

Once done, a folder structure similar to what is shown in the following screenshot will be generated:

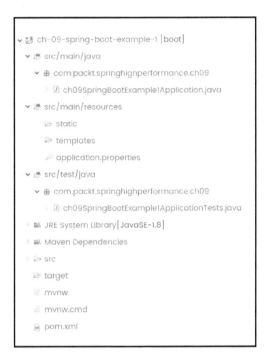

Spring Initializr also supports the command-line interface to create the Spring project configuration. The following command can be used to generate a project configuration:

```
> curl https://start.spring.io/starter.zip -d dependencies=web,jpa -d
bootVersion=2.0.0 -o ch-09-spring-boot-example-1.zip
```

As mentioned earlier, Spring Initializr supports integration with IDE. It integrates well with Eclipse/STS, IntelliJ ultimate edition, and NetBeans with NB the SpringBoot plugin.

Starters with Maven

In the preceding section, we looked at the Spring Initializr tool. It is time to quickly look at the starters or dependencies supported by Spring Boot.

Dependency management becomes challenging as the project grows in complexity. It is recommended not to manage the dependencies manually for a complex project. Spring Boot starters fix a similar problem. Spring Boot starters is a set of dependency descriptors that can be included in Spring-powered applications using starter POMs. It eliminates the need to look for sample code and copy/paste lots of dependency descriptors for Spring and related libraries. As an example, if we want to develop an application using Spring and JPA, we can include the `spring-boot-data-jpa-starter` dependency in the project. `spring-boot-data-jpa-starter` is one of the starters. The starters follow uniform naming patterns, such as `spring-boot-starter-*`, where * denotes the type of application.

Here is a list of some Spring Boot application starters:

Name	Description
`spring-boot-starter`	Core starter provides auto-configuration and logging support.
`spring-boot-starter-activemq`	JMS messaging starter using Apache ActiveMQ.
`spring-boot-starter-amqp`	Spring AMQP and Rabbit MQ starter.
`spring-boot-starter-aop`	Spring AOP and AspectJ starter.
`spring-boot-starter-artemis`	JMS messaging starter using Apache Artemis.
`spring-boot-starter-batch`	Spring Batch starter.
`spring-boot-starter-cache`	Spring Framework's caching support.
`spring-boot-starter-cloud-connectors`	Starter providing support for simplified connections with cloud services using Spring Cloud Connectors in cloud platforms such as Cloud Foundry and Heroku.
`spring-boot-starter-data-elasticsearch`	Starter with support for elasticsearch and analytics engine, and Spring Data Elasticsearch.
`spring-boot-starter-data-jpa`	Spring Data JPA with Hibernate.
`spring-boot-starter-data-ldap`	Spring Data LDAP.
`spring-boot-starter-data-mongodb`	MongoDB document-oriented database and Spring Data MongoDB.
`spring-boot-starter-data-redis`	Redis key-value data store with Spring Data Redis and the Lettuce client.
`spring-boot-starter-data-rest`	Starter providing support for exposing Spring Data repositories over REST using Spring Data REST.
`spring-boot-starter-data-solr`	Apache Solr search platform with Spring Data Solr.
`spring-boot-starter-freemarker`	Starter supports building MVC web applications using the FreeMarker views.
`spring-boot-starter-groovy-templates`	Starter supporting building MVC web applications using the Groovy templates views.
`spring-boot-starter-integration`	Spring Integration.
`spring-boot-starter-jdbc`	JDBC with the Tomcat JDBC connection pool.
`spring-boot-starter-jersey`	Starter supporting building RESTful web applications using JAX-RS and Jersey. It is an alternative to `spring-boot-starter-web starter`.
`spring-boot-starter-json`	Starter supporting JSON manipulation.
`spring-boot-starter-mail`	Starter supporting the use of Java Mail and Spring Framework's email-sending support.

`spring-boot-starter-quartz`	Starter for using Spring Boot Quartz.
`spring-boot-starter-security`	Spring Security starter.
`spring-boot-starter-test`	Support for Spring Boot applications with libraries including JUnit, Hamcrest, and Mockito.
`spring-boot-starter-thymeleaf`	Supports building MVC web applications using the Thymeleaf views.
`spring-boot-starter-validation`	Starter supporting Java Bean Validation with Hibernate Validator.
`spring-boot-starter-web`	Supports building web, including RESTful, applications using Spring MVC. It uses Tomcat as the default embedded container.
`spring-boot-starter-web-services`	Supports use of Spring Web Services.
`spring-boot-starter-websocket`	Supports building WebSocket applications using Spring Framework's WebSocket support.

`spring-boot-starter-actuator` is a production starter for Spring Boot's Actuator tool, which provides support for production-ready features, such as application monitoring, health checks, logging, and beans.

The following list includes a few of the technical starters for Spring Boot:

Name	Description
`spring-boot-starter-jetty`	Support for Jetty as the embedded servlet container. This is an alternative to `spring-boot-starter-tomcat`.
`spring-boot-starter-log4j2`	Starter supporting Log4j 2 for logging. This is an alternative to `spring-boot-starter-logging`.
`spring-boot-starter-logging`	This is the default logging starter using logback.
`spring-boot-starter-tomcat`	This is the default servlet container starter used for `spring-boot-starter-web`. It uses Tomcat as the embedded server.
`spring-boot-starter-undertow`	This is an alternative to `spring-boot-starter-tomcat starter`. It uses Undertow as the embedded server.
`spring-boot-starter-cache`	Spring Framework's caching support.

Creating your first Spring Boot application

In this section, we will look at the prerequisites for developing a Spring Boot application. We will develop a small Spring Boot application to understand the configuration required for a Spring Boot application and the importance of each configuration.

Here is the list of prerequisites for working with Spring Boot:

- Java 8 or 9
- Spring 5.0.4 or later

Spring Boot supports:

- Maven 3.2+ and Gradle 4 for dependency management and explicit builds

- Tomcat 8.5, Jetty 9.4, and Undertow 1.4

Spring Boot applications can be deployed to any servlet 3.0+ compatible servlet container.

The first step in developing a Spring Boot application is to install Spring Boot. It is extremely easy to set up. It can be set up in the same way as other standard Java libraries. To install Spring Boot, we need to include the appropriate `spring-boot-*.jar` library files in the classpath. Any IDE or text editor can be used as Spring Boot does not require any specialized tools.

Though we can copy the required Spring Boot JAR files in the application classpath, the recommendation is to use a build tool, such as Maven or Gradle, for dependency management.

The Maven `groupId` used by the Spring Boot dependencies is `org.springframework.boot`. For Spring Boot applications, the Maven POM file inherits the `spring-boot-starter-parent` project. Spring Boot defines starter projects and it is defined as a dependency in the Spring Boot application's dependencies.

Let's jump on to creating our first Spring Boot application by performing the following steps:

1. Create a kickstarter application using Spring Initializr.
2. Choose **Maven** as the build and dependency management tool.
3. Choose the appropriate **Spring Boot** version.
4. Choose the packaging type as **War**.
5. For the sake of simplicity, we will not include a JPA starter in the application. We will include a web module only to demonstrate the one request-response flow.
6. Download and import the project into STS or Eclipse.
7. In STS, you can run the application as a Spring Boot application whereas in Eclipse, you can choose to run the application as a **Java Application**.

Let's walk through the code snippets now. The following is the sample Maven POM file:

```xml
<?xml version="1.0" encoding="UTF-8"?>
<project xmlns="http://maven.apache.org/POM/4.0.0"
    xmlns:xsi="http://www.w3.org/2001/XMLSchema-instance"
    xsi:schemaLocation="http://maven.apache.org/POM/4.0.0
    http://maven.apache.org/xsd/maven-4.0.0.xsd">
```

```xml
<modelVersion>4.0.0</modelVersion>

<groupId>com.packt.springhighperformance.ch09</groupId>
<artifactId>ch-09-boot-example</artifactId>
<version>0.0.1-SNAPSHOT</version>
<packaging>jar</packaging>

<name>boot-example</name>
<description>Demo project for Spring boot</description>

<parent>
  <groupId>org.springframework.boot</groupId>
  <artifactId>spring-boot-starter-parent</artifactId>
  <version>2.0.0.RELEASE</version>
  <relativePath/> <!-- lookup parent from repository -->
</parent>

<properties>
  <project.build.sourceEncoding>UTF-8</project.build.sourceEncoding>
  <project.reporting.outputEncoding>UTF-
  8</project.reporting.outputEncoding>
  <java.version>1.8</java.version>
  <spring-cloud.version>Finchley.M9</spring-cloud.version>
</properties>

<dependencies>
  <dependency>
    <groupId>org.springframework.boot</groupId>
    <artifactId>spring-boot-starter-web</artifactId>
  </dependency>
  <dependency>
    <groupId>org.springframework.boot</groupId>
    <artifactId>spring-boot-starter-test</artifactId>
    <scope>test</scope>
  </dependency>
</dependencies>

<build>
  <plugins>
    <plugin>
      <groupId>org.springframework.boot</groupId>
      <artifactId>spring-boot-maven-plugin</artifactId>
    </plugin>
  </plugins>
</build>
</project>
```

One of the notable configurations in the preceding configuration file is the parent dependency. As mentioned earlier, all Spring Boot applications use `spring-boot-starter-parent` as the parent dependency in the `pom.xml` file.

The parent POM helps manage the following for child projects and modules:

- Java version
- Version management for included dependencies
- The default configuration for the plugin

The Spring Boot parent starter defines Spring Boot dependencies as the parent POM. So, it inherits dependency-management features from Spring Boot dependencies. It defines the default Java version to be 1.6, but at a project level, we can change it to `1.8`, as shown in the preceding code sample.

Along with the default POM file, Spring Boot also creates a Java class that works as an application starter. The following is the sample Java code:

```
package com.packt.springhighperformance.ch09;

import org.springframework.boot.SpringApplication;
import org.springframework.boot.autoconfigure.SpringBootApplication;

@SpringBootApplication
public class BootExampleApplication {

  public static void main(String[] args) {
    SpringApplication.run(BootExampleApplication.class, args);
  }
}
```

`SpringApplication` is a class responsible for bootstrapping the Spring Boot application.

Spring Boot application developers are used to annotate the main application class with `@Configuration`, `@EnableAutoConfiguration`, and `@ComponentScan` annotations. Here is a brief description for each of the annotations:

- `@Configuration`: This is a Spring annotation and not specific to Spring Boot applications. It indicates that the class is the source for bean definitions.
- `@EnableAutoConfiguration`: This one is a Spring Boot-specific annotation. The annotation enables the application to add beans from the classpath definitions.
- `@ComponentScan`: This annotation tells the Spring application to search for components, configurations, and services in the search path provided.

The following is the definition for the `@SpringBootApplication` annotation:

```
@Target(ElementType.TYPE)
@Retention(RetentionPolicy.RUNTIME)
@Documented
@Inherited
@Configuration
@EnableAutoConfiguration
@ComponentScan
public @interface SpringBootApplication {
......
```

Looking at the previous code, it is clear that `@SpringBootApplication` works as a convenient annotation to define the Spring Boot application instead of declaring three annotations.

The following block shows the log's output when the Spring Boot application is started:

```
  .   ____          _            __ _ _
 /\\ / ___'_ __ _ _(_)_ __  __ _ \ \ \ \
( ( )\___ | '_ | '_| | '_ \/ _` | \ \ \ \
 \\/  ___)| |_)| | | | | || (_| |  ) ) ) )
  '  |____| .__|_| |_|_| |_\__, | / / / /
 =========|_|==============|___/=/_/_/_/
 :: Spring Boot ::        (v2.0.0.RELEASE)

2018-05-23 16:29:21.382  INFO 32268 --- [ main]
c.p.s.ch09.BootExampleApplication : Starting BootExampleApplication on
DESKTOP-4D355MC with PID 32268 (E:\projects\spring-high-
performance\ch-09\boot-example\target\classes started by baps in
E:\projects\spring-high-performance\ch-09\boot-example)
2018-05-23 16:29:21.386  INFO 32268 --- [ main]
c.p.s.ch09.BootExampleApplication : No active profile set, falling back
to default profiles: default
2018-05-23 16:29:21.441  INFO 32268 --- [ main]
ConfigServletWebServerApplicationContext : Refreshing
org.springframework.boot.web.servlet.context.AnnotationConfigServletWeb
ServerApplicationContext@58ce9668: startup date [Wed May 23 16:29:21
IST 2018]; root of context hierarchy
2018-05-23 16:29:23.854  INFO 32268 --- [ main]
o.s.b.w.embedded.tomcat.TomcatWebServer : Tomcat initialized with
port(s): 8080 (http)
2018-05-23 16:29:23.881  INFO 32268 --- [ main]
o.apache.catalina.core.StandardService : Starting service [Tomcat]
2018-05-23 16:29:23.881  INFO 32268 --- [ main]
org.apache.catalina.core.StandardEngine : Starting Servlet Engine:
Apache Tomcat/8.5.28
```

```
2018-05-23 16:29:23.888 INFO 32268 --- [ost-startStop-1]
o.a.catalina.core.AprLifecycleListener : The APR based Apache Tomcat
Native library which allows optimal performance in production
environments was not found on the java.library.path: ...
2018-05-23 16:29:24.015 INFO 32268 --- [ost-startStop-1]
o.a.c.c.C.[Tomcat].[localhost].[/] : Initializing Spring embedded
WebApplicationContext
2018-05-23 16:29:24.016 INFO 32268 --- [ost-startStop-1]
o.s.web.context.ContextLoader : Root WebApplicationContext:
initialization completed in 2581 ms
2018-05-23 16:29:25.011 INFO 32268 --- [ost-startStop-1]
o.s.b.w.servlet.ServletRegistrationBean : Servlet dispatcherServlet
mapped to [/]
2018-05-23 16:29:25.015 INFO 32268 --- [ost-startStop-1]
o.s.b.w.servlet.FilterRegistrationBean : Mapping filter:
'characterEncodingFilter' to: [/*]
2018-05-23 16:29:25.016 INFO 32268 --- [ost-startStop-1]
o.s.b.w.servlet.FilterRegistrationBean : Mapping filter:
'hiddenHttpMethodFilter' to: [/*]
2018-05-23 16:29:25.016 INFO 32268 --- [ost-startStop-1]
o.s.b.w.servlet.FilterRegistrationBean : Mapping filter:
'httpPutFormContentFilter' to: [/*]
2018-05-23 16:29:25.016 INFO 32268 --- [ost-startStop-1]
o.s.b.w.servlet.FilterRegistrationBean : Mapping filter:
'requestContextFilter' to: [/*]
2018-05-23 16:29:25.016 INFO 32268 --- [ost-startStop-1]
o.s.b.w.servlet.FilterRegistrationBean : Mapping filter:
'httpTraceFilter' to: [/*]
2018-05-23 16:29:25.016 INFO 32268 --- [ost-startStop-1]
o.s.b.w.servlet.FilterRegistrationBean : Mapping filter:
'webMvcMetricsFilter' to: [/*]
2018-05-23 16:29:26.283 INFO 32268 --- [ main]
s.w.s.m.m.a.RequestMappingHandlerMapping : Mapped "{[/welcome]}" onto
public java.lang.String
com.packt.springhighperformance.ch09.controllers.MainController.helloMe
ssage(java.lang.String)
2018-05-23 16:29:26.284 INFO 32268 --- [ main]
s.w.s.m.m.a.RequestMappingHandlerMapping : Mapped "{[/]}" onto public
java.lang.String
com.packt.springhighperformance.ch09.controllers.MainController.helloWo
rld()
2018-05-23 16:29:26.291 INFO 32268 --- [ main]
s.w.s.m.m.a.RequestMappingHandlerMapping : Mapped "{[/error]}" onto
public
org.springframework.http.ResponseEntity<java.util.Map<java.lang.String,
java.lang.Object>>
org.springframework.boot.autoconfigure.web.servlet.error.BasicErrorCont
roller.error(javax.servlet.http.HttpServletRequest)
```

```
2018-05-23 16:29:26.292 INFO 32268 --- [ main]
s.w.s.m.m.a.RequestMappingHandlerMapping : Mapped
"{[/error],produces=[text/html]}" onto public
org.springframework.web.servlet.ModelAndView
org.springframework.boot.autoconfigure.web.servlet.error.BasicErrorCont
roller.errorHtml(javax.servlet.http.HttpServletRequest,javax.servlet.ht
tp.HttpServletResponse)
2018-05-23 16:29:26.358 INFO 32268 --- [ main]
o.s.w.s.handler.SimpleUrlHandlerMapping : Mapped URL path [/webjars/**]
onto handler of type [class
org.springframework.web.servlet.resource.ResourceHttpRequestHandler]
2018-05-23 16:29:26.359 INFO 32268 --- [ main]
o.s.w.s.handler.SimpleUrlHandlerMapping : Mapped URL path [/**] onto
handler of type [class
org.springframework.web.servlet.resource.ResourceHttpRequestHandler]
2018-05-23 16:29:26.410 INFO 32268 --- [ main]
o.s.w.s.handler.SimpleUrlHandlerMapping : Mapped URL path
[/**/favicon.ico] onto handler of type [class
org.springframework.web.servlet.resource.ResourceHttpRequestHandler]
2018-05-23 16:29:27.033 INFO 32268 --- [ main]
o.s.j.e.a.AnnotationMBeanExporter : Registering beans for JMX exposure
on startup
2018-05-23 16:29:27.082 INFO 32268 --- [ main]
o.s.b.w.embedded.tomcat.TomcatWebServer : Tomcat started on port(s):
8080 (http) with context path ''
2018-05-23 16:29:27.085 INFO 32268 --- [ main]
c.p.s.ch09.BootExampleApplication : Started BootExampleApplication in
6.068 seconds (JVM running for 7.496)
```

At this point, we have the kickstarter Spring Boot application ready, but we don't have any URLs to be rendered. So, when you access `http://localhost:8080`, a page similar to the one shown in the following screenshot is displayed:

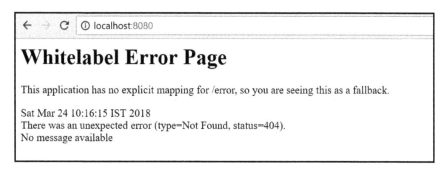

Let's define the Spring controller and default route, and add text content to it. The following is the code snippet for the controller class:

```
package com.packt.springhighperformance.ch09.controllers;

import org.springframework.stereotype.Controller;
import org.springframework.web.bind.annotation.RequestMapping;
import org.springframework.web.bind.annotation.RequestParam;
import org.springframework.web.bind.annotation.ResponseBody;

@Controller
public class MainController {
  @RequestMapping(value="/")
  @ResponseBody
  public String helloWorld() {
    return "<h1>Hello World<h1>";
  }
  @RequestMapping(value="/welcome")
  @ResponseBody
  public String showMessage(@RequestParam(name="name") String name) {
    return "<h1>Hello " + name + "<h1>";
  }

}
```

In the preceding example code, we have defined two routes using the `@RequestMapping` annotation. The following is a list of annotations used in the preceding code block with brief descriptions:

- The `@Controller` annotation indicates that the class is a controller class and may contain request mappings.
- The `@RequestMapping` annotation defines an application URL that the users can navigate to in the browser.
- The `@ResponseBody` annotation indicates that the method return value should be rendered on the page as the HTML content. The value parameter can take the URL path to be navigated.

The following screenshot shows the page displayed or rendered when we hit `http://localhost:8080` in the browser:

We have also defined parameterized request mapping with the value as /welcome. The value of the request parameter will be reflected in the message on the page when we navigate to the URL in the browser. The following screenshot shows how the content is rendered:

We can find the following log entries when the application with these requests mappings bootstraps:

```
2018-03-24 10:26:26.154 INFO 11148 --- [ main]
s.w.s.m.m.a.RequestMappingHandlerAdapter : Looking for
@ControllerAdvice:
org.springframework.boot.web.servlet.context.AnnotationConfigServletWeb
ServerApplicationContext@3c153a1: startup date [Sat Mar 24 10:26:24 IST
2018]; root of context hierarchy
2018-03-24 10:26:26.214 INFO 11148 --- [ main]
s.w.s.m.m.a.RequestMappingHandlerMapping : Mapped "{[/]}" onto public
java.lang.String
com.packt.springhighperformance.ch09.controllers.MainController.helloWo
rld()
2018-03-24 10:26:26.218 INFO 11148 --- [ main]
s.w.s.m.m.a.RequestMappingHandlerMapping : Mapped "{[/welcome]}" onto
public java.lang.String
com.packt.springhighperformance.ch09.controllers.MainController.helloMe
ssage(java.lang.String)
```

At this point, our first Spring Boot application with example request mappings are in place. This section served as a step-by-step guide to Spring Boot application development. In the next section, we will look at more Spring Boot features.

Metrics with Spring Boot Actuator

Before we move any further, it is important to understand what a Spring Boot Actuator is. We will introduce the Spring Boot Actuator in the sections to follow. We will also look at the out-of-the-box capabilities provided by the Spring Boot Actuator. We will also go through examples to understand the configuration and other necessary details.

What is Spring Actuator?

Essentially, the Spring Boot Actuator can be considered a subproject of Spring Boot. It helps bring production-grade features in the application that we develop using Spring Boot out of the box. The Spring Boot Actuator needs to be configured before we can leverage the features exposed by it. The Spring Boot Actuator has been available since Spring Boot first release in April 2014. The Spring Boot Actuator materializes different HTTP endpoints so the development team can perform the following tasks:

- Application monitoring
- Analyzing application metrics
- Interacting with the application
- Version information
- Logger details
- Bean details

Enabling Spring Boot Actuator

Apart from helping in bootstrapping application development, Spring Boot enables a number of features that can be used in the application. These additional features include, but are not limited to, monitoring and managing the application. Application management and monitoring can be done over HTTP endpoints or using JMX. Auditing, health checkups, and metrics can also be applied with a configuration in a Spring Boot application. These are the production-ready features provided by the `spring-boot-actuator` module.

Here is the definition of the Actuator from the Spring Boot reference documentation (`https://docs.spring.io/spring-boot/docs/current/reference/htmlsingle/ #production-ready`):

> *An actuator is a manufacturing term that refers to a mechanical device for moving or controlling something. Actuators can generate a large amount of motion from a small change.*

In order to leverage the features of the Spring Boot Actuator, the first step is to enable it. It is not enabled by default and we have to add the dependency to enable it. It is extremely easy to enable the Spring Boot Actuator in a Spring Boot application. We will need to add the `spring-boot-starter-actuator` dependency in the `pom.xml` file in case we are using Maven for dependency management in the application. The following is the snippet for Maven dependency for the Spring Boot Actuator:

```
<dependency>
  <groupId>org.springframework.boot</groupId>
  <artifactId>spring-boot-starter-actuator</artifactId>
</dependency>
```

As mentioned before, the Spring Boot Actuator enables application monitoring by exposing or enabling endpoints to interact with. The module has a number of out-of-the-box endpoints. It also allows the developer to create their own custom endpoints. We can enable or disable each individual endpoint. This ensures that the endpoint is created in the application and the corresponding bean exists in the application's context.

The endpoint can be accessed remotely by exposing it over JMX or HTTP. Usually, applications expose the endpoints over HTTP. The endpoint URL is derived by mapping the endpoint ID along with the /actuator prefix.

The following is a list of technology-agnostic endpoints:

ID	Description	Enabled by default
auditevents	This endpoint exposes the audio event's information.	Yes
beans	This endpoints shows a complete list of the Spring beans available in the application.	Yes
conditions	This endpoint displays the conditions that are evaluated on configuration and auto-configuration classes.	Yes
configprops	This endpoint shows a list of properties marked with @ConfigurationProperties.	Yes
env	This endpoint displays the properties from Spring's ConfigurableEnvironment.	Yes
flyway	The endpoint shows any flyway database migrations that might have been applied.	Yes
health	This endpoint shows the health information of the application.	Yes
httptrace	This endpoint shows the HTTP trace information. By default, it shows the last 100 HTTP request-response exchanges.	Yes
info	This endpoint exposes application information.	Yes
loggers	This endpoint shows the application logger configuration.	Yes
liquibase	This endpoint displays any liquibase database migrations that might have been applied.	Yes
metrics	This endpoint displays metrics information for the application.	Yes
mappings	This endpoint displays a list of all the @RequestMapping paths.	Yes
scheduledtasks	This endpoint shows the scheduled tasks for the application.	Yes

sessions	This endpoint allows retrieval and deletion of user sessions from a Spring Session-backed session store. It is not available when using Spring Session's support for reactive web applications.	Yes
shutdown	This endpoint allows the application to be shutdown gracefully.	No
threaddump	This endpoint performs a threaddump.	Yes

The following is a list of additional endpoints that are exposed if the application is a web application:

ID	Description	Enabled by default
heapdump	This endpoint returns a compressed hprof heap dump file.	Yes
jolokia	This endpoint exposes JMX beans over HTTP.	Yes
logfile	This endpoint shows the contents of the logfile if the logging.file or logging.path is set in the properties. It uses the HTTP range header to partly retrieve contents of the log file.	Yes
prometheus	This endpoint shows metrics in a format that can be scraped by a Prometheus server.	Yes

Enabling endpoints

With the Spring Boot Actuator, all endpoints are enabled by default, except the shutdown endpoint. In order to enable or disable a particular endpoint, a relevant property should be added in the application.properties file. The following is the format for enabling the endpoint:

```
management.endpoint.<id>.enabled=true
```

As an example, the following property can be added to enable the shutdown endpoint:

```
management.endpoint.shutdown.enabled=true
```

The following log entries can be seen when we bootstrap an application with the default Actuator endpoints enabled:

```
2018-03-24 17:51:36.687 INFO 8516 --- [ main]
s.b.a.e.w.s.WebMvcEndpointHandlerMapping : Mapped
"{[/actuator/health],methods=[GET],produces=[application/vnd.spring-
boot.actuator.v2+json || application/json]}" onto public
java.lang.Object
org.springframework.boot.actuate.endpoint.web.servlet.AbstractWebMvcEnd
pointHandlerMapping$OperationHandler.handle(javax.servlet.http.HttpServ
letRequest,java.util.Map<java.lang.String, java.lang.String>)
```

```
2018-03-24 17:51:36.696 INFO 8516 --- [ main]
s.b.a.e.w.s.WebMvcEndpointHandlerMapping : Mapped
"{[/actuator/info],methods=[GET],produces=[application/vnd.spring-
boot.actuator.v2+json || application/json]}" onto public
java.lang.Object
org.springframework.boot.actuate.endpoint.web.servlet.AbstractWebMvcEnd
pointHandlerMapping$OperationHandler.handle(javax.servlet.http.HttpServ
letRequest,java.util.Map<java.lang.String, java.lang.String>)
2018-03-24 17:51:36.697 INFO 8516 --- [ main]
s.b.a.e.w.s.WebMvcEndpointHandlerMapping : Mapped
"{[/actuator],methods=[GET],produces=[application/vnd.spring-
boot.actuator.v2+json || application/json]}" onto protected
java.util.Map<java.lang.String, java.util.Map<java.lang.String,
org.springframework.boot.actuate.endpoint.web.Link>>
org.springframework.boot.actuate.endpoint.web.servlet.WebMvcEndpointHan
dlerMapping.links(javax.servlet.http.HttpServletRequest,javax.servlet.h
ttp.HttpServletResponse)
```

Looking at the log entries closely, we find that the following endpoints or URLs are exposed:

- /actuator
- /actuator/health
- /actuator/info

Why does the application have three endpoints exposed out of so many listed earlier? To answer this question, the Spring Boot Actuator exposes only three endpoints over HTTP. The rest of the endpoints, listed previously, are exposed over the JMX connection. The following is a list of endpoints and information about whether they are exposed over HTTP or JMX:

ID	Exposed over JMX	Exposed over HTTP
auditevents	Yes	No
beans	Yes	No
conditions	Yes	No
configprops	Yes	No
env	Yes	No
flyway	Yes	No
health	Yes	Yes
heapdump	N/A	No
httptrace	Yes	No

info	Yes	Yes
jolokia	N/A	No
logfile	N/A	No
loggers	Yes	No
liquibase	Yes	No
metrics	Yes	No
mappings	Yes	No
prometheus	N/A	No
scheduledtasks	Yes	No
sessions	Yes	No
shutdown	Yes	No
threaddump	Yes	No

Why does Spring Boot not expose all the endpoints over HTTP by default? The reason is that the endpoints may expose sensitive information. So, a careful consideration should be done in exposing them.

The following properties can be used to change or override the default exposure behavior of the endpoints:

- `management.endpoints.jmx.exposure.exclude`: The endpoint IDs specified in a comma-separated list are excluded from default exposure over the JMX connection. By default, none of the default endpoints are excluded.

- `management.endpoints.jmx.exposure.include`: The endpoint IDs specified in a comma-separated list are included along with the default exposure over the JMX connection. The property can be used to expose those endpoints that are not included in the default list of endpoints. The default value for the property is *, which indicates that all of the endpoints are exposed.

- `management.endpoints.web.exposure.exclude`: The endpoint IDs specified by a comma-separated list are excluded from being exposed over HTTP. Though no default value exists, only `info` and `health` endpoints are exposed. The rest of the endpoints are implicitly excluded for HTTP.

- `management.endpoints.web.exposure.include`: The endpoint IDs specified in a comma-separated list are included along with the default exposure over HTTP. The property can be used to expose those endpoints that are not included in the default list of endpoints. The default value for the property is `info`, `health`.

Health checks

One of the extremely critical aspects of ensuring the high performance of the application is to monitor the health of the application. A production-grade application is always under observation of a specialized monitoring and alerting software. Threshold values are configured for every parameter, whether it be average response time, disk utilization, or CPU utilization. Once the parameter value exceeds the specified threshold value, the monitoring software signals an alert via email or notifications. Development and operations teams take the necessary actions to ensure the application is back to its normal state.

For the Spring Boot application, we can collect health information by navigating to the `/actuator/health` URL. The `health` endpoint is enabled by default. For the application deployed in the production environment, health information gathered using the `health` endpoint can be sent to a monitoring software for alerting purposes.

The information presented by the `health` endpoint depends on the `management.endpoint.health.show-details` property. The following is the list of supported values for the property:

- `always`: It indicates that all the information should be shown to all users.
- `never`: It indicates that the details should never be shown.
- `when-authorized`: This indicates that the details are shown to users with authorized roles only. The authorized roles can be configured using the `management..endpoint.health.roles` property.

The default value for the `show-details` property is `never`. Also, the user can be considered authorized when it has one or more of the endpoint's authorized roles. By default, none of the roles are configured as authorized. So, all authenticated users are considered authorized users.

`HealthIndicator` is one of the important interfaces that provides an indication of application health on different aspects, such as disk space, data source, or JMS. The `health` endpoint collects health information from all the `HealthIndicator` implementation beans defined in the application's context. Spring Boot comes with an auto-configured set of health indicators. The framework is flexible enough to support custom health indicator implementations. The final health status of the application is derived by `HealthAggregator`. The health aggregator sorts statuses from all the health indicators as per the order of statuses that have been defined.

Here is a list of auto-configured `HealthIndicators` by Spring Boot:

- `CassandraHealthIndicator`: Checks whether the Cassandra database is up
- `DiskSpaceHealthIndicator`: Checks whether enough disk space is available
- `DataSourceHealthIndicator`: Checks whether the connection with the data source can be obtained or not
- `ElasticSearchHealthIndicator`: Checks whether the elasticsearch cluster is up
- `InfluxDbHealthIndicator`: Checks whether the Influx server is up and running
- `JmsHealthIndicator`: Checks whether the JMS broker is up and running
- `MailHealthIndicator`: Checks whether the mail server is up and running
- `MongoHealthIndicator`: Checks whether the Mongo database is up and running
- `Neo4jHealthIndicator`: Checks whether the Neo4j server is up and running
- `RabbitHealthIndicator`: Checks whether the Rabbit server is up and running
- `RedisHealthIndicator`: Checks whether the Redis server is up and running
- `SolrHealthIndicator`: Checks whether the Solr server is up and running

These health indicators are auto-configured based on the appropriate Spring Boot starter configuration.

The following is the example disk space health check output when we navigate to the `http://localhost:8080/actuator/health` URL:

```
{
  "status": "UP",
  "details": {
    "diskSpace": {
      "status": "UP",
      "details": {
        "total": 407250137088,
        "free": 392089661440,
        "threshold": 10485760
      }
    }
  }
}
```

We can add additional customized health indicators to include the information we want to see. The customized health indicator will be displayed in the result of the health endpoint. It is super easy to create and register a custom health indicator.

The following is an example of a custom health indicator:

```java
package com.packt.springhighperformance.ch09.healthindicators;

import org.springframework.boot.actuate.health.AbstractHealthIndicator;
import org.springframework.boot.actuate.health.Health;
import org.springframework.stereotype.Component;

@Component
public class ExampleHealthCheck extends AbstractHealthIndicator {
    @Override
    protected void doHealthCheck(Health.Builder builder)
    throws Exception
    {
        // TODO implement some check
        boolean running = true;
        if (running) {
            builder.up();
        } else {
            builder.down();
        }
    }
}
```

We have to create a Java class that extends from `AbstractHealthIndicator`. In the custom health indicator class, we have to implement the `doHealthCheck()` method. The method expects a `Health.Builder` object to be passed. If we find that the health parameters OK, then the `builder.up()` method should be called, otherwise the `builder.down()` method should be called.

The following is the output rendered on the page when the `/actuator/health` URL is hit:

```json
{
  "status": "UP",
  "details": {
    "exampleHealthCheck": {
      "status": "UP"
    },
    "diskSpace": {
      "status": "UP",
      "details": {
        "total": 407250137088,
```

```
            "free": 392071581696,
            "threshold": 10485760
        }
    },
    "db": {
      "status": "UP",
      "details": {
        "database": "MySQL",
        "hello": 1
      }
    }
  }
}
```

The custom health indicator is not required to be registered. The `@Component` annotation is scanned and the bean is registered with the `ApplicationContext`.

So far, we have learned, in detail, about Spring Boot with examples. The following sections will focus on the use of Spring Boot with microservices.

Microservices using Spring Boot

We have a hefty amount of information about Spring Boot now from the previous sections. With the information that we have so far, we are now in a position to build microservices using Spring Boot. Before jumping into the implementation of our first microservice with Spring Boot, to proceed with implementing the first microservice, it is assumed that you know basic information about microservices, including the issues with monoliths, what microservices are, and the features microservices bring to the table.

First microservice with Spring Boot

The following are the details of the microservice that we are going to develop:

- We will implement an accounting service as a microservice.
- The microservice will be REST-based. It is an architectural pattern for developing web services. It focuses on identifying each resource in the application with a unique URL.
- We will identify the Spring Boot starter project that we will need and generate the Maven `pom.xml` file accordingly.
- We will implement an `Account` class with a few basic properties.

- We will implement `AccountRepository` with the find-by-name example method.
- We will implement the controller class, which has a repository auto-wired. The controller exposes the endpoints.
- We will also implement a way to feed the test data into the database.

Let's start!

We will start implementation by generating the Spring Boot application using Spring Initializr. We have to decide on the Spring Boot starter projects to be used. We want to develop a JPA-based web application. For the purpose of storing `Account` data in a database, we can use either MySQL or H2. Usually, H2 is a more convenient option as we don't need to set up anything. We will use MySQL for the examples in this chapter.

The following are the starter projects to be selected:

- Web
- JPA
- MySQL or H2
- REST repositories

We can also add the Spring Boot Actuator for application monitoring purpose but is not mandatory for the example.

The following is the `pom.xml` file that is generated by Spring Initializr:

```xml
<?xml version="1.0" encoding="UTF-8"?>
<project xmlns="http://maven.apache.org/POM/4.0.0"
xmlns:xsi="http://www.w3.org/2001/XMLSchema-instance"
  xsi:schemaLocation="http://maven.apache.org/POM/4.0.0
  http://maven.apache.org/xsd/maven-4.0.0.xsd">
  <modelVersion>4.0.0</modelVersion>

  <groupId>com.packt.springhighperformance.ch09</groupId>
  <artifactId>ch-09-accounting-service</artifactId>
  <version>0.0.1-SNAPSHOT</version>
  <packaging>jar</packaging>

  <name>accounting-service</name>
  <description>Example accounting service</description>

  <parent>
    <groupId>org.springframework.boot</groupId>
    <artifactId>spring-boot-starter-parent</artifactId>
```

```xml
    <version>2.0.0.RELEASE</version>
    <relativePath /> <!-- lookup parent from repository -->
</parent>

<properties>
    <project.build.sourceEncoding>UTF-8</project.build.sourceEncoding>
    <project.reporting.outputEncoding>UTF-
    8</project.reporting.outputEncoding>
    <java.version>1.8</java.version>
</properties>

<dependencies>
    <dependency>
        <groupId>org.springframework.boot</groupId>
        <artifactId>spring-boot-starter-actuator</artifactId>
    </dependency>
    <dependency>
        <groupId>org.springframework.boot</groupId>
        <artifactId>spring-boot-starter-data-jpa</artifactId>
    </dependency>
    <dependency>
        <groupId>org.springframework.boot</groupId>
        <artifactId>spring-boot-starter-data-rest</artifactId>
    </dependency>
    <dependency>
        <groupId>org.springframework.boot</groupId>
        <artifactId>spring-boot-starter-hateoas</artifactId>
    </dependency>
    <dependency>
        <groupId>org.springframework.boot</groupId>
        <artifactId>spring-boot-starter-web</artifactId>
    </dependency>
    <dependency>
        <groupId>org.springframework.data</groupId>
        <artifactId>spring-data-rest-hal-browser</artifactId>
    </dependency>
    <dependency>
        <groupId>mysql</groupId>
        <artifactId>mysql-connector-java</artifactId>
        <scope>runtime</scope>
    </dependency>
    <dependency>
        <groupId>org.springframework.boot</groupId>
        <artifactId>spring-boot-starter-test</artifactId>
        <scope>test</scope>
    </dependency>
</dependencies>
```

```
<build>
  <plugins>
    <plugin>
      <groupId>org.springframework.boot</groupId>
      <artifactId>spring-boot-maven-plugin</artifactId>
    </plugin>
  </plugins>
</build>
</project>
```

Another piece of code that is generated by Spring Initializr is the Spring Boot application:

```
package com.packt.springhighperformance.ch09.accountingservice;

import org.springframework.boot.SpringApplication;
import org.springframework.boot.autoconfigure.SpringBootApplication;

@SpringBootApplication
public class AccountingServiceApplication {

  public static void main(String[] args) {
    SpringApplication.run(AccountingServiceApplication.class, args);
  }

}
```

At this point, we should have our project imported in our IDE of preference.

People, get ready for the hands-on development now. We will start by creating the Account JPA entity class. We will annotate the Account class with @Entity and @Table annotations. The @Table annotation allows us to supply the desired table name. We have one more column, which is accountName. It stores and represents the name of the Account. Basically, the Account entity represents the account type in the real world. One other important attribute that we have added is id. id represents a unique, autogenerated numeric identifier. We can identify each account uniquely using the identifier. The @GeneratedValue annotation lets us supply the way id values will be generated in the database. Keeping it to AUTO defines that it depends on the database to automatically generate id values. The @Column annotation allows us to match the accountName attribute to the ACCT_NAME database field.

The following is the code for the Account entity:

```
package com.packt.springhighperformance.ch09.accountingservice.models;

import javax.persistence.Column;
import javax.persistence.Entity;
import javax.persistence.GeneratedValue;
```

```java
import javax.persistence.GenerationType;
import javax.persistence.Id;
import javax.persistence.Table;

@Entity
@Table(name = "accounts")
public class Account {

  @Id
  @GeneratedValue(strategy = GenerationType.AUTO)
  @Column(name = "ACCT_ID")
  private Long id;

  @Column(name = "ACCT_NAME")
      private String accountName;

  public Account() {
  }

  public Account(String accountName) {
    this.accountName = accountName;
  }

  public Long getId() {
    return id;
  }

  public void setId(Long id) {
    this.id = id;
  }

  public String getAccountName() {
    return accountName;
  }

  public void setAccountName(String accountName) {
    this.accountName = accountName;
  }
  @Override
  public String toString() {
    return "Account{"
        + "id=" + id +
        ", accountName='" + accountName + '\'' +
        '}';
  }

}
```

Spring Data provides a convenient interface to perform common database operations. The interface is called `CrudRepository`. It supports basic `Create`, `Read`, `Update`, and `Delete` operations for a specific type. The interface is inherited by the `JpaRepository` interface, which is a JPA-specific definition of the `CrudRepository` interface. `JpaRepository` also inherits sorting and paging capabilities from the `PagingAndSortingRepository` interface.

With this background, the next task for us is to build an interface to interact with the `accounts` database table. The following is the code for the `AccountsRepository` class:

```
package com.packt.springhighperformance.ch09.
accountingservice.repositories;

import java.util.Collection;

import org.springframework.data.jpa.repository.JpaRepository;
import org.springframework.data.repository.query.Param;
import
org.springframework.data.rest.core.annotation.RepositoryRestResource;

import
com.packt.springhighperformance.ch09.accountingservice.models.Account;

@RepositoryRestResource
public interface AccountsRepository extends JpaRepository<Account,
Long> {

   Collection<Account> findByAccountName(@Param("an") String an);
}
```

In the `AccountsRepository` interface, we have defined a method that is intended to find the `Account` entries from the database based on the `accountName`. The `CrudRepository` interface is very powerful. It will generate the implementation for the `findByAccountName` method. It can generate the implementation for all such query methods that follow the convention, such as `findBy{model-attribute-name}`. It also returns the objects of the `Account` type.

Also, you might have noticed that the use of `@RepositoryRestResource` is provided by the Spring Data REST module. It briefly exposes the repository methods for data manipulation as REST endpoints without any further configuration or development.

Now, we have the entity and repository in place. Next is the controller part of a web application. We have to create a controller class. The following is the code for the `AccountsController` class:

```
package com.packt.springhighperformance.ch09
.accountingservice.controllers;

import java.util.Collections;
import java.util.Map;

import org.springframework.web.bind.annotation.GetMapping;
import org.springframework.web.bind.annotation.PathVariable;
import org.springframework.web.bind.annotation.RestController;

@RestController
public class AccountsController {
  @GetMapping(value = "/account/{name}")
  Map<String, Object> getAccount(@PathVariable String name) {
    return Collections.singletonMap("Account : ", name);
  }
}
```

Three notable annotations from the `AccountsController` code are:

- `@RestController`: This annotation is a combination of the `@Controller` and `@ResponseBody` annotations. If we used the `@RestController` annotation, we don't need to define these two other annotations. The `@RestController` annotation indicates that the class should be treated as a controller and every endpoint method will respond with content as a response body.
- `@GetMapping`: This annotation is used to define a REST GET endpoint mapping.
- `@PathVariable`: This annotation is used to fetch the values supplied in the URL path itself.

Two things are left. One is the database and other important properties, while the other one is a way to populate the initial data in the `accounts` table.

The following is the `application.properties` file that manages the configuration part of the application:

```
spring.jpa.hibernate.ddl-auto=create-drop
spring.datasource.url=jdbc:mysql://localhost:3306/db_example?useSSL=false
spring.datasource.username=root
spring.datasource.password=root
```

From the list of properties, the `spring.jpa.hibernate.ddl-auto` property determines the initial generation of the database based on the database configurations provided. It determines whether the Spring Boot application should create the database schema up on application startup. `none`, `validate`, `update`, `create`, and `create-drop` are the options available for the property.

While booting up the application, we may also receive the following error:

```
Establishing SSL connection without server's identity verification is
not recommended.
```

We can use `useSSL=true` in the database connection URL to overcome this warning, as you can see in the properties in the preceding code example.

Loading sample data into the database

At this point in time, it is necessary to have some initial data in the `accounts` table in the database. It will help us test the account's microservice that we have developed. The Spring modules provide multiple ways to achieve this.

The JPA way of initial data loading

Spring Data JPA provides a way to execute database manipulation commands on the application startup. As the schema will be generated in the database from the JPA entity configuration and `ddl-auto` property value, we have to take care to insert the account records in the `accounts` table only. The following are the steps to accomplish this:

1. Add the following property to the `application.properties` file:

   ```
   spring.datasource.initialization-mode=always
   ```

2. Create a `data.sql` file with `INSERT` queries in the `src/main/resources` folder of the project:

   ```
   INSERT INTO accounts (ACCT_NAME) VALUES
       ('Savings'),
       ('Current'),
       ('Fixed Deposit'),
       ('Recurring Deposit'),
       ('Loan');
   ```

That's it! When we start the application, Spring will automatically insert the data into the `accounts` table in the database.

The ApplicationRunner way of initial data loading

We can also accomplish this using the `ApplicationRunner` interface. This interface is responsible for executing the code defined in the `run` method on application startup.

The following is the code for the `ApplicationRunner` interface's implementation:

```
package com.packt.springhighperformance.ch09.accountingservice;

import java.util.stream.Stream;

import org.springframework.beans.factory.annotation.Autowired;
import org.springframework.boot.ApplicationArguments;
import org.springframework.boot.ApplicationRunner;
import org.springframework.stereotype.Component;

import
com.packt.springhighperformance.ch09.accountingservice.models.Account;
import
com.packt.springhighperformance.ch09.accountingservice.repositories.Acc
ountsRepository;

@Component
public class AccountsDataRunner implements ApplicationRunner {

  @Autowired
  private AccountsRepository acctRepository;

  @Override
  public void run(ApplicationArguments args) throws Exception {
    Stream.of("Savings", "Current", "Recurring", "Fixed Deposit")
    .forEach(name -> acctRepository.save(new Account(name)));
    acctRepository.findAll().forEach(System.out::println);
  }

}
```

We have auto-wired the repository so that we can access the `AccountsRepository` methods for inserting `accounts` records into the database.

Microservice client

Now that we have the microservice in place, we have to look at how to consume it. The plan is to create another web application using Spring Initializr and use the appropriate tools to consume the accounting microservice.

The following is the POM file for the client application:

```xml
<?xml version="1.0" encoding="UTF-8"?>
<project xmlns="http://maven.apache.org/POM/4.0.0"
xmlns:xsi="http://www.w3.org/2001/XMLSchema-instance"
  xsi:schemaLocation="http://maven.apache.org/POM/4.0.0
  http://maven.apache.org/xsd/maven-4.0.0.xsd">
  <modelVersion>4.0.0</modelVersion>

  <groupId>com.packt.springhighperformance.ch09</groupId>
  <artifactId>ch-09-accounting-service-client</artifactId>
  <version>0.0.1-SNAPSHOT</version>
  <packaging>jar</packaging>

  <name>accounting-service-client</name>
  <description>Example accounting service client</description>

  <parent>
    <groupId>org.springframework.boot</groupId>
    <artifactId>spring-boot-starter-parent</artifactId>
    <version>2.0.0.RELEASE</version>
    <relativePath /> <!-- lookup parent from repository -->
  </parent>

  <properties>
    <project.build.sourceEncoding>UTF-8</project.build.sourceEncoding>
    <project.reporting.outputEncoding>UTF-
    8</project.reporting.outputEncoding>
    <java.version>1.8</java.version>
    <spring-cloud.version>Finchley.M9</spring-cloud.version>
  </properties>

  <dependencies>
    <dependency>
      <groupId>org.springframework.boot</groupId>
      <artifactId>spring-boot-starter-actuator</artifactId>
    </dependency>
    <dependency>
      <groupId>org.springframework.boot</groupId>
      <artifactId>spring-boot-starter-web</artifactId>
    </dependency>
```

```xml
    <dependency>
      <groupId>org.springframework.cloud</groupId>
      <artifactId>spring-cloud-starter-openfeign</artifactId>
    </dependency>

    <dependency>
      <groupId>org.springframework.boot</groupId>
      <artifactId>spring-boot-starter-test</artifactId>
      <scope>test</scope>
    </dependency>
  </dependencies>

  <dependencyManagement>
    <dependencies>
      <dependency>
        <groupId>org.springframework.cloud</groupId>
        <artifactId>spring-cloud-dependencies</artifactId>
        <version>${spring-cloud.version}</version>
        <type>pom</type>
        <scope>import</scope>
      </dependency>
    </dependencies>
  </dependencyManagement>

  <build>
    <plugins>
      <plugin>
        <groupId>org.springframework.boot</groupId>
        <artifactId>spring-boot-maven-plugin</artifactId>
      </plugin>
    </plugins>
  </build>

  <repositories>
    <repository>
      <id>spring-milestones</id>
      <name>Spring Milestones</name>
      <url>https://repo.spring.io/milestone</url>
      <snapshots>
        <enabled>false</enabled>
      </snapshots>
    </repository>
  </repositories>

</project>
```

In the preceding `pom.xml` file, we have imported Spring Cloud dependencies using the Maven dependency-management element. We have added the `openfeign` starter project as well. Feign is a client tool to consume web services and provides a REST client templating facility.

The following is the code for the `main` class in our Spring Boot client application:

```
package com.packt.springhighperformance.ch09.accountingclient;

import java.util.Map;

import org.springframework.beans.factory.annotation.Value;
import org.springframework.boot.SpringApplication;
import org.springframework.boot.autoconfigure.SpringBootApplication;
import org.springframework.boot.json.BasicJsonParser;
import org.springframework.boot.json.JsonParser;
import org.springframework.http.ResponseEntity;
import org.springframework.web.bind.annotation.GetMapping;
import org.springframework.web.bind.annotation.RequestParam;
import org.springframework.web.bind.annotation.RestController;
import org.springframework.web.client.RestTemplate;

@SpringBootApplication
public class AccountingServiceClientApplication {

  public static void main(String[] args) {
    SpringApplication.run(AccountingServiceClientApplication.class,
    args);
  }
}

@RestController
class MainController {

  @Value("${accounting.service.url}")
  private String accountingServiceUrl;

  @GetMapping("/account")
  public String getAccountName(@RequestParam("id") Long id) {
    ResponseEntity<String> responseEntity = new
    RestTemplate().getForEntity(accountingServiceUrl + "/" + id,
    String.class);
    JsonParser parser = new BasicJsonParser();
    Map<String, Object> responseMap =
    parser.parseMap(responseEntity.getBody());
    return (String) responseMap.get("accountName");
  }
```

```
}
```

We have defined the REST controller in the same Java file.

The following is the `application.properties` file that defines the microservices URL and defines the `server.port` for running the client application:

```
accounting.service.url=http://localhost:8080/accounts/
server.port=8181
```

Microservices with Spring Cloud

Spring Cloud provides a declarative approach to building cloud-native web applications. Cloud-native is an application development paradigm to encourage adoption of value-driven development best practices. Spring Cloud is built on top of Spring Boot. Spring Cloud provides a way for all components in a distributed system to have easy access to all features.

Spring Cloud provides:

- Git-managed versioning of centralized configuration data
- Pairing with Netflix Eureka and Ribbon for application services to discover each other dynamically
- Pushing away load-balancing decisions from a dedicated proxy load balancer to client services

Externalized configurations is one of the major advantages of Spring Cloud. In the next section, we will develop an example to showcase the externalized configuration for the Spring Boot application.

Spring microservice configuration example

For the externalized configuration to work, we need to set up a centralized configuration server. The configuration server will store and provide configuration data for the registered Spring Boot applications. In this section, we will develop a configuration server, and the accounting service that we developed earlier will serve as the configuration client.

The following is the POM file for the Spring Boot config server:

```
<?xml version="1.0" encoding="UTF-8"?>
<project xmlns="http://maven.apache.org/POM/4.0.0"
```

```
  xmlns:xsi="http://www.w3.org/2001/XMLSchema-instance"
  xsi:schemaLocation="http://maven.apache.org/POM/4.0.0
  http://maven.apache.org/xsd/maven-4.0.0.xsd">
<modelVersion>4.0.0</modelVersion>

<groupId>com.spring.server.config</groupId>
<artifactId>spring-config-server</artifactId>
<version>0.0.1-SNAPSHOT</version>
<packaging>jar</packaging>

<name>config-server</name>
<description>Example spring boot config server</description>

<parent>
  <groupId>org.springframework.boot</groupId>
  <artifactId>spring-boot-starter-parent</artifactId>
  <version>2.0.0.RELEASE</version>
  <relativePath /> <!-- lookup parent from repository -->
</parent>

<properties>
  <project.build.sourceEncoding>UTF-8</project.build.sourceEncoding>
  <project.reporting.outputEncoding>UTF-
8</project.reporting.outputEncoding>
  <java.version>1.8</java.version>
  <spring-cloud.version>Finchley.M9</spring-cloud.version>
</properties>

<dependencies>
  <dependency>
    <groupId>org.springframework.cloud</groupId>
    <artifactId>spring-cloud-config-server</artifactId>
  </dependency>

  <dependency>
    <groupId>org.springframework.boot</groupId>
    <artifactId>spring-boot-starter-test</artifactId>
    <scope>test</scope>
  </dependency>
</dependencies>

<dependencyManagement>
  <dependencies>
    <dependency>
      <groupId>org.springframework.cloud</groupId>
      <artifactId>spring-cloud-dependencies</artifactId>
      <version>${spring-cloud.version}</version>
      <type>pom</type>
```

```xml
          <scope>import</scope>
        </dependency>
      </dependencies>
    </dependencyManagement>

    <build>
      <plugins>
        <plugin>
          <groupId>org.springframework.boot</groupId>
          <artifactId>spring-boot-maven-plugin</artifactId>
        </plugin>
      </plugins>
    </build>

    <repositories>
      <repository>
        <id>spring-milestones</id>
        <name>Spring Milestones</name>
        <url>https://repo.spring.io/milestone</url>
        <snapshots>
          <enabled>false</enabled>
        </snapshots>
      </repository>
    </repositories>
</project>
```

Two configurations should be noted from the preceding dependencies:

- `spring-cloud-dependencies`: It provides a set of dependencies necessary for Spring Cloud projects
- `spring-cloud-config-server`: This is the Spring Cloud starter project for Spring Boot

The following is the `application.properties` file:

```
spring.application.name=configserver
spring.cloud.config.server.git.uri:${user.home}\\Desktop\\config-repo
server.port=9000
spring.profiles.active=development,production
```

The `spring.cloud.config.server.git.uri` property points to a Git-based directory where the configurations are stored. The versioning is maintained by Git itself.

The `spring.profiles.active` denotes profiles to be used by applications. It is a common use case for development teams to have multiple environments in place. In order to have separate configurations for each environment, we can use this property.

The @EnableConfigServer annotation is provided by the Spring Cloud starter project. It marks the class as the configuration server. The following is the code for the Spring Boot application main class:

```
package com.spring.server.config;

import org.springframework.boot.SpringApplication;
import org.springframework.boot.autoconfigure.SpringBootApplication;
import org.springframework.cloud.config.server.EnableConfigServer;

@SpringBootApplication
@EnableConfigServer
public class ConfigServerApplication {

  public static void main(String[] args) {
    SpringApplication.run(ConfigServerApplication.class, args);
  }
}
```

Once this is done, the configuration server is ready to be run. In the Git repository, we have created an accountingservice.properties file with the following contents:

```
server.port=8101
```

Once the application is started, we can navigate to http://localhost:9000/accountingservice/default. As we do not have profile-specific files for the accountingservice application in the configuration server, it picks up the default profile. The contents of the page are as shown here:

```
{
    "name": "accountingservice",
    "profiles": [
        "default"
    ],
    "label": null,
    "version": "ddc6d770dfdd94f69029ec3a456657ac66ac7211",
    "state": null,
    "propertySources": [
        {
            "name": "C:\\Users\\baps\\Desktop\\config-repo/accountingservice.properties",
            "source": {
                "server.port": "8101"
            }
        }
    ]
}
```

As we can see, the `server.port` property value is rendered on the page.

The next step is to build a client that utilizes the centralized configuration defined in the configuration server. We have to create a Spring Boot starter application with web dependency.

The following is the POM file for the configuration server client:

```xml
<?xml version="1.0" encoding="UTF-8"?>
<project xmlns="http://maven.apache.org/POM/4.0.0"
    xmlns:xsi="http://www.w3.org/2001/XMLSchema-instance"
    xsi:schemaLocation="http://maven.apache.org/POM/4.0.0
    http://maven.apache.org/xsd/maven-4.0.0.xsd">
  <modelVersion>4.0.0</modelVersion>

  <groupId>com.packt.springhighperformance.ch09</groupId>
  <artifactId>ch-09-accounting-service</artifactId>
  <version>0.0.1-SNAPSHOT</version>
  <packaging>jar</packaging>

  <name>accounting-service</name>
  <description>Example accounting service</description>

  <parent>
    <groupId>org.springframework.boot</groupId>
    <artifactId>spring-boot-starter-parent</artifactId>
    <version>2.0.0.RELEASE</version>
    <relativePath /> <!-- lookup parent from repository -->
  </parent>

  <properties>
    <project.build.sourceEncoding>UTF-8</project.build.sourceEncoding>
    <project.reporting.outputEncoding>UTF-
    8</project.reporting.outputEncoding>
    <java.version>1.8</java.version>
  </properties>

  <dependencies>
    <dependency>
      <groupId>org.springframework.boot</groupId>
      <artifactId>spring-boot-starter-actuator</artifactId>
    </dependency>
    <dependency>
      <groupId>org.springframework.boot</groupId>
      <artifactId>spring-boot-starter-web</artifactId>
    </dependency>
    <dependency>
```

```
      <groupId>org.springframework.boot</groupId>
      <artifactId>spring-boot-starter-test</artifactId>
      <scope>test</scope>
   </dependency>
   <dependency>
      <groupId>org.springframework.cloud</groupId>
      <artifactId>spring-cloud-starter-config</artifactId>
      <version>2.0.0.M9</version>
   </dependency>
</dependencies>

<build>
   <plugins>
      <plugin>
         <groupId>org.springframework.boot</groupId>
         <artifactId>spring-boot-maven-plugin</artifactId>
      </plugin>
   </plugins>
</build>
</project>
```

As we can see in the preceding Maven file, we need to add the `spring-cloud-config-starter` project as the dependency. The project provides the necessary configuration for the application to be registered as a config server client.

The following is the `application.properties` file:

```
management.endpoints.web.exposure.include=*
server.port=8888
```

For the application to be registered as a client to the configuration server, we have to enable management web endpoints. The server will be running at port `8888`, as per the configuration in the `application.properties` file.

Spring Cloud operates on an additional context, known as the **bootstrap** context. The bootstrap context is the parent to the main `ApplicationContext`. The responsibility of the bootstrap context is to load configuration properties from external sources into local external configurations. It is advisable to have a separate properties file for the bootstrap context.

The following are the properties from the `bootstrap.properties` file:

```
spring.application.name=accountingservice
spring.cloud.config.uri=http://localhost:9000
```

We have defined the application name that matches the name of the configuration properties file stored in the Git directory on the configuration server. The `bootstrap.properties` file also defines the URL for the Spring Cloud configuration server.

This is all for the client to register with the Spring Cloud configuration server. The following log entries can be seen upon server startup:

```
2018-04-01 16:11:11.196 INFO 13556 --- [ main]
c.c.c.ConfigServicePropertySourceLocator : Fetching config from server
at: http://localhost:9000
....

2018-04-01 16:11:13.303  INFO 13556 --- [            main]
o.s.b.w.embedded.tomcat.TomcatWebServer  : Tomcat initialized with
port(s): 8101 (http)
....

2018-04-01 16:11:17.825  INFO 13556 --- [            main]
o.s.b.w.embedded.tomcat.TomcatWebServer  : Tomcat started on port(s):
8101 (http) with context path ''
```

As you can see, though we have defined the server port for the client application to be 8888, it fetches the `server.port` property from the configuration server and starts Tomcat on port 8101. The following is what the page looks like when we render the `/accounts` URL:

```
←  →  C  ⓘ localhost:8101/accounts

{
    "_embedded": {
        "accounts": [
            {
                "accountName": "Savings",
                "_links": {
                    "self": {
                        "href": "http://localhost:8101/accounts/1"
                    },
                    "account": {
                        "href": "http://localhost:8101/accounts/1"
                    }
                }
            },
            {
                "accountName": "Current",
                "_links": {
                    "self": {
                        "href": "http://localhost:8101/accounts/2"
                    },
                    "account": {
                        "href": "http://localhost:8101/accounts/2"
                    }
                }
            },
            {
                "accountName": "Fixed Deposit",
                "_links": {
                    "self": {
                        "href": "http://localhost:8101/accounts/3"
                    },
                    "account": {
                        "href": "http://localhost:8101/accounts/3"
```

This section described step-by-step ways to create a simple configuration server and a client that uses the configuration server. In the section to follow, we will see a way to monitor Spring microservices.

Monitoring microservices with Spring Boot admin

Spring Boot admin is an application that facilitates monitoring and managing of Spring Boot applications. The latest version of the Spring Boot admin application is not yet compatible with Spring 2.0.0. For the purpose of examples showcased in this section, we have used the Spring Boot 1.5.11 snapshot. The Spring Boot admin version is 1.5.4.

The Spring Boot client applications register themselves with the Spring Boot admin application via HTTP. It is also possible that admin applications discover client applications using the Spring Cloud Eureka discovery service. The Spring Boot admin user interface is built in AngularJS over Actuator endpoints.

That should be enough for the introduction part as examples will provide more insight. Let's build the Spring Boot admin server first.

`spring-boot-admin-server` is the dependency for building the admin server application. The Spring Boot admin application can have multiple Spring Boot applications registered, so, it becomes necessary for the Spring Boot admin application to be secure. That is the reason we have added the Spring Security starter project dependency. We will incorporate basic authentication for the purpose of this application, but it is not a limitation. We can add advanced security mechanisms, such as OAuth, for securing applications. The following is the POM file for the Spring Boot admin server:

```xml
<?xml version="1.0" encoding="UTF-8"?>
<project xmlns="http://maven.apache.org/POM/4.0.0"
    xmlns:xsi="http://www.w3.org/2001/XMLSchema-instance"
    xsi:schemaLocation="http://maven.apache.org/POM/4.0.0
    http://maven.apache.org/xsd/maven-4.0.0.xsd">
  <modelVersion>4.0.0</modelVersion>

  <groupId>com.spring.admin</groupId>
  <artifactId>admin-server</artifactId>
  <version>0.0.1-SNAPSHOT</version>
  <packaging>jar</packaging>

  <name>admin-server</name>
  <description>Demo project for Spring Boot</description>

  <parent>
    <groupId>org.springframework.boot</groupId>
    <artifactId>spring-boot-starter-parent</artifactId>
    <version>1.5.11.BUILD-SNAPSHOT</version>
    <relativePath /> <!-- lookup parent from repository -->
```

```
    </parent>

    <properties>
        <project.build.sourceEncoding>UTF-8</project.build.sourceEncoding>
<project.reporting.outputEncoding>UTF-8</project.reporting.outputEncodi
ng>
        <java.version>1.8</java.version>
    </properties>

    <dependencies>
        <dependency>
            <groupId>org.springframework.boot</groupId>
            <artifactId>spring-boot-starter-web</artifactId>
        </dependency>
        <dependency>
            <groupId>de.codecentric</groupId>
            <artifactId>spring-boot-admin-server</artifactId>
            <version>1.5.4</version>
        </dependency>
        <dependency>
            <groupId>de.codecentric</groupId>
            <artifactId>spring-boot-admin-server-ui</artifactId>
            <version>1.5.4</version>
        </dependency>
        <dependency>
            <groupId>org.springframework.boot</groupId>
            <artifactId>spring-boot-starter-security</artifactId>
        </dependency>
        <dependency>
            <groupId>de.codecentric</groupId>
            <artifactId>spring-boot-admin-server-ui-login</artifactId>
            <version>1.5.4</version>
        </dependency>

        <dependency>
            <groupId>org.springframework.boot</groupId>
            <artifactId>spring-boot-starter-test</artifactId>
            <scope>test</scope>
        </dependency>
    </dependencies>

    <build>
        <plugins>
            <plugin>
                <groupId>org.springframework.boot</groupId>
                <artifactId>spring-boot-maven-plugin</artifactId>
            </plugin>
        </plugins>
```

```xml
    </build>

    <repositories>
      <repository>
        <id>spring-snapshots</id>
        <name>Spring Snapshots</name>
        <url>https://repo.spring.io/snapshot</url>
        <snapshots>
          <enabled>true</enabled>
        </snapshots>
      </repository>
      <repository>
        <id>spring-milestones</id>
        <name>Spring Milestones</name>
        <url>https://repo.spring.io/milestone</url>
        <snapshots>
          <enabled>false</enabled>
        </snapshots>
      </repository>
    </repositories>

    <pluginRepositories>
      <pluginRepository>
        <id>spring-snapshots</id>
        <name>Spring Snapshots</name>
        <url>https://repo.spring.io/snapshot</url>
        <snapshots>
          <enabled>true</enabled>
        </snapshots>
      </pluginRepository>
      <pluginRepository>
        <id>spring-milestones</id>
        <name>Spring Milestones</name>
        <url>https://repo.spring.io/milestone</url>
        <snapshots>
          <enabled>false</enabled>
        </snapshots>
      </pluginRepository>
    </pluginRepositories>
  </project>
```

The `application.properties` file is where we define the security credentials for accessing the admin application. The following is the contents of the `application.properties` file:

```
security.user.name=admin
security.user.password=admin
```

`@EnableAdminServer` is provided by the Spring Boot admin server dependency. It indicates that the application works as a Spring Boot admin application. The following is the code for the Spring Boot application `main` class:

```
package com.spring.admin.adminserver;

import org.springframework.boot.SpringApplication;
import org.springframework.boot.autoconfigure.SpringBootApplication;

import de.codecentric.boot.admin.config.EnableAdminServer;

@SpringBootApplication
@EnableAdminServer
public class AdminServerApplication {

  public static void main(String[] args) {
    SpringApplication.run(AdminServerApplication.class, args);
  }
}
```

The next step is to build a sample application that will be registered with the Spring Boot admin application. The following is the POM file:

```
<?xml version="1.0" encoding="UTF-8"?>
<project xmlns="http://maven.apache.org/POM/4.0.0"
    xmlns:xsi="http://www.w3.org/2001/XMLSchema-instance"
    xsi:schemaLocation="http://maven.apache.org/POM/4.0.0
    http://maven.apache.org/xsd/maven-4.0.0.xsd">
  <modelVersion>4.0.0</modelVersion>

  <parent>
    <groupId>org.springframework.boot</groupId>
    <artifactId>spring-boot-starter-parent</artifactId>
    <version>1.5.11.BUILD-SNAPSHOT</version>
    <relativePath /> <!-- lookup parent from repository -->
  </parent>

  <properties>
    <spring-boot-admin.version>1.5.7</spring-boot-admin.version>
  </properties>

  <dependencies>
    <dependency>
      <groupId>de.codecentric</groupId>
      <artifactId>spring-boot-admin-starter-client</artifactId>
    </dependency>
    <dependency>
```

```
        <groupId>org.springframework.boot</groupId>
        <artifactId>spring-boot-starter-actuator</artifactId>
    </dependency>
    <dependency>
        <groupId>org.springframework.boot</groupId>
        <artifactId>spring-boot-starter-security</artifactId>
    </dependency>
</project>
```

We have to define the following properties:

- `spring.boot.admin.url`: The URL points to the Spring Boot admin application.
- `spring.boot.admin.username`: It is necessary for the admin client to access the admin application using security credentials. This property specifies the username for the admin application.
- `spring.boot.admin.password`: This property specifies the password for the admin application.
- `management.security.enabled`: This property denotes whether security is enabled for the client application or not.
- `security.user.name`: This property defines the username for accessing the client application.
- `security.user.password`: This property specifies the password for accessing the client application.

The following is the `application.properties` file:

```
spring.boot.admin.url=http://localhost:8080
server.port=8181
spring.boot.admin.username=admin
spring.boot.admin.password=admin
management.endpoints.web.exposure.include=*
security.user.name=user
security.user.password=password
management.security.enabled=false
```

The following is the code for the simple Spring Boot application class:

```
package com.spring.admin.client.bootadminclient;

import org.springframework.boot.SpringApplication;
import org.springframework.boot.autoconfigure.SpringBootApplication;

@SpringBootApplication
public class BootAdminClientApplication {

  public static void main(String[] args) {
    SpringApplication.run(BootAdminClientApplication.class, args);
  }
}
```

It is also possible to add customization to default web security configurations provided by Spring Security. The following is an example that demonstrates allowing all requests for authorization:

```
package com.spring.admin.client.bootadminclient;

import org.springframework.context.annotation.Configuration;
import
org.springframework.security.config.annotation.web.builders.HttpSecurit
y;
import
org.springframework.security.config.annotation.web.configuration.WebSec
urityConfigurerAdapter;

@Configuration
public class SecurityPermitAllConfig extends
WebSecurityConfigurerAdapter {
  @Override
  protected void configure(HttpSecurity http) throws Exception {
    http.authorizeRequests().anyRequest().permitAll().
    and().csrf().disable();
  }
}
```

At this point, we are ready to start both the Spring Boot admin and client applications. When we navigate to the Spring Boot admin application URL, the following screen is shown with a list of all the registered applications:

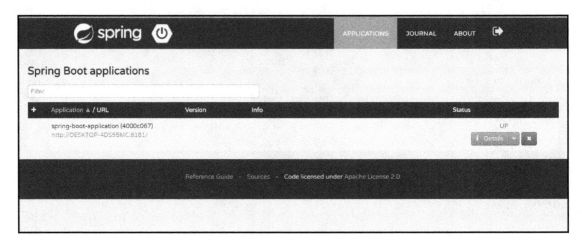

Clicking on the **Details** button on the right side of the application name will bring up an interface similar to the one shown here. The **Details** tab shows the health of the application, memory and JVM statistics, and garbage collector details:

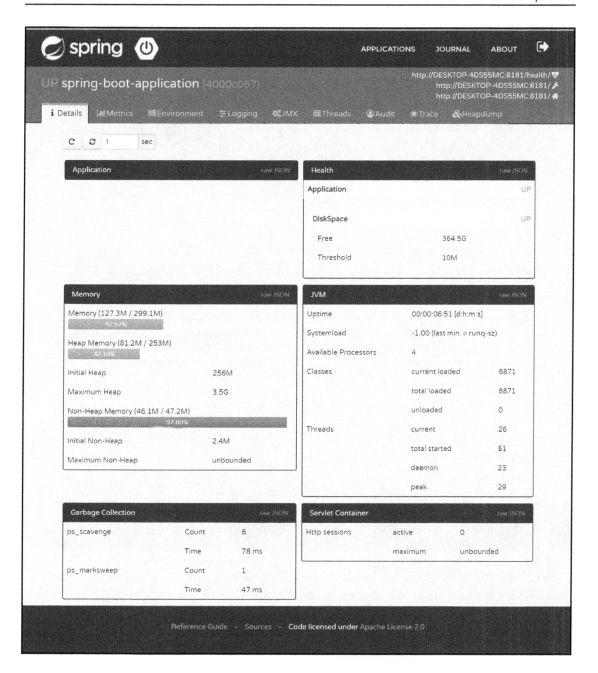

The **Logging** tab for the application details and displays a list of all the configured loggers. It is possible to change the log level. The following is the interface for **Logging**:

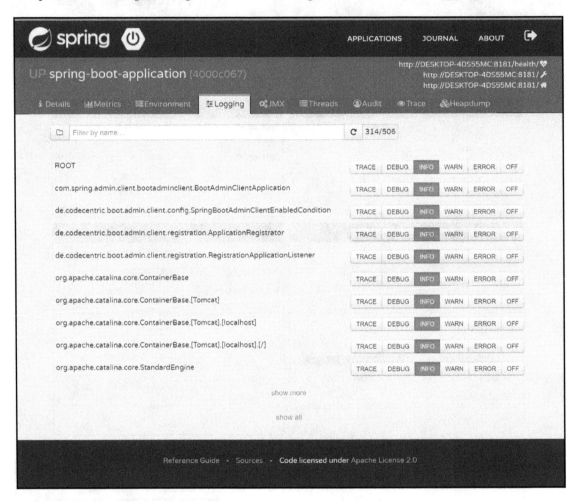

That's all for the Spring Boot admin application. It provides a production-grade interface and details for monitoring Spring Boot applications. The next section provides performance tuning for Spring Boot applications.

Spring Boot performance tuning

Spring Boot is a great tool to bootstrap and develop the Spring Framework-based application really quickly. The vanilla version of the Spring Boot application provides high performance without a doubt. But as the application starts to grow, its performance starts to be a bottleneck. This is a normal scenario for all web applications. The performance hit is observed when the different features are added and incoming requests are increasing day by day. We will learn the performance optimization techniques for Spring Boot applications in this section.

Undertow as an embedded server

Spring Boot provides embedded servers that can run web applications in a JAR file. A few of the available embedded servers for use are Tomcat, Undertow, Webflux, and Jetty. It is advisable to have Undertow as the embedded server. Undertow provides more throughput and consumes less memory compared to Tomcat and Jetty. The following comparisons may provide some insight:

- Throughput comparison:

Server	Samples	Error %	Throughput
Tomcat	3000	0	293.86
Jetty	3000	0	291.52
Undertow	3000	0	295.68

- Heap memory comparison:

Server	Heap size	Used	Max
Tomcat	665.5 MB	118.50 MB	2 GB
Jetty	599.5 MB	297 MB	2 GB
Undertow	602 MB	109 MB	2 GB

- Threads comparison:

Server	Live	Started
Tomcat	17	22
Jetty	19	22
Undertow	17	20

From the preceding comparisons, Undertow looks like the obvious choice for an embedded server in Spring Boot applications.

Overhead with the @SpringBootApplication annotation

The `@SpringBootApplication` annotation is a provision for the developers who used to annotate Spring classes with `@ComponentScan`, `@EnableAutoConfiguration`, and `@Configuration`. So, the `@SpringBootApplication` annotation is equivalent to using three annotations with default configurations. The implicit `@ComponentScan` annotation scans the Java classes defined in the base package (package for the Spring Boot application main class) and all subpackages. This slows down the application startup when the application has grown significantly in size.

To overcome this, we can replace the `@SpringBootApplication` annotation with individual annotations where we provide package paths to be scanned with `@ComponentScan`. We can also consider using the `@Import` annotation to import only the required components, beans, or configurations.

Summary

This chapter started with insightful details on Spring Boot, Spring Cloud, microservices, and all of these together. We covered the details of Spring Initializr, Spring Boot starter projects, and learned how to create our first Spring Boot application. Then, we learned about the Spring Boot Actuator and the production-grade features provided by the Actuator. The details on the application health checks and endpoints are important for production-ready applications.

Later in the chapter, we migrated to the world of microservices. We learned how Spring Boot can leverage features for the benefit of building microservices. We developed a microservice with Spring Boot and Spring Cloud with support for externalized configurations. We also looked at the integration of the Spring Boot admin for monitoring Spring Boot applications. Last but not least, we learned a few techniques to improve the performance of Spring Boot applications. Pretty huge stuff, isn't it?

At this point, you have a very good understanding of performance assessment and performance tuning for Spring and, in essence, any Java-based web application. This is all for the scope of this book. A step forward, you can learn the JVM class-loading mechanism, Spring Batch framework, design patterns for microservices, microservices deployment, and **Infrastructure as a Service (IaaS)**. We hope you will find these helpful.

Other Books You May Enjoy

If you enjoyed this book, you may be interested in these other books by Packt:

Spring Security - Third Edition
Mick Knutson, Robert Winch, Peter Mularien

ISBN: 978-1-78712-951-1

- Understand common security vulnerabilities and how to resolve them
- Learn to perform initial penetration testing to uncover common security vulnerabilities
- Implement authentication and authorization
- Learn to utilize existing corporate infrastructure such as LDAP, Active Directory, Kerberos, CAS, OpenID, and OAuth
- Integrate with popular frameworks such as Spring, Spring-Boot, Spring-Data, JSF, Vaaden, jQuery, and AngularJS.
- Gain deep understanding of the security challenges with RESTful webservices and microservice architectures
- Integrate Spring with other security infrastructure components like LDAP, Apache Directory server and SAML

Mastering Spring 5.0

Ranga Karanam

ISBN: 978-1-78712-317-5

- Explore the new features in Spring Framework 5.0
- Build microservices with Spring Boot
- Get to know the advanced features of Spring Boot in order to effectively develop and monitor applications
- Use Spring Cloud to deploy and manage applications on the Cloud
- Understand Spring Data and Spring Cloud Data Flow
- Understand the basics of reactive programming
- Get to know the best practices when developing applications with the Spring Framework
- Create a new project using Kotlin and implement a couple of basic services with unit and integration testing

Leave a review - let other readers know what you think

Please share your thoughts on this book with others by leaving a review on the site that you bought it from. If you purchased the book from Amazon, please leave us an honest review on this book's Amazon page. This is vital so that other potential readers can see and use your unbiased opinion to make purchasing decisions, we can understand what our customers think about our products, and our authors can see your feedback on the title that they have worked with Packt to create. It will only take a few minutes of your time, but is valuable to other potential customers, our authors, and Packt. Thank you!

Index

www.ingramcontent.com/pod-product-compliance
Lightning Source LLC
Chambersburg PA
CBHW060651060326
40690CB00020B/4599